CRUMPLED PAPER BOAT

CRUMPLED PAPER BOAT

EXPERIMENTS IN ETHNOGRAPHIC WRITING

Anand Pandian and Stuart McLean, editors

A SCHOOL FOR ADVANCED RESEARCH ADVANCED SEMINAR

DUKE UNIVERSITY PRESS *Durham and London* 2017

© 2017 Duke University Press
All rights reserved
Printed in the United States of America on acid-free paper ∞
Designed by Amy Ruth Buchanan
Typeset in Quadraat by Westchester Publishing Services

Library of Congress Cataloging-in-Publication Data
Names: Pandian, Anand, editor. | McLean, Stuart (Stuart John), editor.
Title: Crumpled paper boat : experiments in ethnographic writing /
Anand Pandian and Stuart McLean, editors.
Other titles: School of American Research advanced seminar series.
Description: Durham : Duke University Press, 2017. | Series: School
for Advanced Research Advanced Seminar | Includes bibliographical
references and index.
Identifiers:
LCCN 2016040907 (print)
LCCN 2016041332 (ebook)
ISBN 9780822363293 (hardcover : alk. paper)
ISBN 9780822363408 (pbk. : alk. paper)
ISBN 9780822373261 (e-book)
Subjects: LCSH: Ethnology—Authorship. | Anthropology—
Authorship. | Ethnology in literature. | Anthropology in literature.
Classification: LCC GN307.7.c78 2017 (print) | LCC GN307.7 (ebook) |
DDC 808.06/63—dc23
LC record available at https://lccn.loc.gov/2016040907

Poems in Chapter 5, "Milk," "Mud," "Lost Boy," "War
Metaphysics for a Sudanese Girl," "The Unraveling Strangeness,"
"Bus Station, Kampala, Uganda," "Skull Trees, South Sudan,"
and "Opening Day, Mukaya," are by Adrie Kusserow, from *Refuge*.
Copyright © 2013 by Adrie Kusserow. Republished with the
permission of The Permissions Company, Inc., on behalf of BOA
Editions, Ltd., www.boaeditions.org
Chapter 9 was originally published in *Reel World* from Duke
University Press. Copyright © 2015, Anand Pandian.

CONTENTS

ACKNOWLEDGMENTS

This volume emerged from an Advanced Seminar at the School for Advanced Research (SAR), Santa Fe, New Mexico, titled "Literary Anthropology." Convened by Anand Pandian and Stuart McLean, the seminar met from Sunday, April 21, to Friday, April 25, 2013. We wish to thank the administration and staff of SAR for their hospitality and unstinting support, most especially Lynn Baca, James Brooks, Michael Brown, Jason Ordaz, Leslie Shipman, and Nicole Taylor. We are deeply grateful to the participants in the seminar, the contributors to this volume, for their generous spirit of collaboration and the wonder of their words. We wish to express our gratitude to Katie Stewart for her profound and illuminating afterword. Thanks are also due to Dominic Boyer, Lawrence Cohen, Vincent Crapanzano, Val Daniel, Elizabeth Davis, Bob Desjarlais, Denielle Elliott, Abou Farman, Brian Goldstone, Cymene Howe, Tim Ingold, Eduardo Kohn, Jean Langford, Natasha Myers, Kirin Narayan, Juan Obarrio, Beth Povinelli, Hugh Raffles, Pete Skafish, Mick Taussig, Rane Willerslev, Boris Wiseman, and Helena Wulff, who have provided much inspiration and encouragement over the years. Parts of chapter 1 appear in an earlier form in "The Blue Years: An Ethnography of a Prison Archive," *Cultural Anthropology* 31, no. 4 (November 2016), and parts of chapter 19 appeared in a different form in Lisa Stevenson's book *Life beside Itself*. Finally, we thank Duke University Press (in particular, Ken Wissoker) and two anonymous reviewers for their enthusiasm and support for this book.

Prologue

ANAND PANDIAN AND STUART McLEAN

An ethnography carries beings of one world into another one. This is a promise that our writing shares with fiction, poetry, cinema, and most other expressive arts. It is also a capacity we share with more literal modes of transport: the flatbeds, planes, ships, and mobile devices that take us in and out of the field, put our interlocutors in motion, and allow our stories to travel from place to place on their own. When it comes to such movements, we get caught up too often in ideas of origin and destination—where someone is coming from, where a text must go. The "how" of transportation is easily lost: the means of conveyance, the transformative potential of movement, the techniques our works rely on in taking their readers elsewhere. Writing is a transitive process of communication, a material practice no less participatory and dynamic than ethnographic fieldwork itself. This is a volume of experimental ventures in anthropological writing, attempts to explore and extend both the medium and its basic modes of displacement.

Our title is borrowed from a phrase in Paul Schmidt's translation of "The Drunken Boat," a poem composed by Arthur Rimbaud in 1871. Here's how the poem ends:

> If I long for a shore in Europe,
> It's a small pond, dark, cold, remote,
> The odor of evening, and a child full of sorrow
> Who stoops to launch a crumpled paper boat.
>
> Washed in your languors, Sea, I cannot trace
> The wake of tankers foaming through the cold,

Nor assault the pride of pennants and flags,
Nor endure the slave ship's stinking hold.

The "I" of the poem, "a little lost boat," is set loose on a river by "howling Indians," winding up adrift amid the waters, flotsam, and mythical beasts of "the Poem of the Sea."[1] Its travails embody the famous formula for poetic displacement, "I is another," that Rimbaud declared in a letter written earlier that year, the phrase that Claude Lévi-Strauss would cite a century later as the very essence of the anthropological endeavor.[2] We find, in this image of a frail vessel adrift, a sense of the peril that can come with such exit from oneself. There is a sense here of the frustrations that lead writers to crumple and scrap the slips of paper on which they work. But there is also the sense of writing as a material adventure, a casting off, the idea of a text cut loose as a thing in the world, something delicate that might yet float to unforeseen and unforeseeable destinations—like the paper boat we are launching here, this volume.

Like so many European adventurers of his era, Rimbaud set sail to seek his fortune in the Orient, serving in the Dutch colonial army in Java and dealing in arms in the Yemeni port of Aden, only to succumb to illness within a decade.[3] Lévi-Strauss, later confronting the rubble of that colonial world, would lament in *Tristes Tropiques* that "journeys, those magic caskets full of dreamlike promises, will never again yield up their treasures untarnished."[4] Certainly, the early twenty-first century seems even less a time to celebrate adventures on ramshackle vessels. Journeys are at once more commonplace and more desperate, as attested by the plight of refugees, itinerant people, and undocumented migrants. Nonetheless, even if anthropologists and their interlocutors travel today along less exotic pathways, our writing remains a charged form of voyaging. The idea of a transformative passage remains essential to the critical promise of ethnography, a promise embodied most fully in the form and force of ethnographic writing—a medium imbued with both potentiality and risk.[5]

As we know very well now, there has always been something peculiar about this genre, ethnography, claimed by anthropology as its own, yet forever edging close to travelogue, literature, and memoir.[6] Think of Bronislaw Malinowski's experiments with narrative point of view—"Imagine yourself suddenly set down . . ."—in *Argonauts of the Western Pacific* or Raymond Firth's effort to conjure the "unreal perspective" of a shoreline encounter at the outset of *We, the Tikopia*. Think of what happens to the integrity of the author's voice in Vincent Crapanzano's *Tuhami* or to the clarity of that being in Jeanne Favret-Saada's *Deadly Words*. To be sure, certain ideas of science and suspicions of rhetoric have weighed down such literary flights. Ruth Benedict and David Sapir kept their poetry to themselves, and the ethnographic novels of Laura Bohannon, Hilda Kuper, and many others since have often held a tenuous place in the official canons of the discipline.[7] And yet the literary impulse has persisted in anthropology as an "uncanny" presence, "both desired and dreaded," as E. Valentine Daniel and Jeffrey Peck have put it, promising to reveal a more intractable and encompassing form of truth—that of the fieldwork encounter with an alien reality.[8]

This was one of the central challenges that motivated the "experimental moment" of the 1980s, George Marcus and Michael Fischer argued in *Anthropology as Cultural Critique*, a time of heightened reflexive attention to the difficulty of ethnographic understanding and the textual devices available for such pursuits. Marcus has since suggested that ethnographic texts may have exhausted this experimental potential.[9] But it seems to us that certain more radical possibilities for experimentation with ethnographic writing remain unexplored, even in the wake of anthropology's "reflexive" turn. Imagine, for example, a spirit of textual adventure that took writing as a practice immanent to the world, rather than as a detached reflection upon the world and itself. Imagine the novel possibilities for thought and action that might come with a deferral of critical distance, in pursuit of a less guarded, even reckless contamination by circumstance. Imagine ways of writing that might put ourselves more deeply at risk than what we have tried till now. What could such experiments look like, and what, if anything, might they achieve?[10]

"In the act of writing, as in spirit possession, sexual ecstasy, or spiritual bliss, we are momentarily out of our minds," Michael Jackson reflects. "We shape-shift. . . . We stretch the limits of what is humanly possible."[11] Jackson's words speak to what can happen in both the writing and the reading of an ethnographic work, through the encounter, that is, with a literary force that is metamorphic by nature, acting in and upon the world and its beings. This is not the familiar image of a knower examining the things of the world at a safe remove, or the idea of a text as a representation that stands apart from the world that it depicts. Instead, what is conveyed here is the chance for something more profound and unsettling to happen through the play of image, voice, character, and scene, a transgression of the limits of individual identity and the fixity of the reality at hand. "Writing is inseparable from becoming," Gilles Deleuze writes, "always incomplete, always in the midst of being formed."[12] We ask, with this book, what might become of anthropology if we cultivated such literary powers more assiduously.

This book grows out of a weeklong seminar in the spring of 2013, hosted by the School for Advanced Research in Santa Fe. That seminar, "Literary Anthropology," brought together a group of anthropologists—mostly younger, and one younger at heart than all of us—who shared a commitment to the practice of writing and a frustration with the limits of conventional scholarly prose. We shared a sense that explanations came too quickly and easily in the social sciences, stripped of the dense and deeply mortal flesh of life. We all described a desire to convey more elusive truths in experience, as well as a feeling of having been taken there by language at times in a manner that we could scarcely make sense of ourselves. We wrote on topics as disparate as roadkill in suburban America and madness in a Moroccan city, mustering resources from literary genres as diverse as epistolary memoir and apocalyptic fiction, philosophical poetry and cinematic scriptwriting. Still, what we held in common was the conviction that such elements could sustain a more lucid and convincing mode of anthropological thought and expression, rather than serving merely as literary props or aesthetic embellishments.

In the French anthropological tradition, Vincent Debaene has shown, scholarly books have always been shadowed by literary works like *Tristes Tropiques*, "experiences made with writing and through writing [as] a true continuation of fieldwork."[13] The chapters that follow similarly take up experimental modes of writing as ways of lingering with the vicissitudes and implications of empirical encounters. In Todd Ramón Ochoa's essay, for example, rhythms of praise for the dead in Cuba compose a narrative topography of undulating pleats, folds, waves, and rolls. For Daniella Gandolfo, a conversation with a hunter on the car radio lights up the carcasses littering a parkway, pulsing all of a sudden with sentiments of both fascination and revulsion. Michael Jackson is caught up in a frustration to recall the details of another radio episode, until that feeling itself opens into an appreciation for the resistance to closure that ethnography demands. Writing thus becomes a means of marking and maintaining an openness to events, surprises, and contingencies, to a reality that is as much a source of questions and provocations as of answers.

"Anthropology has always been vexed about the question of vulnerability," Ruth Behar observes.[14] In what follows, we take this vexation as an incitement to write more faithfully to life, to its ambiguity, uncertainty, and existential risk, however difficult that task may be. Take Angela Garcia's effort to care for an archive of personal letters from the midst of New Mexico's heroin epidemic, a condition of deep and often painful implication that leads her to pursue "writing as a site of intimacy and struggle, mourning and survival." Then there is what happens in Anand Pandian's recounting of the tempestuous desires that propel a scene of filmmaking in India, a torrent of feeling that passes through his essay as a single delirious sentence. One might take such pursuits as a sacrifice of anthropological knowledge to inchoate feelings. But, as Stefania Pandolfo shows in her sensitive reflection regarding a painting born of madness in Morocco, there is a crucial philosophical horizon to such endeavors—writing with the force of passage is what equips us to think otherwise, to bend our concepts to the concepts of others.

All of these essays also share an interest in the craft of writing, an emerging focus of attention in contemporary anthropology, as seen in books such as Kirin Narayan's Alive in the Writing (2012) and the collection Anthropology Off the Shelf (2011) and in the recent series of writers' workshops curated by the anthropology blog Savage Minds.[15] Here, we consider how problems of understanding force a deflection in written form: into narrative prose fiction, the principal reference point for discussions of ethnographic writing, and also into other literary modes. For Tobias Hecht, the appeal of ethnographic fiction—as with his wrenching stories here from the early years of the AIDS epidemic in South Africa—lies in its ability to reveal possible worlds lodged within the apparent banality of the actual. Adrie Kusserow, meanwhile, turns to the "nomadic vagrancy" of poetry as a way of conveying concretely the liminal and unsettled state of Sudanese refugees. Lisa Stevenson's essay, seeking to alight upon the delicate presence of the dead in the life of contemporary Canadian Inuit, assembles a montage of spectral images and nearly inaudible voices. In each of the works to come, the craft of writing is engaged as a material practice, a way of making and unmaking worlds, as attested by Stuart McLean's experimental poem of islands of the North Atlantic, its juxtaposed fragments evoking debris descending from the familiar surface of narrative discourse to the obscurity of the ocean floor.

Any craft demands attentive labor as well as deference: a willingness to allow what is made to find its form, to seek the body that its materials can sustain, to exceed the intentions of its makers. This kind of attunement to the emergent potential of a process was something we often spoke of in Santa Fe, a spirit reflected not only in the substance of what each of us wrote but even in the unfolding of the workshop itself. The momentum of the conversations quickly overtook what the two of us as conveners initially had in mind, and all of us found ourselves swept up by a current of activity that pulled us along without divulging its ultimate direction. This unexpected collective energy provoked various experiments that have since found a place in this book. For example, the chapter that comes immediately after this one is a collaborative work written by all ten of us who participated in the workshop. We had decided, on the spur of the moment, to try out some writing exercises on a collaborative online platform, which we continued to revisit in the months that followed. "Archipelagos" is a text stitched together from those exercises, its sentences formed of fragmentary thoughts and queries hazarded and completed in so wild a manner that none of its ideas can be assigned to any one of us alone.

As a collaborative introduction, "Archipelagos" aims to be faithful to the mood of this book, a place to linger at greater length on the interwoven problems of writerly heritage, craft, consequence, and responsibility that propelled our conversations. Then there are the interludes that follow each of the essays, growing once again out of a vision for the volume as a collective endeavor, as something more than an aggregate of individual contributions. These brief reflections, authored variously, pick up specific themes in the essays as openings into problems of method and technique in ethnographic writing: the challenge of working with care and fidelity, of writing through intercessors and other worlds, of wrestling with excess and the otherwise. Our hope is that these interludes will amplify and extend what is at stake, both conceptually and practically, in the writerly interventions made by the book's essays. They may also communicate the polyphony we hoped to orchestrate by throwing these disparate pieces together. As Kathleen Stewart observes in her luminous epilogue, "There is room in this writing for voices to come and go. . . . Necessarily recursive, it fashions itself like a tuning fork that learns its note through small, incremental experiments made in fits and starts."

This book is composed with the conviction that these notes we hone do indeed matter. Questions are constantly raised these days regarding the relevance of anthropology. This has something to do with our habits of writing; as Orin Starn notes in a recent commemoration of the twenty-fifth anniversary of *Writing Culture*, "We tend not to be very good storytellers."[16] But there is also the difficulty of what anthropology aims to do with experience, the difficulty of thinking creatively and effectively with such tales and other forms. Indeed, in an era of Big Data the insistent particularism of ethnographic research and writing can provoke and disconcert. Witness, for example, the accusations of adventurism and worse that greeted Alice Goffmann's recent effort to record the precarious lives of young African American men in a neighborhood of West Philadelphia. The controversy surrounding Goffmann's book concerned not only the ethics and positionality of the white, Ivy League–educated ethnographer's foray into the worlds of urban black youth, but also its alleged blurring of documentary and fictional modes.[17]

The relationship between reality and fiction has become ever more fraught in the United States in the wake of the 2016 presidential election, widely seen to herald an alarming new era of deliberate falsehoods peddled as "alternative facts." The Oxford English Dictionary actually declared *post-truth* the word of the year in 2016, "denoting circumstances in which objective facts are less influential in shaping public opinion than appeals to emotion and personal belief."[18] Critics have rightly challenged such claims in the political sphere, insisting on the objective reality of things like climate change, or the absence of any evidence tying refugees from certain countries to terrorism in the United States. But we ought also to ask whether it suffices to fall back on such truths in the face of persuasive stories of foreign menace and threat, which have become such powerful forces in contemporary American politics and elsewhere. For it is undeniable that such tales have the capacity to remake reality itself, to reshape the very substance of the here-and-now and the ways in which human actors engage the world at hand. All too often such attempts insist dogmatically upon their own authoritative status, seeking to displace or exclude other possible accounts of what is or might be. Anthropology can help in making sense of how such narratives, mythical and otherwise, act upon the world and its inhabitants. And, in the midst of these perilous and uncertain circumstances, ethnographic writing has a crucial role to play in setting loose other kinds of compelling tales.

In what follows, some of us take experimental writing as a way of lending greater nuance and sensitivity to the project of ethnographic understanding, and thus of entering more profoundly into the lives and worlds of others. Other contributors to this book seek, in writing, new means of breaking with conventional notions of representation and subjectivity, putting the anthropological category of the "human" itself into question. We float this volume with the faith that inventive, appealing, and intellectually adventurous writing can serve both of these ends, while also reaching out to wider and more diverse audiences. We hope to show that such experimentation is essential to anthropology's role in the contemporary world, and that it is one of our most powerful means of engaging it.

At the outset of an important collective effort from the 1980s to think between poetry and anthropology, Stanley Diamond mused that "the writing of poetry has turned into a particular, personal, and exhausting effort, which must fight every moment against the gravity of civilized language." Diamond had in mind the impoverishment of everyday language in the modern world, denuded of expressive richness, depth, and rhythm. "If anthropologists were Zulus, or Eskimo, or Seneca, or Pawnee," he wrote, "the language of everyday life . . . would make it possible for everyone to speak poetry, as many anthropologists have the imagination and experience to understand."[19] Diamond's sober judgment notwithstanding, this book rests on the idea that ethnography can infuse language with the presence of other lives and the density of their worlds, that we can indeed learn (or learn again) to speak such poetry—not as Zulus or Inuit, or even as anthropologists per se, but as living beings in the process of becoming others whose identities remain fundamentally unresolved.[20] Such is the promise of an approach to writing that acknowledges the deep intertwining of language and life, image and experience, thought and the world in which it finds a body.[21]

These ventures, as experiments, may not work for everyone. But we hope they may carry a generative spark, provoking further explorations of the creative and transformative potentials of anthropological writing, further experiments, further castings off—more or less crumpled as they may be, still drifting all the same, uncertain of whom or what they will encounter.

Notes

1. Rimbaud, *Complete Works*, 120–23. The image that we borrow for the title from Schmidt's translation was expressed otherwise by Rimbaud—"Un bateau frêle comme un papillon de mai." But, as Schmidt explains with regard to his method, "What remained for me . . . was to wrestle with Rimbaud's poetry the way an actor wrestles with a part, to perform what his words revealed. To arrange it? To impose order on his derangements? No. Simply to speak it in my own language, to say what he wrote, to tell what appears to have happened within the periods that Rimbaud himself has set, the seasons that obsessed him" (xv).

2. Lévi-Strauss, "Jean-Jacques Rousseau."

3. Taminian, "Rimbaud's House in Aden, Yemen."

4. Lévi-Strauss, *Tristes Tropiques*, 37.

5. "The travel writer's transient and literary approach, sharply rejected in the disciplining of fieldwork, has continued to tempt and contaminate the scientific practices of cultural description. Anthropologists are, typically, people who leave and write," James Clifford observes. Clifford, *Routes*, 65.

6. Essential reflections on the writing of ethnography include Marcus and Cushman, "Ethnographies as Texts"; Clifford and Marcus, *Writing Culture*; Clifford, *Predicament of Culture*; Geertz, *Works and Lives*; Tedlock, "From Participant Observation to the Observation of Participation"; Rapport, *Prose and the Passion*; and Daniel and Peck, *Culture/Contexture*.

7. Schmidt, "Ethnographic Fiction."

8. Daniel and Peck, "Culture/Contexture: An Introduction," 1.

9. Reviewing the legacies of the hugely influential *Writing Culture*, which he coedited with James Clifford, Marcus has argued that "the classical ethnographic textual form—even as amended since the 1980s, and given its learned pleasures—is a very partial and increasingly inadequate means of composing the movements and contests of fieldwork—both naturalistic and contrived, collaborative and individualistic—that motivate it, and on which it is intended to report." For Marcus, the locus of experimentation has shifted to other media and sites of collaboration such as studio, lab, and design spaces. Marcus, "Legacies of *Writing Culture*," 432.

10. Recent and inspiring examples of such efforts, for which a space has always existed in the discipline of anthropology, include Michael Taussig's *Law in a Lawless Land* (2003), Kirin Narayan's *My Family and Other Saints* (2007), Kathleen Stewart's *Ordinary Affects* (2007), Hugh Raffles's *Insectopedia* (2010), Robert Desjarlais's *Counterplay* (2011), Ruth Behar's *Traveling Heavy* (2013), Renato Rosaldo's *The Day of Shelley's Death* (2013), Lucas Bessire's *Behold the Black Caiman* (2014), and Paul Stoller's *Yaya's Story* (2014), not to mention the work of the contributors to this volume.

11. Jackson, *Other Shore*, 3.

12. Deleuze, "Literature and Life," 225.

13. Debaene, *Far Afield*, x.

14. Behar, *Vulnerable Observer*, 5.

15. A second edition of John Van Maanen's *Tales of the Field: On Writing Ethnography* was also published by the University of Chicago Press in 2011. Published most recently, in 2016, was *The Anthropologist as Writer*, edited by Helena Wulff.

16. Starn, "Introduction," 9.

17. Goffmann, *On the Run*; Gideon Lewis-Kraus, "The Trials of Alice Goffmann," *New York Times*, January 12, 2016.

18. "Word of the Year: Post-truth," English: Oxford Living Dictionaries, accessed February 7, 2017, https://en.oxforddictionaries.com/word-of-the-year/word-of-the-year -2016.

19. S. Diamond, "Preface," 131.

20. What Steven A. Tyler wrote of postmodern ethnography remains deeply compelling to us: "It is, in a word, poetry—not in its textual form, but in its return to the original context and function of poetry, which, by means of its performative break with everyday speech, evoked memories of the *ethos* of the community and thereby provoked hearers to act ethically," breaking from reality and returning to a commonsensical world "transformed, renewed, and sacralized." Tyler, "Postmodern Ethnography," 125–26.

21. See Lavie, Narayan, and Rosaldo, *Creativity/Anthropology*.

Introduction

_____

ARCHIPELAGOS, A VOYAGE IN WRITING

PAPER BOAT COLLECTIVE

For a long time I've thought about writing as a kind of sorcery.

Stories give us hints as to how they need to be written.

It seemed to me that a certain kind
of overt interest in writing caused
people not to take you seriously.

Why should an account of human life, which is,
after all, the most interesting thing on earth, be
rendered in such uninteresting ways?

I can sometimes just be so thrilled by a turn of phrase.

Something happens to break down the integrity of the reader
and the text—what the text is, and what it isn't, somehow
become undecidable.

For me it's important in the writing to convey a lifeworld
but also a world of thought and the possibility of new
thought, new concepts, new worlds that can open up.

What are the ethics of writing, of working
with the words of another, whether those
words are spoken or written?

In some weird way, the dead are an audience, always.

I hope at the end of this I'll still want to write poetry.

Writing

We came here to talk about writing. Here—an adobe bungalow on Garcia Street in the high reaches of Santa Fe, New Mexico. The mud-walled compound once belonged to two wealthy sisters from New York, Martha and Elizabeth White, who named it El Delirio, "the madness," after a bar they chanced upon during a vacation in Seville, Spain. The sisters were known both as enthusiastic patrons of archaeology and native arts and as the hosts of lavish costume parties, where guests would dance the night away dressed as ancient Mayans.[1] A cemetery for their beloved breed dogs lies undisturbed in a quiet corner of the property. Now, as the School for Advanced Research, the compound plays host to the more muted, professionally sanctioned revelries of visiting anthropologists.

Beyond the compound lie the high desert and the southernmost subrange of the Rockies, the Sangre de Cristo Mountains, formed around twenty-seven million years ago. The Spanish colonists who arrived here in the early seventeenth century saw blood in the reddish alpenglow of these peaks at sunrise and named them accordingly. They struggle still for control of the region's resources: descendants of these settlers, the Native Americans they displaced, and the Mexican and American settlers who came after them. Just thirty-odd miles north of Santa Fe's shops and galleries lies the Los Alamos National Laboratory, where the world's first atomic weapons were developed and manufactured. The setting is one where beauty and violence have long commingled and as such is replete both with reminders of the short-lived and transitory character of the human presence in the region and with intimations of the disquieting prospect of a posthuman future—a suggestive place, in other words, to think about the contemporary stakes of anthropological writing.

It is well known that anthropologists write, and write a lot: notes and transcriptions, proposals and reports, books and articles, sometimes even drama, fiction, and poetry. For the most part still, these exercises are evaluated with a narrow standard of accuracy in mind: how closely they "represent" some other world out there, how faithfully they mediate between that world and those who make and consume anthropological texts. Beyond the fulfillment of this expectation, writing in anthropology tends to be seen as an aesthetic adornment, a hobby pursued by those with the time and inclination to do so, a diversion from the more serious business of conveying content and information.

*Someone recalls—What bothered me when I came to anthropology was that
so many people said, "You'll have to leave the poetry behind now." There was
a sense that social science required a distance from direct testimony or direct
engagement in people's lives, in order to have some kind of authority. I detested
the whole idea of this authority—it seemed to me that a text didn't have authority, it had authenticity.*

How to tell a story and tell it well? Why do we as anthropologists feel
so constrained in the face of this question, in contrast to the freedom that
writers of fiction or literary essays seem to enjoy? This difficulty has much
to do with the specific demands that our subject matter places on our writing: honoring our subjects, honoring the lifeworlds we write about. The
literary in its popular sense is all about inventing, making things up, but as
ethnographers we have the sense also of wanting to do the right thing by
the people we're writing about. A consciousness of this responsibility often
stays our hand when it comes to experimental writing. But should it always?
Might our encounters with others demand on occasion that we experiment?

We struggle here with the limits of a writing that isn't subtle enough or
rich enough to do justice to the realities that we encounter, realities that are
turned so often into generic ABCs in what we read about them. Experimental
writing, sometimes errant, at times even literary, can also *know* something
of the world—something that has no less of a claim on the truth of the world
than the sciences or the social sciences, perhaps even a great deal more to
claim than some institutionalized forms of knowledge. Literature forces us
to ask what it means to "convey" something in the first place. Language is
more than an empty vehicle to carry over information, for the medium has
an ineradicable presence in the act of saying something: the density of certain words that cannot be substituted by other words, turns of phrase that
cannot be altered or expressed otherwise. Such elements work to produce
worlds of life, worlds of thought, through a convergence of the literary and
the lived, the philosophical and the aesthetic.

"Yes, happily language is a thing," Maurice Blanchot wrote—"it is a written thing, a bit of bark, a sliver of rock, a fragment of clay in which the reality
of the earth continues to exist."[2] In this book, we think of writing as a generative practice, a tangible presence, part of the stuff of the worlds it seeks to
engage, working with powers and potentialities always present in language,
always at work in the world. Writing, as a mode of expression, shares its

creative energy with the milieus from which it emerges. This emphasis on the materiality of expression also leads us to a particular understanding of ethnography, as a way of participating in the activity of the world, a making and remaking of instances of life entangled with moments of thought, its writing as a form of sorcery, a conjuration of powers both generative and destructive.

For such sorcery is a vexed thing: it can harm and it can heal. Betrayal is inescapable, in this practice of working with words that are not our own. A world comes back into being through the debris of language, in the form of residues and detritus: buried stories, forgotten images, diary entries, fragments of verse. How effectively do these elements engage the lives of the people we work with? What is it to know by means of the narrative shards and broken dreams that compose the archive of anthropology? Ethnographies always alter and transfigure the worlds that motivate them, illuminating and occluding the lives and stories with which they are suffused.

Michel de Certeau suggests that writing begins in loss.[3] We work here with voices that seek a place but never settle, voices unmoored and apart from the integrity of body and identity, voices that pass through ethnography without the security of anchor and harbor. We pursue ethnographic experiments with altered states of feeling: dream, reverie, revelation, visceral forces of self-estrangement and becoming-otherwise.

(Even these words, here, to whom do they belong? We can't say—they weave between and among us.)

Such writing puts both exteriority and interiority into play. At stake in this book is the depth of anthropology's commitment to the world beyond itself, as well as its willingness to court a dissolution of itself in pursuit of the unknown.

Writing is hazardous, a practice of submission and surrender, engaging always with something larger and more unsettling than the being of the writer or ethnographer. "In truth it is the world that has the edge and calls the final shot," writes Michael Jackson.[4] With this acknowledgment comes a way of tapping into the radical potential of worldly energies, potentials domesticated all too often, potentials that the writing here seeks instead to restore and intensify. Critical scholarship still trades too much in defensive irony and detachment. With this volume and its experiments, we pursue writing that is captivated, vulnerable, and implicated, writing nurtured in pain and fear, writing that courts joy and seeks knowledge in the uncertainty and excess of attachment, writing that puts its authors, its readers, even itself, at risk.

Craft

Echoes of costume parties and the blood-red mountains in the distance— or the pet cemetery somewhere on these grounds—are not the only presences from the past to reckon with in this adobe bungalow. The ghosts of seminars past gaze down from framed photographs on every wall: some ancestors venerated still, others long since forgotten. We joke uneasily about how to make our peace with these presences. Genuflect? Ignore? Position ourselves in relation to them, as readers of an introduction such as this one might expect? Or simply watch and wait until the passage of time causes them to mutate and become protean, even monstrous, beyond their own and our wildest imaginings? Children too have their place as witnesses among the gods—creators, lawbreakers, and monstrous offspring themselves. Aren't we ethnographers always like children at the door, playing with its size, weight, and sound, the rush of wind as it slams? Invariably, fingers get caught. The child screams, is reprimanded, but soon enough, stealthily and crafty still, drifts back to the door.

Thirty years ago, in the same bungalow, another group of ten gathered to discuss the making of ethnographic texts, producing a volume—*Writing Culture: The Poetics and Politics of Ethnography*—that remains one of the most influential works of anthropological scholarship to this day. Contributors to that seminal work had much to say about the rhetorical construction of anthropological texts and their embeddedness within "larger contexts of systematic power inequality, world-systems constraints, and institutional formations that could only partly be accounted for by a focus on textual production."[5] But with hindsight, the moment in the 1980s that gave rise to *Writing Culture*—a culmination of the "linguistic turn" pervasive in the humanities and social sciences—seems marked most especially by a heightened suspicion of writing. That volume had surprisingly little to say about writerly powers and affects that could upturn the political and epistemic status quo.

As a critique of the "politics of representation," *Writing Culture* positioned itself in the gap between dominant representations and what they purported to represent: a distance that underpins not only the scholarly claim to describe and interpret the world in an accurate and authoritative manner, but also the critical method that consists in showing how particular representations are unwittingly enmeshed in various relations of power. When the force of texts is taken primarily as a vehicle of domination and mystification, however, it becomes more difficult to see what else they might do, what other effects they might produce. All too often what remains is a narrative mood of irony, pursued in a spirit of professional civility and urbanity, and anchored in a distance immune to surprise, shock, and the horror of derailment.

The feminist, antiracist, and postcolonial critiques of anthropological knowledge that provoked *Writing Culture*, nevertheless, have also incited other radical responses in the history of anthropology. Long before the manifestly experimental ventures of recent decades, there existed a heterogeneous corpus of writings marginal to the established canons of the discipline: memoirs, life histories and ethnographic novels, sometimes pseudonymously published, often the work of women or people of color, like Franz Boas's onetime students Ella Deloria and Zora Neale Hurston, neither of whom succeeded in finding positions in the academy.[6] These writings make up less a "little tradition" than a "minor literature," subsisting alongside anthropology's defining voices and textual monuments and occasionally succeeding in pulling the latter temporarily into their own orbit, as with Maya Deren's evocative and influential *Divine Horsemen*.[7]

"You take up the pen when you are told," Hurston says about writing *Their Eyes Were Watching God*—"the force from somewhere in Space which commands you to write in the first place, gives you no choice."[8] Such reflections convey a power of writing born of its own excessive and transgressive exteriority: a writing that generates worldly effects that inevitably overflow the conscious intentions of the one who writes, a writing that plunges its own writer into the midst of hazards and potencies that can never be definitively mastered. Writing can indeed be conscripted as a tool for the legitimation of power, but only because it can also exceed such appropriations. How best to nurture these unruly capacities to challenge existing orders of meaning and feeling?

This possibility, we suggest, is ultimately a matter of craft. The word *craft* may call up certain associations, such as a sense of craftiness—of cunning, skill at deception, even witchcraft. After all, idioms of wizardry and enchantment have often pervaded the archive of responses to "vivid" ethnographic writing, as though the vitality of such writing were seen to depend upon a sleight of hand: seeming to bring something inanimate to life, or to draw upon the forces of animate objects to do something unexpected to living beings. As Vincent Crapanzano writes of George Catlin, for example, "his aim is to impress his experience of what he has *seen* so strongly, so vividly, on his readers that they cannot doubt its veracity."[9] Play with such powers often elicits a response of suspicion, most especially when they appear to play a constitutive role in the making, unmaking, and remaking of worlds. The English term *craft* derives from the Old High German *Kraft*, meaning strength or power.

But to speak of the craft of writing is also to suggest an artisanal endeavor. We might think of writing as akin to woodworking, calling attention to the rhythms of a practice, to the way that a body can come, over time, into proximity with something else being honed. Consider the kind of power that a chisel or rasp may exercise with respect to a plane of wood, trying, failing, working, trying, coming back around again. Such engagements, Tim Ingold argues, demand acknowledgment that "materials are active" rather than "dead or inert matter."[10] These are not antagonistic relations, or a straightforward matter of domination, but have everything to do with the way that the potential forces of the tool handler find ways of speaking with the potentials of that material. There is a braiding together of activity and passivity, agency and patiency, the development of a capacity to be acted upon, even as one acts, a capacity akin to what Georges Bataille, in a very different context, called "the mastery of non-mastery."[11]

> How is the text receptive? someone asks. What array of receptors have been written into it, so that it might find future partners? Hooks are meant to change natures, to change the nature of the reader, to change the nature of the writing, to give us different eyes. That's a Nietzschean idea: nature isn't fixed, it's more likely to shift and transform into something new if it grips and connects to something else.

Writerly craft—the practice, for example, of thinking in images, writing in images, releasing some vector of vital force through the honing of an artful turn of phrase. There are times when stating something directly, affirming something explicitly, may not be as effective as presenting a more equivocal scene or story. Montage can bring things into tension and let them spark. So can the attachments and vagaries of a narrative presence caught up in the momentum of such scenes—such implication can be productive, bringing things that exist into new alignments, new arrangements, giving a new concreteness to objects and feelings below the threshold of perception.

All writers engage a particular face of an object, the side of it that engages, enthralls, or repels. At stake here is an "expressive" relationship between work and world, something more proximate and intimate than we are accustomed to acknowledging.[12] Our language works with the substance of the world, as the Roman poet and atomist philosopher Lucretius recognized long ago in his only surviving work, De Rerum Natura, identifying the letters of his own verse with the aggregating and disaggregating atoms forming the physical universe.[13] The craft of writing engages with transformative potentials already present in the environment at hand—"fragments of cloth," as James Agee put it, "bits of cotton, lumps of earth, records of speech, pieces of wood and iron, phials of odors, plates of food and excrement."[14]

Reality

Michael Taussig is in Medellín, Colombia—maybe in Medellín, maybe just passing through. As his taxi speeds into the pitch black of a freeway tunnel, he spots a man and woman beside the canyon walls of the tunnel entrance. She is sewing that man into a white nylon bag, the anthropologist thinks, the kind of bag in which Colombian peasants heap their potatoes and corn. He has three seconds to take in this arcane pair. He cranes his neck, writes in his notebook. Later, he adds a sentence—"I swear I saw this"—followed by a watercolor sketch.[15]

Taussig's story reminds us of a conceit essential to ethnographic writing: that of reporting faithfully and rationally on the circumstance of our encounters, of making the "incorrigible assertion," as Clifford Geertz put it, that we have truly "been there."[16] There is that familiar commitment to writing as a kind of mimesis, a practice of "stating the facts" without addition or embellishment. But there is already more to Taussig's account than just this. "It is a seeing that doubts itself," he observes—the sketch redoubles those words, but the event remains elusive.[17] What these field recordings want is less belief than a willingness to live with uncertainty: less a conquering of doubt than an acknowledgment of its necessity. An account becomes a tale.

Questions arise here concerning the fundamental task of writing in anthropology, but also the nature of the reality that we take this writing to address. "Somewhere, somehow, real reality breaks through the scrim," Taussig writes—but what is this thing, this condition or effect that can burst beyond the fabric of the text?[18] Take "reality" as a name for the here and now, what is given to immediate and tangible experience, and our task may indeed be to report on it, to reproduce it, to document its present actualities, to try to copy down and transmit further the most essential aspects of its givenness.

But suppose instead, as the doubt that suffuses Taussig's seeing suggests, that reality is always suffused with something more, some other face, some other dimension, something intangible, evanescent, resistant to analytical decomposition. Gilles Deleuze called it the virtual, borrowing a formula from Proust: "real without being actual, ideal without being abstract."[19] Or think of the in-between spaces of the barzakh that Vincent Crapanzano describes in Imaginative Horizons, shoal after shoal of spectral horizons, in-between and looking beyond, presences one is not quite there with.[20] What would it mean to be faithful to this other face of reality: to do justice to it, to complement it, to reveal aspects of the real at the very limits of the perceptible?

This has long been the promise, largely implicit, of anthropology itself: to affirm that actual, existing circumstances are always imbued with the possibility of being otherwise—that actuality is never coincident with itself, that the real is always more than what is actually present somewhere. Ethnography is wagered on the possibility that a given reality's difference from itself—and the kind of empirical commitment this expectation demands—can be revealed most powerfully through writing. Bronislaw Malinowski penned an inkling of this promise into his Trobriand diaries:

> The sea is blue, absorbing everything, fused with the sky. At moments, the pink silhouettes of the mountains appear through the mist, like phantoms of reality in the flood of blue, like the unfinished ideas of some youthful creative force. You can just make out the shapes of the islands scattered here and there—as though headed for some unknown destination, mysterious in their isolation, beautiful with the beauty of perfection—self-sufficient.
>
> Here and there flat coral islands, like enormous rafts gliding over the smooth water. Occasionally these forms take on life, passing for a moment into the realm of [crude] reality. A pale silhouette suddenly turns into a rocky island. Gigantic trees rise right out of the sea, set on an alluvial platform.[21]

Such visions, however, would win only a tenuous and irregular place in the avowedly scientific works that followed.

The question of writing's fidelity to the real cannot be adjudicated on the basis of conventional distinctions between "documentary" and "fictional" registers. Instead, we need to approach an ethnographic mode that somehow presses—in Michel Serres's terms—closer to the turbulence preceding the emergence of an intelligible, discursively knowable world.[22] Literary writing, Serres argues, in its capacity to body forth this aspect of the world at its limits, may be no less truthful than science. In fact, insofar as such writing evokes more effectively the becoming of the world—its processual transformation, its perennial noncoincidence with itself—we might take it to be *more* faithful to the real, committed to a different kind of knowing more profound than either science or philosophy.

> *Ethnography should also work as a story, someone insists. Not like these books you can't open, you can't read, unbearable in some way, badly told or that just don't work. The problem that anthropologists face is not a lack of reality, but what to do with it. Through artifice, you can get closer to the real.*

"Man must be a liar by nature, he must be above all an artist," Friedrich Nietzsche wrote in *The Will to Power*.[23] With art, Nietzsche had in mind ways of grappling creatively with dissonant forms of worldly potential. We pull closer here to the original sense in Latin of "fiction"—*fingere*, to form, mold, shape—and, indeed, fiction too can be taken as an artifice that preserves and sustains the life of thought by perturbing its settlement into taken-for-granted truths. Think of what Bataille said of poetry: that which moves away from us, what is left of language as subjectivity passes into wordless anguish or delight—a boundary stone, a pale, beyond which remain laughter, tears, and silence.[24] By skirting this boundary, writerly knowing attests to the creative power of what is real.

The making of literary fictions has been typically conceived as an exclusively human affair. "Only a few have ventured into the depths of inanimate nature," Walter Benjamin has observed, sketching a portrait of the storyteller as someone who draws authority instead from a natural history in which death and life are inseparably conjoined as moments of a single process.[25] The reality of which the story speaks, for Benjamin, is not the reality of everyday life as humans experience it. Rather, the storyteller conveys a reality as seen from the point of view of a life beyond: the real of rocks and inanimate things; the real of mountains and forests, of the stars in the wake of their explosive birth; the real of an ancestral humanity lost to verifiable science; the real of more contemporary others, suppressed, dispossessed, and exterminated everywhere, as were the people who lived in these mountains of what is now known as New Mexico.

Much of this reality is beyond our capacity to witness, to respond, and to acknowledge, at least through conventional forms of selfhood and sociality. There is, therefore, a visionary horizon to experimental forms of ethnographic expression: the capability to dwell for some time beyond present human consciousness, to subsist within neglected and other-than-conscious forms, to receive the world—as does a film like Leviathan by Lucien Castaing-Taylor and Verena Paravel—as seen and experienced by gulls and fish, or as revealed by their dying in the nets of a fishing trawler.[26] Such work can lead us beyond a time of human thoughts and deeds alone, into the untimeliness that all of us confront with the darkening horizon beyond the reign of anthropos, this Anthropocene.[27]

Take the reality of this book too as something tangible, tactile, materially present, something like the sea, perhaps even a marine jelly, stirred by tremors and undulations, always in motion, perpetually liable to mutual transformation with its readers. Take this text as a surface of openings, channels, wormholes, ways into a reality that remains elusive and unmade. Ethnographic writing is a field of physical and embodied sensations, inextricable from the inchoate nature of experience itself. Experimental moments are those times in which reality is felt to seep beyond itself.

Responsibility

Horses were turned loose in the child's sorrow. Black and roan, cantering
through snow.
The way light fills the hand with light, November with graves, infancy with white.
White. Given lilacs, lilacs disappear. Then low voices rising in walls.
The way they withdrew from the child's body and spoke as if it were not there.
—CAROLYN FORCHÉ, "Sequestered Writing," in Blue Hour

Most everything here trespasses the perimeters of scholarly prose: those familiar lines between reality and fiction, representation and invention, responsibility and irreverence. Is such writing a means to an end, or an end in itself? What of the goal, the end, the purpose of ethnography? The stakes are always high, too high, in the kind of work that we do in anthropology. Ethnography is often a site of expression for politics, economics, justice, and the ethical, and rightly so. Are we retreating from heroin, colonialism, psychosis, AIDS, and dispossession into a realm of indulgence? Or might we be drawing closer to these realities in a way that only a sustained attentiveness to writing as a material practice could allow?

If writing involves risk, does it not also entail responsibility? If the possible and the impossible, the factual and the counterfactual, the present and the absent, the living and the dead all belong equally to life's reality, where does this leave our responsibility to be faithful? In what ways are we responsible, for example, to those whose lives we seek to write about? Should our writing emerge, in the first instance, out of our solidarity with our informants, as a response to the demands they place upon us? Should those demands set limits on the writerly impulses we are willing to arrogate to ourselves? Or should they be taken as an impetus to push boundaries, to explore to the fullest extent the possibilities of writing differently? Does responsibility reside in the acknowledgment that these questions can never be definitively answered, that they demand rather to be continuously reengaged, through the practice, say, of writing itself?

> Someone interjects—I've written about people who live thirty miles away from here. If I were to write about them in a book that they would want to open and close immediately, I couldn't show up at the barbecue.

We ought to distinguish among the various implications of diverse styles of expression. It is not exactly the same to say "I witnessed this" (as classic ethnographies often do) and "I could have witnessed something like this" (as a fiction writer might claim). Not being sure if you saw something and knowing that you didn't are also different from each other. Passing fiction off as fact in a court of law is perjury; passing it off as truth to your lover's demand is betrayal. Then again the lover and the court of law expect very different things when it comes to reality. And explanations that come too quickly, as they often do in the social sciences, court another kind of betrayal: injustice to the complexity of the world, an explaining away of things and details that don't quite fit. Fidelity to the real may consist in acknowledging that it will always exceed the accounts we are able to give of it.

The multifaceted character of life leads us to deploy different forms and techniques to engage with different aspects of being. This is a pragmatist argument for turning to poetry or discursive prose, depending on the situation we are trying to cope with or do justice to. Simply writing ethnography poetically, without taking the situation at hand into account, is pointless. At stake also, however, is an ontological commitment to enacting and exploring our immanent participation in a world that inevitably surpasses us. Being faithful to reality is a matter of taking part in it, of allowing it to take part in us, rather than making a pronouncement on it. The salient distinction is whether a form of writing is alive or dead to the activity of the world, whether it emerges *from* or seeks to preside *over* a world that doesn't sit still. Lest we forget, fiction can be as much a dead letter as academic prose.

"Human beings can only bear so much reality," T. S. Eliot once said.[28] Literary devices, then, can be taken as "simplifying betrayals," means of coping with the great expanse of the world. Such coping can mean many things—it's not as though the "hard facts" of death and suffering should somehow stop the possibility of a creative response in its tracks. There are moments in which we demand other kinds of "truth." Think, for example, of the Chilean poet Raúl Zurita, whose poetry is an extraordinarily powerful response to the fact of missing bodies during the Pinochet dictatorship. Zurita writes, "Each one of us is more than an I, each one is a torrent of the deceased that ends in our life just as we end in our descendants. This is what's meant by a tradition and culture; that all those who have preceded us return to speak when we speak, they return to see when we see, feel when we feel. Each one of us is the resurrection of the dead and that miracle is achieved in each second of our lives."[29]

Zurita's declaration of faith in poetry's capacity to speak for the dead, or, more precisely, to speak the dead, deserves to be taken absolutely literally. Poetry speaks not only the named and individuated dead, not only the dead en masse, but also through and along with them the immense, indifferent, inhuman materiality of the universe that is the precursor and successor of all life, human or otherwise. Poetry, one might say, makes the dead matter.

This encounter with the dead often occurs in reading and writing, always wrapped up in the voices of others, in appropriations and deletions. There is both responsibility and delicacy in this task of taking up the speech and silence of others, and then giving those elements the reach of another world. We often work with those who lack the most basic freedoms that we enjoy, those that enable our travel and our questions, lacks that demand some kind of acknowledgment or response. Our words stand as restitution for what we owe, but they also transfigure what we have seen. How do we grapple with the pain that such endeavors can also produce?

When we think of the politics of writing, we often think of the demands made by a particular moment, and the actors at work in a set of circumstances: the imperative to say something about what is happening, and to do so in response to, in dialogue with, the human protagonists of that event. The writer's relationship with the world she writes about is, no doubt, always an intersubjective matter, directly comparable to the calling or summons we feel as parents, spouses, or as members of a polis. But the writer is obliged to meet the demands of her child as well as to assist the child's passage from home into the world, where the child will have a life of its own, independent of the one who gave it life. The letting go that this necessarily involves is itself another kind of responsibility and another kind of risk.

Linger on the debts that writing carries, and you might be left with an image of aporia: the pathless path, the ship's wake that marks the sea, only to be erased so quickly by the waters that survive beyond its cut. Our writing may not always return us to the world that occasioned it, and we may not always have the last word on what everything means, how it should be seen, how it should be responded to. But such moments of indistinction, when our powers of articulation fail us, may also allow other powers to emerge. The narratives and counternarratives that we throw out into the world take part in its ceaseless remaking. As James Joyce reminds us in *Finnegans Wake*, a text that unfolds in a time of dreams neither present nor past but both and more besides, "the world, mind, is, was and will be writing its own wrunes for ever."[30]

Islands in the Desert

All of this is beginning to happen around a pitted wooden table in that mud-walled bungalow in New Mexico: ten anthropologists, five men and five women, variously connected by birth or ancestry to Britain, India, Canada,

Italy, New Zealand, Mexico, Peru, and the United States. There are moments of consensus. There are disagreements. Sometimes there are tears, in this dreaming of islands, the high desert caving into the floor of the sea.

If I could, someone says to herself, I would take a deep breath and dive down, swim north in search of cooler water. Then the one next to her bolts for a pad of paper. This text is an archipelago, he says, sketching—there are spaces or worlds of exploration, a journey from island to island. These conversations are seas in which we drift together.

Archipelagos are chains of minor islands, dotting every map with hardly any mass to speak of, except for the things they accrete: shells, piles of washed-up debris, broken bits of fossilized animals, plastic detritus, and bits of seaweed. The archipelago as we learned it looks to a major island where the runway would be, where the colonial administration would make its home. But then it scatters into islands too tiny to be called islands, masses disappointing to the projects of a land-bound consciousness, surfacing sometimes above the tideline, falling sometimes below.

Is it any accident that anthropologists have been drawn so often to such places? Islands are spaces of both utopian imagining and banishment: think of the Trobriands, to which the Polish-born Malinowski was consigned as a suspicious alien by the British colonial authorities at the outbreak of the First World War; or the Andaman Islands as described by Radcliffe "Anarchy" Brown, home to a penal colony built to house political prisoners, where inmates died in their thousands; or even Robinson Crusoe, castaway and empire builder in miniature, whom James Joyce (an Irish islander in continental exile) would identify as the prototypical figure of the British colonist.[31] Islands have long incited dreams of conquest and settlement.

Islands are imagined as bounded, walled, and self-enclosed, yet open all the same into a fluid medium of connection and displacement (island = I-land? Eye-land? I'll and?). "And deeper than did ever plummet sound / I'll drown my book," says Shakespeare's Prospero, both exile and colonist, consigning the words that have underwritten his power as a magician to watery oblivion, as he prepares to resume his former life far from the sea as Duke of Milan.[32] Other voyagers, meanwhile, have found ultimate refuge in the offshore depths to which islands can serve as stepping stones. In Inuit storytelling traditions, Sedna, the daughter who refuses to marry, cast overboard by her father, takes up residence at the bottom of the sea, the island of all islands perhaps, as the spirit mistress of the marine mammals on which Inuit hunters depend for their survival.[33]

The ethnographic archipelago—a place where writing is tried, sentenced, cast away. We tend to think that things may be stranded on such islands, stuck within the boundaries of the knowable and sayable. But we tend to forget that things left here can also go wild, rising, expanding, transmogrifying, growing over and becoming unrecognizable to themselves, like the singular flora and fauna of the Galápagos. Accretions of words, soaked through and waterlogged by rain and sea, by the dead and all those who came before, clinging to the slivers of earth that remain behind from the subsidence of tectonic plates. Accretions of all those who may have come but didn't stay. They plot; they figure out a way to float off together, or to disappear altogether beneath the water's surface.

Continents, continent—temperate, moderate, and chaste. What we want is an incontinent writing, words that face up to the threat of overflowing, the danger of being overrun. There is safety in the continents of discourse, in the security of their containment. Not so the island, especially at the tail of its archipelago, incontinent witness to the coming and going of meaning, truth, politics, value. Even here, between and among these fragments of writing, our words are always flowing into each other.

> Islands appear only in my dreams, someone says. She speaks of a beach, of walking down a flight of steps, of lingering for a moment on the stairs before descending into the sand. There was water underground, sweet water at the threshold of the seawater, but reaching it meant to cease living in this form, to abandon the world as it is, to remember the forgotten as forgotten. The bottom of the dream was like the bottom of the sea, she says. The poets of Morocco call this the aferdu, the place where the staircase of poetry sinks into the ground. Perhaps only myth can capture the sense of this form.

Islands are scenes of appearance and disappearance, rising from the depths on a tide of submarine magma, only to be eroded once more by the sea. "Islands are either from before or for after humankind," writes Deleuze—they attest to both the emergence and the ultimate vanishing of the human.[34] Islands remind us that impermanence and precarity are the conditions with which all writing grapples. They are also the lived realities of so many of those that we as anthropologists write about. Tuvalu and Kiribati face the threat of an imminent inundation. Thousands seek to pass into Europe through the islands of the Mediterranean, many to wash ashore with no prospect of passage or return. A paper boat on turbulent waters, our writing struggles to respond to lives and worlds that are at constant risk of being swept away.

Notes

1. Stark and Rayne, El Delirio.
2. Blanchot, Work of Fire, 327–28.
3. De Certeau, Writing of History.
4. Jackson, Other Shore, 173.
5. Clifford and Marcus, Writing Culture, vii–viii.
6. Hurston, Mules and Men; Deloria, Waterlily. See also Cotera, Native Speakers.
7. The phrases "little tradition" and "minor literature" were put forward, respectively, by Robert Redfield's Little Community, and Kafka by Gilles Deleuze and Félix Guattari.
8. Hurston, Dust Tracks on a Road, 212–13.
9. Crapanzano, "Hermes Dilemma," 57.
10. Ingold, Being Alive, 16.
11. Bataille, Accursed Share, 209.
12. Spinoza, Ethics; Deleuze, Expressionism in Philosophy.
13. Lucretius, On the Nature of the Universe.
14. Agee, Let Us Now Praise Famous Men, 13.
15. Taussig, I Swear I Saw This, 1.
16. Geertz, Works and Lives, 5.
17. Taussig, I Swear I Saw This, 2.
18. Taussig, I Swear I Saw This, 5.
19. Deleuze, Bergsonism, 96.
20. Crapanzano, Imaginative Horizons, 39–65.
21. Malinowski, Diary in the Strict Sense of the Term, 98.
22. Serres, Troubadour of Knowledge, 65.
23. Nietzsche, Will to Power, 451.
24. Bataille, Impossible.
25. Benjamin, "Storyteller."
26. Castaing-Taylor and Paravel, Leviathan.
27. See Cymene Howe and Anand Pandian, "Lexicon for an Anthropocene Yet Unseen," Theorizing the Contemporary, Cultural Anthropology, July 12, 2016, https://culanth.org/fieldsights/803-lexicon-for-an-anthropocene-yet-unseen.
28. Eliot, Four Quartets, 14.
29. Zurita, Dreams for Kurosawa, 48.
30. Joyce, Finnegans Wake, 19.
31. See Ram Kapse, "A Hundred Years of the Andamans' Cellular Jail," Hindu (Chennai), December 21, 2005; Joyce, "Daniel Defoe." Such adventures though don't always

turn out as expected, as in Michel Tournier's subversive retelling of the Crusoe story, in which the island itself ("Speranza") features as an animate, feminized presence, by which Crusoe and later Friday are—literally—seduced. Tournier, *Friday*.

32. Shakespeare, *The Tempest*, 155.

33. Laugrand and Oosten, *Sea Woman*.

34. Deleuze, *Desert Islands*, 9.

The Ambivalent Archive

ANGELA GARCIA

Letter to Eugenia:

April 7, 2006

I am doing my best to keep my mind so it means a lot to know that you are doing ok. Everything is the same but I have blisters on my wrist. My skin hurts. I was upset at the c/o for not taking me to the infirmary. She ignores me everyday. I told her the yard had no shade and my skin was burning. I walked up to her and showed her my arms. She ignored me and looked the other way and I started yelling and waving my arms. I didn't hit her but my mind was saying STOP but I couldn't stop. She ignores me. I need my cream. Can you please let them know? PLEASE. She ziptied my hands behind my back. She made me sit in the yard even when everyone else was called inside. She separated me. I was afraid I would go to Level 5 because she threatened. I just had to sit in the sun like that for hours. Even though it was cold the sun burned.

I feel like I'm shouting and no one hears. It's hard to write because it hurts. I have to be honest with you. It bothers me my cellmate gets more visits from her family even though they live in Window Rock. I think that is further away. That's what she said but maybe she's just trying to get me. She's seems pretty nice though. She reminds me of Piñon because she is so short and round. Why don't you come? You can ask Laura to give you a ride. Her sister is in Level 3 and I heard from Brenda who is here too that she comes at least once a month.

You are in my prayers. Please keep me in your prayers. Please don't forget me. b.

This is an account of my encounter with a collection of letters written by three generations of female kin in New Mexico. It is a story about the pressures through which these letters emerged and the processes through which they were eventually shaped by me into an archive. I am not a historian and I am not specifically trained in archival methods, so I use the term *archive* with some reservation. Nevertheless, I call the collection of letters an archive and not, for example, an album or a scrapbook because I believe that the stories that inhabit it deserve to be taken seriously as historiography. I also want to underscore the materiality and meaning of the archive to illuminate writing as a site of intimacy and struggle, mourning and survival, both for the authors of the archived writing and for the anthropologist who engages it at a later moment.

This struggle is multisited. In *Archive Fever*, Jacques Derrida notes that the word *archive* stems from the Greek *arkhē*, the place where things begin and where power is exercised. The meaning of the word *archive* is traced to the house of citizens with the power to watch over and signify the documents therein.[1] This definition is unsettling to me but instructive, for the archive that I discuss here is located, literally, within my home. Over the last four years, it has traveled with me from New Mexico to Los Angeles to Oakland, has moved from a garage to a bedroom closet to a cabinet in a home office. No matter where I am within my home I am aware of its presence. The archive watches over me as much as I watch over it.

It's hard to write because it hurts.

These are Bernadette's words, written while she was incarcerated for a drug-related offense. Intended as private correspondence to her mother, her words seek to maintain a connection to life under the shadow of loss and isolation. The letter was eventually given to me, a kind of message in the bottle seeking an afterlife. I can only make sense of why this occurred within the context of broader relations that have connected lives and texts across time.

Anthropology is a part of this story. More than a "discipline," it is involved in the process of creating the connections between life and text, opening them up to new cadences and horizons. I have released these connections into their own materialization, into this ethnography—another kind of archive. My ethnography affirms, rather than covers up, its own ambivalences, in order to hold open the possibility of a return, a response, through which the archive is woven.

Why don't you come?

I met Bernadette in 2004, shortly after I returned to northern New Mexico's Española Valley. I have roots in the valley and had lived there as a child. I returned as an adult to conduct ethnographic fieldwork on heroin addiction; the Española Valley suffers one of the highest rates of heroin addiction and heroin-induced death in the United States.[2] Several of my relatives and schoolmates died of heroin overdose; still others struggle with the disease. Each week, I read the online version of the obituary section of the local paper, scouring names and photographs of the deceased, looking for old friends. These deaths haunt me and have prompted me to return (again and again) to the Española Valley and to the question of immemorial loss and the recovery of loss. What has been at stake for me is engaging loss as a form of relationality, which moves one toward the anticipation of an unknown future. The archive of letters I discuss in this chapter is one site for the development and enunciation of this melancholic movement.

The Rhythm of Writing

In *The Writing of History*, Michel de Certeau notes, "Writing speaks of the past only to inter it."[3] The rhythm of writing is the rhythm of mourning, which transforms absence into an enduring presence. The losses tied to Bernadette's letter are tied to my own. The archive materializes Bernadette's loss and opens up a space for my return.

Please don't forget me.

In 2004, Bernadette was ordered to attend a drug recovery program in the Española Valley, where I worked as an ethnographer and clinical staff. I observed her monthlong stay during my work on the night shift and often attended to her basic needs, like providing her food or medications or dialing the telephone for her outgoing calls. We were close in age and got along easily—so well we wondered whether we were friends as young children.

Having been a patient at the clinic before, Bernadette was used to the routine of rehab and avoided conflict with the other patients or staff. I was new and the only staff on duty at night, which often felt overwhelming. Without my ever asking, Bernadette helped me wash the evening dishes, sweep the floors, or fold the bedclothes. In casual conversation, I learned that her mother, Eugenia, was also addicted to heroin and suffered from depression. I also learned that Bernadette had two children, an estranged teenage son who lived with a distant relative and a young daughter named Ashley who had lived with her until her arrest.

On the day of Bernadette's departure from the clinic, an electronic monitoring bracelet was attached to her ankle and she was confined to her trailer until her impending trial date. Her only legal time away from home was to meet with her drug counselor or to attend recovery meetings. Still, she would steal a few moments between these meetings to visit her daughter, who was under the care of another relative, or her mother, who lived only a few miles away from her own. Mostly, however, Bernadette waited at home, alone.

I started yelling and waving my arms.

I visited her often during this period, making the short drive from my village to hers. I brought her groceries and cigarettes and she told me stories about her life. Often these stories centered on "another time," well before she started using heroin, when she and Eugenia lived in their ancestral village, in their ancestral home where Eugenia was born and where her own mother died. Bernadette spoke nostalgically about the home and the events that took place within it: birthday parties, Christmases, picking fruit from the apple and apricot trees on the surrounding land. But the bucolic image of the house and the quaint memories of it stood in tension with the other stories Bernadette would eventually tell me: stories of her mother's addiction and mental state, their deepening poverty, and her own growing loneliness and worry.

During an especially difficult time, Eugenia sold the beloved ancestral home, and the two relocated to a rented trailer in the town of Española. At the age of thirteen, Bernadette worked in the evenings and on weekends in order to contribute to the running of the new household. There were very few mental health or addiction services in the area, despite the growing drug problem. The profound stigma attached to being a heroin-addicted woman, especially a mother, made accessing these limited services even more challenging for Eugenia. Mother and daughter thus crafted their own services by caring for each other, often obtaining *medicina* (heroin) to relieve Eugenia's pain. Such work is typically conceived as an effort to provide care and protection, as well as a means to live.

Bernadette once described how when her mother was high, things would go back to normal. Eugenia would stop hurting or crying and would be released into feelings of love and tranquility, feelings Bernadette also craved and needed. But such feelings diminished as Eugenia's state worsened. Heroin soon became a medicine Bernadette needed too.

Sepia Tone

A childhood memory returns. I am at the weekly swap meet with my own mother on a hot summer afternoon. Neighbors become shop owners for a few hours, selling old tools, mixing bowls, outgrown clothes. There's the old man selling watermelons blessed by Jesus, the old woman with the live chickens squawking in their metal cages. Heat bounces off the black tarmac. I want to go home but my mother's not finished searching for something . . . *what*? I pull at her shirt. I am seven, maybe eight years old.

My mother gives me a dollar to buy a snack or books, to leave her in peace. I take the money and wander, watching my feet pass discarded household goods for sale. I peer over foldout tables where the finer objects are on display: jewelry, calculators, typewriters. I stop at a table covered with small, cardboard boxes juxtaposed like puzzle pieces. Each box contains photographs, many of them from bygone days. One of the boxes of photos captures my interest: it holds about two dozen images featuring the same family. They are on holiday somewhere far away from New Mexico.

The photos are small, no larger than the palm of my hand. The women have short bobbed hair and wear old-fashioned bathing suits or wide-legged pants and fitted blouses. The men wear neckties. Everyone is attractive and smiling, posing confidently by the beach, in front of a stately fountain, beside an elegant automobile. The old man selling the photos tells me they are his relatives. He is dark, Mexicano; the people in the image are white. I ask him how much the box of photos costs—he quotes me two dollars but accepts my one. I keep the photos hidden from my family.

In 2005, Bernadette was convicted of a felony-level drug crime and was given a five-year sentence at a women's prison located about 150 miles from home. Anticipating her conviction, she had already made arrangements to place her personal belongings into one of the many self-storage facilities in the Española Valley. Initially, Eugenia paid the monthly fee. When she fell behind in the payments, the contents of Bernadette's unit were auctioned off or destroyed by the facility management.

I visited Bernadette in prison many times. We'd sit together in the brightly lit visitation room amid families huddled over small metal tables bolted to the floor. Blue jumpsuits and shackled ankles and wrists differentiated prisoners from those in the free community. Although these visits were designated "open contact," meaning prisoners were not separated by a screen or intercom system, touch was prohibited. Bernadette was untouchable.

There were excruciating stretches of silence during our visits, which lasted several hours. I often thought of leaving, mentally counting to three, then to five, then to ten, trying to muster my body for exit. Bernadette may well have done the same. In any case, for likely very different reasons, we waited it out, saying good-bye only when the visitation guard demanded it.

Bernadette was paroled in 2009. She returned to the Española Valley and lived with her mother and daughter. Their housing situation was unstable: Bernadette couldn't find a job and Eugenia's monthly Social Security check barely covered the rent for their efficiency apartment. During a visit, I found their residence worryingly empty. I was concerned Bernadette might relapse, which seemed related to living with Eugenia, and suggested alternative living arrangements for her and her daughter. Bernadette was patient with my worries but said that there was nowhere else in the world she would rather be, or even could be. After such a long and painful period of separation, she had no intention of leaving.

Before we said good-bye, Bernadette asked me if I would do her a favor and presented me with a large box. She asked me to store it for her, explaining that she didn't want the contents around her or her daughter any longer, but that she didn't want to lose them either. I told her I needed to know what was inside before I could agree. She set the box on the floor and ripped off the tape that sealed its worn edges. She reached in and pulled out handful after handful of paper, letting them fall around her feet like leaves. "They're just letters," she said. "Nothing illegal, nothing to worry about." The following afternoon I carried the box back home with me to Los Angeles for what Bernadette called safekeeping.

Convergence

Another memory. We are heading south, caravanning down Interstate 25— my mother's yellow Volkswagen Bug, followed by her boyfriend's van and my uncle's pickup truck. Each vehicle is stuffed with our belongings. The dishes rattle in their boxes while my mother talks about a fresh start. My face presses against the backseat passenger window as I whisper good-bye to my friends, the juniper-covered hills, the river. My little sister squirms in my lap. My older brother squeezes his eyes shut, feigning sleep. Our mother pleads with us. *Look,* she says, *I've got to get out of there. One day you will understand.*

We arrive in Albuquerque. I can't decide if the distance between the two places is great or short. The two-bedroom house my mother arranged for us feels no different from our old house, and the new neighborhood looks just like the one up north. I tell my mother this but she insists that we are a world away. To prove her point she drives us to the west mesa. We climb onto the hood of the car and watch the city stretching below. Dusk turns to night and the amber lights of Albuquerque shimmer thickly. But we live south of the river, in darkness.

Blue Years

For several months, the box of letters sat undisturbed in my office. Then one morning I opened it, only partly by accident. I pulled out one letter and began to read, and then another, and so on. The basic plot was familiar to me: a mother's mistakes, a daughter's loneliness and worry. Reading the letters felt like weaving together the connective tissues of lives, images, and emotions that had been forced apart.

I wanted to read them all, felt I shouldn't, but did. Multiple calls to Bernadette after my period of passionate reading went unanswered. I flew to Albuquerque, drove north to Española, knocked on her apartment door, not knowing if she had moved on. After a couple of unsuccessful visits, I finally found Bernadette inside, visibly loaded. The box of letters was far from her mind.

The very first letter I drew from the box was undated and addressed to Eugenia. It says, "As long as you keep writing back I'll be OK. *Pero los días que no me escribes se sienten lonely. Se sienten azules . . .* [But the days you don't write me feel lonely. They feel blue . . .]" Bernadette's description of waiting and longing assumed the form of a haunting image—the image of lonely days, blue days. I still dwell in the density of feeling in this fragment and its palpable sense of loneliness and longing. The fragment carried excruciating affective intensity, in part because the letter's material texture makes legible the constraints that shaped Bernadette's words; the paper she used to write was the prison's blue-tinted stationery. Thus, the blueness of days is not only a melancholic account of Bernadette's interior world, but also an expression of the institutional barriers that structured her writing of despair.

Possession

Letter to Eugenia:

[undated excerpt]
I hope you are OK. How is mi'jita? I miss her so much. So much. So much. I am just trying to stay out of people's way so I can get back home. It is turning winter already. Sometimes I can smell firewood in my mind. Thanksgiving is coming. We're making decorations like we did when I was a kid, but they don't let us touch scissors. All the ladies are trying to make the best of it. What else can we do?

In 2006, a communications representative gave me a guided tour of the prison. I never saw Bernadette's cell, never saw where she slept, or wept, or wrote. Although I sent her letters and wired money at her request, I never received a letter from her. So I was surprised when I first saw Bernadette's broad and looping script, how her words shifted back and forth from print to cursive, English to Spanish—fashioning an intimate, bilingual language caught within the monolingual grammar of the prison. Toward the end of the letter excerpted above, Bernadette writes: "How is my little Ashley? I miss her so much. . . . *Cuídala bien, mamá. Cuídate bien.* [Take good care of her, mama. Take good care of yourself.]" She closes with "I know you can't come. *Pero* send me a little something? *Necesito escuchar tu voz* [I need to hear your voice]."

The address of emotion between mother and daughter, and Bernadette's struggle to maintain her own status as a mother, is entangled with the logics of power, displacement, and labor. Indeed, the paper that enabled Bernadette's writing was not free. Alongside the limited selection of junk food, toiletries, and menstrual products at the prison commissary was paper, at a cost of five cents per sheet, which, in the carceral economy, is more akin to one dollar, if not more.

But what are the costs, really, of writing, and what are the costs of not? How does connection and narration coexist with dislocation and silence? In what ways do Bernadette's letters sustain these equivalences and reframe our understanding of the relationship between history, human interiority, and narratability?

The process by which I have come to preserve, organize, and study the letters is neither direct nor simple. "Nothing could be at once more intimate and more alienable," Terry Eagleton writes. The letter is "part of the body which is detachable: torn from the very depths of the subject."[4] Eagleton's metaphor of tearing resonates with my own ambivalence in being keeper and curator of the archive. I have struggled with the idea of writing about it, sharing a fear that Roland Barthes describes as "making literature" out of private grieving.[5] That this danger suddenly seems more *real* to me now than it did before—that is, before I held the contents of Bernadette's thoughts and feelings (as compared to when she "told" me)—speaks, perhaps, to the kinds of seductions inherent in archival research.[6] It also raises important questions about the varying sensibilities we bring to different genres of ethnographic documentation, as well as the radically different insights these genres enable.

Over the past few years, I have returned to the letters and have occasionally written about them with feelings of uncertainty and inadequacy. I have also written about Bernadette and her family without saying anything about the letters, feeling that a key resource for my thinking was hidden from view.[7] In these other writings, I have given much attention to their history of economic and personal loss, and I draw, in part, on this history to account for Bernadette's desire for safekeeping.

Six months after she was released on parole, Bernadette discovered that Ashley saved the letters she sent from prison, even those letters written during the years Ashley could not yet read. Bernadette found the letters wrapped in plastic shopping bags beneath the bed they shared. This striking encounter might be richly analyzed in any number of ways and I frankly hesitate to analyze it at all. Yet I am reminded of Julia Kristeva's conception of maternal love and loss in relation to language. Kristeva writes, "It is being separated from his mother, despairingly, with no going back, that prompts [the child's] attempts to recuperate her, along with other objects, in his imagination and, later, in words."[8] From this perspective, Ashley's own safekeeping of Bernadette's letters might be said to represent her recuperation of her mother via words and dreams, which may have afforded her sorrowful pleasure at a time of painful separation.

Double Narrative

As it turns out, Ashley wasn't the only one to recuperate and imagine, for Bernadette also saved many of the letters that Eugenia and, eventually, Ashley wrote to her. But as prisoners are only allowed to keep a limited number of personal items, Bernadette was forced to part with many letters in order to make room for new ones. Bodies of correspondence that work as relations and shared history are thus curtailed, pointing to the inherently partial and political nature of any archive. In a recent interview with me, Bernadette described the fraught practice of sorting through letters and determining which ones she could part with.

> I had two piles [of letters]. One was letters I would trade in. They were old or maybe seemed unimportant. Or I memorized them and just didn't think I needed them no more. The other pile I wanted to keep no matter what. . . . I checked those two piles all the time. I worried I put one in the wrong place, you know, the wrong pile. Like I accidentally was getting rid of something that I really wanted to keep, and when I checked through the piles I was always changing my mind about the ones I thought I could get rid of because they all seemed important again.

Referring to the constant sorting and self-doubt, Bernadette described sometimes feeling like she was going crazy. At the same time, the ritual of sorting was one practical, if enforced, mechanism of preserving her severed connection, and perhaps even her sanity. She eloquently and painfully underscored how the structures that surround an archive's production and preservation are just as important as the documents themselves.

After nearly two years of anxious sorting, a more experienced cellmate suggested that Bernadette instruct family members to write on only one side of each sheet of paper, thereby leaving the other side blank. In this way, Bernadette could respond on the blank page, send the letter back, thereby saving both letters and precious money. But this epistolary practice raised different anxieties, such as whether her unstable mother would manage to keep the letters she sought to preserve. (At the time she did not know her daughter was performing this function.) Still, Bernadette tried this new method and a few dozen of the letters in the archive are, in fact, two.

In the shared gesture of writing and saving, narrative is always double narrative, and the relation between self, text, and time is entangled. Ashley and Bernadette's appropriation of the archive expands the signifying capacities of language, endowing new meaning and significance to these texts. I, the most recent curator of these letters, am now implicated in this process too.

The Act of Binding

In 2010 I hired a young women's studies major to help organize the letters. I wanted them to be taken care of, to acquire respectability. I thought I knew what that would look like and created an organizational system, at which point I began calling them an archive.

My assistant's first task was to photocopy each letter three times. She neatly numbered each duplicate in pencil based on the thematic system I devised and began filing the duplicates accordingly. Watching her handle the letters (that is, their duplicates), I became anxious and possessive. I soon had her do unrelated work. My feelings were stirred less by her reading or conceiving the letters as, for example, sites of memory or contestation, but in her encountering them physically. It was as if the letters were alive, vulnerable to a stranger's touch.

Three years later, the copies of the letters are separated into folders that hang in a wood filing cabinet in my home. The originals are preserved in plastic sleeves, tightly bound in three-ring folders. I pull the metal rings of one binder open and take a letter out of its plastic sleeve. It is thin and wrinkled, torn-edged, yellowed. The letter "pricks me . . . bruises me" like a photograph.[9] It is not just the text but also the image of the text—the uncertain print script, the misspellings—as well as the image of one letter isolated from another. I carefully slip it back in the sleeve and snap the metal rings shut.

Perhaps the hurt is not the letter, or what it is witness to, but the archival process itself: the process of copying, separating, and staging. I consider taking the letters out of their sleeves, tossing them into the air, letting them fall where they may. An intricately entangled web of hurt and hope, a closer approximation to the complicated story the letters weave. But this is not a story of chance.

I try treating the sleeves in the binder like pages from a book—a more conventional means to explore relations of dislocation and connection, loss and longing, how power is embedded and contested by the writing of letters. Yet, as Maurice Blanchot emphasizes, the act of writing, the desire and necessity of it, cannot find its fulfillment in a book.[10] I consider the fragment, a representational form akin to the personal and social fragmentation that structured this particular history. But related to this fragmentation is a desire for cohesion; indeed, the archive was made by and through this desire. What form, then, should guide the creation and interpretation of an archive whose texts are tied both to the longing for connection and the experience of isolation?

Voice on the Skin

It is unknown how many letters were intercepted, destroyed, or lost, although Bernadette frequently wrote about this concern, particularly during stretches of unrequited communication. For example, in a passage in a letter to her mother written in November 2006, she states, "I feel like shit. You haven't written in a long time. I think they have it out for me. Someone here doesn't like me. Or maybe you are forgetting me?" Bernadette also expressed these concerns during our phone conversations. She was convinced that letters written by and addressed to her were being blocked. The holidays were approaching and she was anxious and depressed. My first impulse was to write her regularly, as if letters from me, a prisoner pen pal, might ease her loneliness. But I also worried that a letter from me might exacerbate the absence of writing she longed for.

I visited Bernadette around Christmas. She was noticeably heavier, downcast, and extremely anxious. It had been several weeks since she had seen or heard from her mother or daughter and she worried that they had forgotten about her. What if her mother moved away? What if she did not regain custody of her daughter? How would she, Bernadette, live? I tried to soothe her worries with updates from family members and friends and by offering empty assurances that things would be okay. In response, Bernadette placed her cuffed hands on the small table in the visitation room and spread her fingers, revealing raw, bitten skin. "I am eating myself," she said.

Self-mutilation provides a "voice on the skin" when the actual voice is forbidden or constrained.[11] A gestural modality of language, it expresses the boundary between existence and nonexistence, self and other, pain and relief. Maurice Merleau-Ponty writes that gestural language "makes its appearance like the boiling point of a liquid, when in the density of being, volumes of empty space are built up and move outwards."[12] Drawing on this metaphor, one might say that her unrequited letters nullified Bernadette's possibility of speech. But her need to speak swelled. Constrained by the physical and social constraint of incarceration, Bernadette's speech was forced back into herself, eventually breaking out through self-injury. She compulsively bit her fingers day and night, eliciting and then tending to her own wounds.

Bernadette blamed the biting on insomnia. She told me that when her fingers had become badly infected, the prison infirmary treated her with antidepressants. Given her status as an "addict," she was denied prescription medication that might have helped her sleep. The antidepressants leveled off the problem temporarily, but the biting eventually returned, and with renewed urgency. The infirmary supplied gloves that prison guards locked onto her hands at night. Bernadette described the gloves as a kind of torture, a double imprisonment. Gloves locked on, her sores began to blister and her sleeplessness worsened. Eventually, the infirmary's nurse gave up and, in Bernadette's words, told her to eat herself to the bone.

Several weeks after my visit with Bernadette, Eugenia wrote her daughter the following letter.

Mija,

I know you are angry. Ashley is too. It is a long way and the pressure on me is heavy. *I am going to meetings 2 or 3 times a week and am just trying to make*

ends meet. I'm barely making it. I have a new job. It isn't much but I am hoping to buy us a car to make travel easier. Hopefully you will be out soon
right? That is what I hear.

We stopped *celebrating the holidays after my mother died.* Maybe that is why
I was not a good mother to you or there like you need me. *I'm sorry.* Ashley knows she has a mother. It is not the same. She made a pretty card
for you, its very pretty and she can write now. I want to send it but you
think you will not receive it so I am saving it for you for when you return.
Unless you want me to send it. Tell me.

I am sorry for all of the pain I caused you mija. I am trying to make it up
now. I promise to write more and visit more. I am trying to get another
phone plan so that I can receive your calls. Be strong. You are always in
my thoughts.[13]

Horizon

In June 2012, I returned to the Española Valley, the archive packed in a suit-
case. My motel room was dark and depressing but offered a glimpse of the
Sangre de Cristo Mountains. Bernadette visited me there during the day. We'd
each sit on one of the full-sized beds, surrounded by the letters. Bernadette
helped provide context, interpretation, and sequence. She modified my
filing system by adding themes that I overlooked, such as men, money,
and dreams. These additions were also interventions that called into question my own thematic desires and logics, as well as our differences in social
class.

At night, we went to the Dreamcatcher cinema and took in a movie—
usually a loud Hollywood blockbuster that erased the heaviness of our day's
work. Sometimes Ashley joined us, but Eugenia never did. She was sick
again and unable to engage in conversation or entertainment.

During our time working together, Bernadette expressed her desires for
the archive. Sometimes, she said I could "do whatever" with the letters, as
if they were a burden she no longer wanted to think about. On a few occasions, she wondered if we might make a book out of them. But as soon as
she began to imagine it, she began to question the point of it and doubted
whether she (or her mother or daughter) had written anything worth
reading.

One afternoon I suggested the idea of an archival website that, in addition to presenting their letters, would enable other users to share their stories and, hopefully, create a community of writers and readers. Bernadette was intrigued by this idea but ultimately couldn't imagine how such a project might work. Where would it be, she asked? Who would find it? She reminded me that she, and many women like her, have limited access and experience with the technology. Her question about form, audience, and accessibility was a critique of the social implications of constructing an archive and also the act of reading it.

In the shadow of these discussions, the archive remains in its wood filing cabinet. My charge remains to hold on to it, care for it, for reasons that sometimes feel obvious, other times ambiguous; it's sometimes a privilege, other times a burden. Still, the archive's endurance suggests the possibility of being drawn upon, understood and related to, well into the future.

Notes

Parts of this chapter appear in "The Blue Years: An Ethnography of a Prison Archive," *Cultural Anthropology* 31, no. 4 (November 2016): 571–94.

1. Derrida writes that the concept of the archive "shelters in itself . . . this memory of the name. But it also *shelters* itself from this memory." Derrida, *Archive Fever*, 2.

2. Heroin addiction in the Española Valley primarily affects the Hispano population, which traces its ancestry back to the Spanish colonialists. Among Hispanos, addiction is commonly shared across multiple generations of kin, who often live in a single, shared household. This arrangement reflects Hispano traditions and ideals of family as cohesive, self-reliant, and enduring. It also reflects—and, to a degree, offsets—conditions of poverty, which include high rates of unemployment, addiction, and chronic illness and the pervasive incarceration of kin. For more on this topic, see Garcia, *Pastoral Clinic*.

3. De Certeau, *Writing of History*, 101.

4. Quoted in Steedman, *Dust*, 74.

5. Barthes, *Mourning Diary*, 23.

6. Freshwater, "Allure of the Archive."

7. As Michael Jackson notes, letter writing between anthropologists and subjects, often long after fieldwork is "completed," is fairly common. With a few notable exceptions, these letters rarely make it into the explicit production of ethnographic writing. While not letters per se, João Biehl's engagement with the writings of Catarina presents an evocative example of the centrality of writing in the lives of others and how this "other" writing might be epistemologically and aesthetically engaged in our own. See Biehl, *Vita*.

8. Kristeva, *Tales of Love*, 5.
9. Barthes, *Camera Lucida*, 53.
10. Blanchot, *Writing of Disaster*.
11. McLane, "Voice on the Skin," 107.
12. Merleau-Ponty, *Phenomenology of Perception*, 196.
13. The portions in italics have been translated from the Spanish.

2

WRITING WITH CARE

MICHAEL JACKSON

At the end of our first day of discussions, we strolled down to the center of Santa Fe. Angela knew the town all too well. She grew up in northern New Mexico and had left when she was seventeen. In her prizewinning book on dispossession and heroin addiction in the Española Valley she writes of the years in which she kept her memories of the beautiful desert landscapes and the dark history of the region separate in her mind until she returned to New Mexico to begin fieldwork in January 2004 and recognized the inextricable connections between these physical and social worlds.[1] Angela's comments on the poverty and despair that pervade this idyllic region echo observations by other writers who have chronicled the lives of artists and seekers who, throughout the twentieth century, sought in the Southwest oracular wisdom and utopian communities only to visit upon local Hispanics and Native Americans further acts of social violence.[2] Thus, Lois Palken Rudwick broaches the same question that Angela addresses in *The Pastoral Clinic*, namely the way that romantic art and literature systematically mask "the acts of violence that [have] punctuated this seeming rural paradise," ignoring "the interethnic, racial and class strife that has been a persistent reality of the region."[3]

We approached the plaza as sightseers, along a street of Disneyfied[4] tourist boutiques, crammed with expensive ethnic souvenirs. At the center of the plaza, and directly in front of the old Palace of the Governors, stood an obelisk—called the Soldier's Monument—commemorating the "brave victims who have perished in the various wars with the savage Indians." In 1974, in broad daylight, a young man stepped over the low fence around the monument and chiseled out the word "savage." But despite calls for the complete removal of the monument, including a petition in 2000 by the National Association for the Advancement of Colored People, the monument stays put—a bone of contention between Hispanic locals and "Anglos," residents and tourists, non-Indian street merchants and the New Mexican Historical Society and souvenir stores, teenagers and the city government, "and between those who want to be rid of the obelisk and the historic preservation establishment that likes to point out that the obelisk is about the only thing of historic value left on the Plaza."[5]

There is another side to this question of what we choose to see and not see—landscapes of "deep and troubled beauty"[6] in which poor pueblos are hidden from the highways, through which a dying river flows, in which are strewn thousands of used syringes, and where ruins and ghosts remind all those, like Angela, who leave the beaten track, that history is not past; it is inscribed and reinscribed in the bodies and souls of the living. This is the question of what we write, and how we write. For Angela Garcia, it is a matter of "writing with care"—not simply taking precautions against revealing the identities of one's interlocutors or betraying confidences shared in a clinical setting, but a concern to "capture the humanity, vulnerability, and hopefulness" of lives that are so readily written off in the discourse of the state and public media.[7]

This question of existential care—of a desire to do justice to the other[8]—also finds expression in my own work. The ethnographic encounter, I have long found, is a transitional space, a "place where we live."[9] Echoing the image of the American Southwest as a borderlands, D. W. Winnicott's notion of a transitional space suggests a safe place where people can free themselves from old attachments, obsessions, and addictions and come into their own, realizing hitherto suppressed potentialities. This is at once a location in which the lives of those we study may be changed and where we ourselves are changed. To cite Winnicott again, it is a "holding environment," reminiscent of the intimate space where a mother holds and handles her baby, meeting its needs, giving it comfort and care, allowing it to find its voice, to explore the world around, and finally to walk out into this world on its own two feet.[10] Surely it is not too far-fetched to speak of ethnographic writing as a transitional space or holding environment in which the voices of one's interlocutors can be heard, where their presence can be felt, and where the writer refuses to cast too long a shadow, dominate the conversation, or hog the limelight. And surely this touches on the struggle of which Angela speaks in "The Ambivalent Archive," where she is charged with the task of holding in safekeeping these orphaned letters, taking it upon herself to do justice to Bernadette's correspondence in the way she writes in response. "The archive watches over me as much as I watch over it."

In this subjective in-between, there can be no final conclusion, no closure, for the relationship is perpetually open to revision, and any text that is born of this relationship will inevitably invite critique.[11] One can *show* something, but one may not *know* anything with complete certainty. It is in this sense that the ethnographer is more like a witness than an analyst or activist. One testifies to things one does not necessarily know what to do about. But through one's writing, the reader may be moved to see the world in a new way and to act differently within it.

Notes

1. Garcia, *Pastoral Clinic*, 6.
2. Rudwick, *Utopian Vistas*, 16.
3. Rudwick, *Utopian Vistas*, 16, 9–10.
4. Weigle, "From Desert to Disney World."
5. Mitchell and Staeheli, "Turning Social Relations into Space," 362.
6. Garcia, *Pastoral Clinic*, 210.
7. Garcia, *Pastoral Clinic*, 34–35.
8. Garcia, *Pastoral Clinic*, 205.
9. Winnicott, *Playing and Reality*, 122.
10. Winnicott, *The Maturational Processes and the Facilitating Environment*, 46.
11. Garcia, *Pastoral Clinic*, 205.

3

After the Fact: The Question of Fidelity in Ethnographic Writing

MICHAEL JACKSON

"Well! I've often seen a cat without a grin," thought Alice; "but a grin without a cat! It's the most curious thing I ever saw in my life!"
—LEWIS CARROLL, *Alice in Wonderland*

When Anand Pandian and Stuart McLean invited me to join a four-day seminar on literary anthropology at the School for Advanced Research (SAR) in Santa Fe, I was both flattered and wary. For though I had long been convinced that clear thinking required lucid writing, I had an aversion to ethnographies that were gratuitously literary, or in which the line between the documented and the invented was blurred. I was troubled by the idea of a grin without a cat! It was all very well borrowing narrative conventions, figurative language, and montage from fiction, poetry, and cinema in order to give life to a text and counter the deadening effects of academic jargon and abstraction. But such experimentation should not, in my view, annul the distinction between literature, which freely invents other worlds and other lives, and ethnography, which seeks to do justice to real people in real lifeworlds. Despite these reservations, I felt that literary anthropology might offer new ways of addressing the unresolved relationship in sociocultural anthropology and Western thought in general, between being and thought—sometimes phrased as a contrast between the empirical and the theoretical. As such, the challenge of ethnographic writing might be construed as the development of new techniques for integrating the arts of showing with the sciences of knowing.

Techniques of showing and knowing have typically invoked notions of truth as a kind of fidelity: fidelity to the facts, fidelity to genre conventions and disciplinary boundaries, fidelity to the people whose lives we write about, fidelity to certain standards of logical rigor, scientific impartiality, or proper conduct. Accordingly, ethnographers often find themselves ambivalent about what it may mean, ethically, empirically, and epistemologically, to do justice to life.

Fidelity and Authenticity in Anthropology

A few months ago, I was describing to a colleague my research on the life of Leoš Janáček. I was fascinated, I told Michael Lesley, by the love story that had inspired some of Janáček's greatest compositions—and the way it broached the issue of marital infidelity (since many of his late works were inspired by his "love affair" with a woman thirty-eight years his junior), as well as Janáček's use of peasant songs and dances in his own compositions. Did these borrowings involve betrayals—a cruel indifference to his wife's feelings in the first instance and a blatant exploitation of peasant creativity in the second? And I mentioned other composers, including Dvořák, Kodály, Bartók, and Vaughan Williams, who used folk music as the basis for their own compositions, often without specific acknowledgment of their sources. Undoubtedly, my misgivings reflected my own anxieties as an ethnographer, recording oral traditions, interrogating informants, and collecting the stories of strangers. Even when given carte blanche by those who allowed me to live among them and know their secrets, I was often unable to rid my mind of the thought that I was profiting from things that did not, strictly speaking, belong to me. There lurked a suspicion that I was part of an underhanded and ongoing Western tradition of pilfering and piracy, and that this was somehow connected with what I construed as the impertinent jargon of anthropology itself.

Michael offered to send me a CD in which the Romanian folksongs recorded by Béla Bartók in 1910 and 1912[1] alternated with the orchestral compositions he based on them, and he suggested that listening to these recordings might help answer my questions.

Over the next few days, I played the *Muzsikás* CD many times—on my car stereo, in the solitude of my study. The folksongs affected me deeply. Bartók's Romanian Dances had been the background music to my life at twenty-one. But now, hearing these poignant, heartrending voices from a hundred years ago, from a world one knows will be largely obliterated in the mid-twentieth century, I was overwhelmed. These blackbirds whistling in a summer forest, that remote voice struggling to be heard above the static of an inadequate recording machine: the tragedy and passion of European history were not only conveyed in these fugitive sounds, but also made me aware that even though our lives become lost in the ocean of history, something of our lifeworld survives, albeit fragmented, mutilated, transformed.

I also felt this way when, years ago, I heard an old BBC recording of a nightingale in a Surrey wood, its trills and cadences overshadowed by the pulsing drone of German bombers high overhead, moving en masse toward London. At such moments I am filled with wonderment that these beautiful, melodic, or ambiguous things somehow survive the ravages of time—like the thumbprint of a potter on a piece of terra-cotta tile from the site of a Roman villa in southern England, a bone flute unearthed from a Paleolithic grave, or the fragment of a manuscript from two thousand years ago on which is written the earliest and most discussed phrase in the history of philosophy.

My thoughts went back to my first years of fieldwork in northern Sierra Leone. There were compelling echoes of Bartók's Romanian songs in the songs I recorded in remote Kuranko villages over forty years ago. Many of these songs are sung without instrumental accompaniment; others require the beat of drums, or the music of xylophones, flutes, or harps, recalling the deeds of illustrious chiefs and courageous hunters. Still other songs mark critical junctures in Kuranko stories, and the recurring themes of these stories—the betrayal of friends, the neglect of orphans, the unjust treatment of a junior wife or younger sibling, the fickleness of women—brought me back to the theme of faithlessness that had emerged in the course of my research on Leoš Janáček, not to mention the questions Michael Lesley had broached regarding the monstrous betrayals that marked the history of the twentieth century.

For positivist social science, fidelity immediately suggests faithfulness to the facts, but as Edmund Husserl pointed out in *The Crisis of European Sciences and Transcendental Phenomenology* a narrow empirical measure of truth "on the plane" is a truth of surfaces, of what appears to be self-evident, "objective," "natural," and within the reach of reason. But this conflation of the rational with the objective and the natural blinds us to deeper, more "spiritual" dimensions of human experience.[2] Within a year of Husserl's death in 1938, the implicit connection that he had hinted at—between the "crisis of European science" and the rise of fascism—became all too clear.[3]

The notion that thought can either betray life or be faithful to life informs the work of many writers in the phenomenological tradition, who also share a commitment to the craft of writing as a way of making conceptual thought do justice to lived experience. For John Berger, "Authenticity comes from a single faithfulness: that to the ambiguity of experience. Its energy is to be found in how one event leads to another. Its mystery is not in the words but on the page."[4] For Jacques Derrida, ambiguity is also of the essence. One thinks and writes at the limit of what it is possible to say. Philosophy exists in relation to what lies beyond philosophy, in the margins, in the penumbra of what is visible, at the limits of what can be heard.[5] Hence Derrida declares, "I dream of a writing that would be neither philosophy nor literature, nor even contaminated by one of the other, while still keeping—I have no desire to abandon this—the memory of literature and philosophy."[6] These allusions to the irreducibility of experience to the words with which we describe it or the analytical means with which we comprehend it strengthen the case for *verisimilitude*, which moves beyond the epistemological question of fidelity to the methodological question as to how one can best create the *appearance* of truth or reality without, however, abandoning the ethical and political demands that even appearances may be judged by. Consider storytelling, which is an art of fabulation and make-believe that often succeeds in making life more edifying and bearable than the "truest" doctrine or most "proven" fact. Hannah Arendt speaks of "the ancient fear" or "nightmare" that has haunted humankind even before philosophy and natural science exacerbated it—the fear that our senses cannot be trusted, that reality and truth lie behind a screen of appearances, and that what seems to us to be solid and incontrovertible is a deception perpetrated by some evil spirit, or simply a dream.[7] Perhaps literary anthropology holds out the promise that we may finally do justice to appearances and find virtue in verisimilitude without the fear that we are behaving unprofessionally, or repudiating science.

New Morning

Although my paper was scheduled for discussion on the first morning of the seminar, I was dissatisfied with the binaries I had invoked in writing it—showing versus knowing, fidelity versus infidelity, anthropology versus literature. So when my shuttle from Albuquerque dropped me off at the SAR on the evening before the seminar began, and I entered a room where several participants were already getting acquainted, I wondered, like Alice, if I had come to the wrong place or had come to the right place on false pretenses.

At some time during that first evening, someone said, "It's like that Luis Buñuel movie, *The Exterminating Angel*"—a group of aristocrats finding themselves trapped in a room where they have gathered after an evening at the opera, and unable to lift the curse or break the spell they seem to be under. *The error is reification*, I thought to myself. The sclerotic tendency of thought to block the arteries along which the lifeblood of the world travels from heart to brain, and the analogous tendency of social systems to seal off openings that allow the flourishing of new life, particularly among the oppressed or marginalized. In Buñuel's film, the imprisoned dinner guests are forced to drop the masks and mannerisms of their privileged world and come to terms with their brute humanity. And as my colleagues began to share their experiments and experiences in ethnographic writing, I asked myself why I should persist in policing the borderlands they were crossing, insisting on a strict separation of poetry and ethnography, keeping them on either side of the tracks, as it were, like the rich and the poor in and around Santa Fe. Whence this inner voice of caution?

In the late 1970s I wrote an "ethnographic novel."[8] It took me ten years to find a publisher, by which time I was unemployed and unable to find work because, as I was told during one job interview, "the consensus . . . [is] that you are not really committed to anthropology."[9] As for my poems, though many had been directly inspired by my fieldwork in Sierra Leone,[10] I had learned to keep my poetic work strictly separate from my academic publications, aware that the former was regarded as inimical to the latter. Was it because my ethnographic work had been derided and invalidated for so many years as overly literary—and, by implication, empirically flawed— that I now sought to protect myself from accusations of unprofessionalism or poetic license by inadvertently adopting the conservative mask I had for so long held in contempt?

On the first morning of the seminar I woke before sunup, dressed quickly, and walked out onto Garcia Street. A sandy trail ran parallel to the paved road, and I hoped it would lead out of town and into the desert. There was not a cloud in the sky. Birds were singing. The sun was rising over a distant hill. Though I did not yet know the names of the sage-green, spindly plants alongside the trail—juniper, barberry, gambel oak, banana yucca, wax currant, buffalo berry—I felt immediately at home in this bleached and rose-hued landscape. Comparable places came to mind. The Greek island of Aegina in the Saronic Gulf. The Tanami Desert in Central Australia. But then I heard the muffled cor coro coo of a ringdove and declared aloud, "My God, it's the south of France!"

Thirty years ago, I spent ten months in Menton on a literary fellowship, and I wrote my first novel. I had waited a long time for a chance to take a break from ethnography and try my hand at fiction, and I did not want this sabbatical to end. But my wife, Pauline, fell gravely ill, and we left precipitously for England where she was diagnosed with cancer. Six months later she died.

Tears scalded my eyes as I remembered our days in the south of France and contemplated the poignant and unpredictable course of every human life—punctuated by exhilarating beginnings and devastating endings, by attachment, separation, and loss.

Hannah Arendt speaks of the new as natality—the "startling unexpectedness" that "is inherent in all beginnings and all origins" and occurs "against the overwhelming odds of statistical laws and their probability, which for all practical, everyday purposes amounts to certainty." When I first met Pauline, it was such a moment. Whatever my life had been until that point, it would never be the same again. But if every new departure appears "in the guise of a miracle,"[11] so too does every ending. Both take us by surprise, breaking with everything we assumed to be constant. Yet most of us go on. Life is renewed. Though we may wish to keep faith with what has been, memorializing and idealizing the past, life, like a great river, sweeps us away into another sea. And so we find ourselves torn between the old and the new. This is why, when I fell in love again, I felt for some time that I was betraying Pauline, just as when I turned to writing fiction in Menton I felt that I was betraying the people to whom I was beholden as an ethnographer. How else can I explain the dreams that tormented me during my first weeks in Menton, when Kuranko friends appeared to me, demanding to know why I had forsaken them by not returning to Sierra Leone?

The week before I flew to New Mexico, I had delivered my final lecture in a course I had been teaching at Harvard on "The Shock of the New." At the heart of this course was the mystery of human bonds—the bonds of love between family or friends; the bonds of memory that bind us to the past, connect us to a natal place or certain landscapes; ties with a homeland or heirloom; the bonds we form with religious or political figures, imaginary friends, utopian ideals, ancestors, mentors, and guides; or the double binds that oblige us to recapitulate the prejudices of the class or culture in which we were raised, even as we pay lip service to another worldview. The course was also about how we sometimes break such bonds—in leaving home, in forging a life for ourselves, in converting to a new faith or losing an old one—or cope with the trauma of events we would not wish on anyone, when the bonds that define our identity and give us security are shattered by the loss of a loved one, a war that turns us into refugees, or a natural disaster, events that mark forever a line between life before and life after. But the impact of life-altering and earth-shattering events may be both terrible and wonderful, and I had explored the theme of human resilience: how new growth may follow destruction and life can be renewed through death.

Yet it was only now, as I stumbled out into the desert, that I began to connect the theme of my course with the critical events of my own life and the research I had recently completed with migrants from three African countries (Sierra Leone, Burkina Faso, and Uganda) in three European cities (London, Amsterdam, and Copenhagen).

When I summarized my paper later that morning, I was at pains to point out that the migration stories that would appear in my forthcoming book, *The Wherewithal of Life: Migration, Ethics and the Question of Well-Being*, were allegories of life itself, in which reconciling the old and the new is always problematic. And I said that I wanted to link the ethical dilemmas of going beyond our natal world to build a new life in another with the vexed issue in literary anthropology of how exact science can be reconciled with creative art, and whether we place at risk our obligations to our subjects when we exercise literary license in ethnographic work.

In his *Essays in Radical Empiricism*, William James deploys the term *experience* to cover both concept and life. *Experience*, he notes, is a double-barreled word. It covers the planted field and the person who plants it—what is acted upon and who is acting, the field and the fieldworker.[12] There are therefore always two aspects to any experience, and the objective *what* and the subjective *who* are inextricably connected and mutually determining. Yet anthropology often assigns a superior explanatory value to the impersonal political, cultural, or genetic forces that shape *who* we are, effectively reducing the human subject to a mere epiphenomenon. Despite paying lip service to agency, anthropologists frequently find themselves in an epistemological quandary as they struggle to achieve the classical scientific goal of identifying the causes and conditions that shape an individual life while keeping faith with the humanistic impulse to recognize the capacity of people to live their lives on their own terms. Can one do justice to both scientific and humanistic aspirations, or will one be inevitably biased toward one extreme or the other?

One answer to this dilemma is to bracket out all a priori notions of what is "scientific" or "humanistic" and to explore the life situations that typically give rise to the different modes of human experience that become reified in these ways. What are the ontological origins of the view that some things are outer or objective and other things are inner or subjective? When do we focus on what is what and when do we focus on who is who? In a recent book, entitled *Between One and One Another*, I had argued that human consciousness constantly oscillates between egocentric and sociocentric extremes, one moment self-absorbed and the next alert to the voice and needs of another. This sense that the other is never entirely identical with oneself and that one can never be known by the other in the same way that one knows oneself produces an intersubjective aporia that is almost impossible to bridge. As with intersubjectivity, so with our relations with the world at large. There is always a tension, Gabriel Marcel observes, between problems that admit of a solution and mysteries that defy our best attempts to fathom them.[13] While the romantic is prepared to leave everything in the realm of mystery, and the person of faith allows God to have the final say, the scientist puts his trust in instruments and methods that neutralize observer bias and promise certain knowledge. Yet all these different worldviews may be regarded as strategies or defense mechanisms for overcoming the existential uncertainties and aporias to which I have alluded.

Aporia literally means "lacking a path" (*a-poros*), a path that is impassable. In particular, *poros* connotes a sea-lane or river road—passages that leave no permanent trace, surfaces "widowed of routes," where there are no stable landmarks and every trail must be blazed anew.[14] An aporia is where we find ourselves out of our depth, in difficulties, all at sea. "The sea is . . . the aporetic space *par excellence*," writes Sarah Kofman, "and it is still the best metaphor for the aporia of discourse."[15] More generally, an aporia is a "puzzle," a "question for discussion" or "state of perplexity," and the aporetic method for broaching problems without offering immediate solutions is exemplified by the Socratic method and the philosophical skepticism of thinkers such as Pyrrho, Timon, Arcesilaus, Diogenes, and Sextus Empiricus. Influenced by Pyrrho, Montaigne advocated that we accept both good and ill since both "are one substance with our life"—a life that is "composed, like the harmony of the world, of discords as well as of different tones, sweet and harsh, sharp and flat, soft and loud."[16]

This brings me back to Janáček, whose passionate yet unrequited love affair with Kamila Stösslová, who was thirty-eight years younger than the composer and married with two children, inspired some of his greatest music, including the famous String Quartet Number 2 (subtitled *Intimate Letters*). To read some of the seven hundred letters Janáček wrote to his "gypsy muse" over the last ten years of his life is to be reminded that love, paradoxically, brings together in the lovers' hearts and minds a sense of being certain that one knows the other completely *and* a sense that neither can adequately explain the attraction between them—since "elective affinities," as Goethe observed, resemble certain chemical bonds in which unity and disunity are curiously copresent, and "antithetical qualities make possible a closer and more intimate union."[17] There are echoes here of what John Keats called a "negative capability" of "being in uncertainties, Mysteries, doubts, without any irritable reaching after fact & reason."[18]

In negative capability, fidelity and infidelity are not necessarily antithetical. Let me explain, or rather show, what I mean.

Constant Craving

Some years ago, I heard a talk on National Public Radio by A. Scott Berg, whose biography of the legendary American editor Maxwell Perkins was published in 1978. The subject of Berg's talk bore an uncanny similarity to the story of Janáček and Stösslová that I had researched and written about in *The Other Shore*,[19] and something of the same romantic hope informed the epistolary friendship between Maxwell Perkins and Elizabeth Lemmon— the relationship that Berg had made the focus of his talk.

In researching his biography, Berg had worked through a long list of names of individuals associated with Perkins, leaving the seemingly least significant until last. Among the barely mentioned names in the Perkins archive was the name of Elizabeth Lemmon, and when Berg traveled to

Virginia to pay her a visit he was convinced that his trip would be a waste of time.

In her youth, Lemmon had studied operatic singing, and in her old age she liked to listen to an opera in the afternoons. She invited her guest to join her. Though Berg politely sat through the opera, he had already lost interest in pressing this eighty-four-year-old woman to explain her relationship, if any, with the subject of his biography. As he was preparing to leave, he was therefore surprised when his elderly hostess asked if he would be interested in seeing Max's letters. Lemmon then went to her bedroom and returned with a shoebox full of carefully preserved, chronologically ordered, and neatly bundled letters. "These are Max's love letters to me," she told Berg. "I was Max's confidante. . . . Ours was a secret love."

Berg instantly realized that he had stumbled on a treasure, and that these letters revealed a dimension of Perkins's life of which he knew nothing.

Lemmon would not allow Berg to take the letters away, though she invited him to visit her again, which he did several times, listening to an opera with her before spending several hours reading through the letters and taking notes for the biography he had, until this encounter, considered effectively finished.

There remained, however, the mystery as to what kind of love affair it had been. The letters provided no clear answer, despite their deeply confessional character, and once again Berg was loath to ask Lemmon a direct question.

Aware of what Berg must be wondering but reluctant to broach, Lemmon took the initiative. One day, as Berg was leaving the house, she declared, "I never slept with Max. I never kissed him."

Indeed, they met only rarely.

The first meeting was in April 1922. Max had been married to Louisa Saunders Perkins for twelve years, and they had five daughters. A devoted mother, Louisa also had a career as an actor/director and writer. This may have contributed to the growing distance between husband and wife, though the seeds of their incompatibility were probably there from the beginning, and only their shared Catholicism and devotion to their daughters sustained the marriage. Elizabeth was a close friend of Louisa's. Both were socialites who enjoyed financial security and had attended the best schools. But when Louisa introduced her husband to her friend, she realized that Max had not only been moved and entranced; he had fallen in love.

The pretext of Max's first letter to Elizabeth was an almost empty, cream-colored box of Turkish cigarettes that she had happened to leave behind.

Dear Miss Lemon:—

When I found these cigarettes you had left I thought at first to keep them as a remembrance. But I am far from needing a remembrance. I then recalled that you had said you meant to stop smoking because cigarettes of this brand were no longer made & I thought I must save you from that dreadful heart-broken feeling you have when you don't smoke, at times, if only for the brief space these two cigarettes would last. If you have stopped, I feel as I have felt. This brief reprieve will make you think of me with extraordinary gratitude. Maybe that's too much to hope; but short of that, these cigarettes have given me a chance to say something too trivial to say without an excuse. It is, that I had just the faintest fear you might really think me so pusilanimous as to have been offended that you "could not bear the sight of me." I guess not though.

Next year, please remembe[r] I sent these & thank me. And I now thank you for all the pleasure you gave me—&, I suppose, everyone else in the neighbourhood—by being here this year[.]

Sincerely yours

Maxwell E. Perkins

I always greatly liked the phrase "dea incessu patuit."[20] But I never really knew its meaning till I saw you coming toward me through our hall the other night.

When one has been smitten, one is torn between a desire to confess one's feelings and a need to err on the side of caution, lest one's feelings are unrequited or come across as maudlin, inappropriate, or downright offensive. One writes to relate, but one is terrified that a careless word or clumsy gesture will destroy the bridge before a single step has been taken across it. In fact, Perkins's adoration was less than fully reciprocated, and to protect himself as well as his marriage he ensured that his friendship with Elizabeth would be conducted at a safe distance, through letters. They wrote to each other for twenty-five years but avoided face-to-face meetings. In 1943, however, twenty-one years after their first exchange of letters, they met at the

Ritz Bar in New York City. They sat at a small table and their talk touched on their relationship.

"Oh, Elizabeth," Max said, reaching his hand toward hers, "it's hopeless." Elizabeth agreed. She withdrew her hand. "I know," she said.

It was the last and only conversation on the subject they ever had.[21] In a letter she wrote him after returning home, she said, "I wish I could have seen you again while I was in New York, but the time was so short and so crowded."[22] The fact is that a prolonged meeting would have accomplished nothing. And everything points to the probability that there was no room in Elizabeth's life for love or marriage.

In order to reconstruct this story, I needed details that could not be found in Berg's biography of Perkins, and so I tracked Scott down on the Internet and explained in an email how moved I had been by his radio talk. Could he help me locate a transcript of it? Scott replied to my email immediately, thanking me for my comments. "There is, to my knowledge, no published source for the talk because—to tell you the truth—it was delivered without a text. I invariably speak only from rough notes (as I did on that occasion); and unless somebody later transcribed it, there would be no printed account of my lecture. It was, of course, recorded—hence, your hearing it . . . so all I can suggest would be your tracking it down through NPR." Scott added that I seemed to have remembered the talk better than he had, an observation that only made my task more difficult, mindful as I was of the fallibility of memory.

Although my desire to be faithful to the facts was frustrated by my hazy recollections of Scott's talk, and by my failure to locate a transcript of the original talk on NPR, I consoled myself with the thought that the fate of the original story obliquely illuminated the significance it had for me when I first heard it. For this story brought home to me that we sometimes keep faith with another person not by presuming to know her but by maintaining a respectful distance from her. To do justice to an event may require a similar resolve not to close the gap between what can be described and what can be explained.

Ethnography is always haunted by the hubris of reductionism, which is why sound ethnographic writing often involves a resistance to closure, a resolve to *suggest* meaning rather than spell it out. The discreet distance that Perkins and Lemmon kept between them may have preserved the illusion of Perkins's marital fidelity, but what fascinates me about this love story is the way in which the mystery of human affinities and affections defies our attempts to explicate it.

In the course of my fieldwork in Sierra Leone, I repeatedly fell into the trap of trying to penetrate the mystery of what my interlocutors thought or felt about themselves and their neighbors, only to be repeatedly reminded that one cannot know what is in another person's "belly" (we would say "heart" or "mind"). What is implied here is something more than the well-known phenomenological uncertainty about the nature of other minds, for our focus is shifted from questions of abstract knowledge to questions of social adroitness. By relinquishing claims to *know* what governs or causes the emotions, thoughts, or actions of other people, our emphasis is placed on the *practical* measures people take to coexist with one another and work out a modus vivendi for social being. Indeed, this emphasis explains why, for Mande-speaking peoples, *societas* is achieved not in talking together, as academics typically do, but by sitting together or eating together in amicable silence. Hence the following adages:

Speech dispersed the world, silence reassembles it.
If speech burned your mouth, silence will heal you.
Silence gave birth to the serious, speech to diversion.
Marriage is made in silence, free love in amusement and noise.[23]

It is this shift from speech to silence that makes the meeting between Max Perkins and Elizabeth Lemmon in the Ritz Bar in 1943 so moving. It marks an unspoken moment in which they recognize that their relationship will be consummated in physical separateness rather than intimacy, through exchanging letters rather than making love.

Discovering how one may strike a balance between a romantic urge for empathy, participation, and union, and a scientific insistence on detachment, observation, and neutrality is a key issue for literary anthropology. In this matter, I am reminded of Aleksandr Romanovich Luria's resistance to the notion that one can understand the human brain without reference to the lived experience of actual persons. In developing his conception of "romantic science," Luria argued that traditional empiricists tend to "single out important units and elements until they can formulate abstract, general laws," thereby reducing "lived reality with all its richness of detail to abstract schemas." By contrast, romantic scholars seek "neither to split living reality into its elementary components nor to represent the wealth of life's

concrete events in abstract models that lose the properties of the phenomena themselves."[24]

Judging when to define one's task as one of creating order, identifying
causes, and connecting facts (i.e., knowing, explaining, or interpreting the
world) or as one of describing, narrating, and communicating the experience
of life as lived becomes a crucial issue. While the positivist undoubtedly
produces a consoling illusion of certainty and gains an aura of authority
from appearing to have resolved mysteries that ordinary mortals cannot
hope to penetrate, the romantic gains an aura of authenticity by appearing to
write "from the heart." Hence John Berger's claim that authenticity comes
from a faithfulness to the ambiguity of experience.

But if the search for *auctoritas* is under the sway of a desire for knowledge as power, the search for authenticity may be faulted for its exagger-
ated emphasis on affect. Accordingly, I prefer to see ambiguity not as a sign
of conceptual indeterminacy or affective confusion but as intrinsic to the
human condition in which we are perennially in two minds, struggling
to achieve clarity, direction, and certainty in the face of forces that cause
bewilderment, insecurity, and despair. Under these conditions, neither the
possession of knowledge nor the virtue of authenticity may help a person
overcome or endure adversity. What matters most is one's ability to live without certainty, and to find the *practical* means of going on—shelter, food,
water, and succor for oneself and those one loves.

The Embourgeoisement of Anthropology

This emphasis on what can be practically rather than intellectually
accomplished—on meaning as a matter of being able to do something even
when one does not really know what to do—calls into question many
bourgeois assumptions about what makes life worth living, as well as the
bourgeois concept of culture that has long been foundational for American
anthropology.[25]

At the beginning of this chapter I drew a comparison between European
composers who used peasant melodies in their own compositions and the
work of ethnographers, suggesting that the production of classical music
and anthropological texts shares a common origin in Europe's mercantile
and imperial exploitation of the third world for its own gain. One illuminating if troubling commentary on this subject is Steven Feld's notable essay

on the social life of a Ba-Benzélé musical composition from the Central African Republic, recorded and distributed on a 1966 ethnomusicological LP entitled *The Music of the Ba-Benzélé Pygmies*. The opening track of the LP alternates voice with the sound of a single-pitch papaya stem whistle (*hindewhu*), and it was this track that was "adapted," unacknowledged, by Herbie Hancock on his 1973 Columbia LP *Headhunters* and later by Madonna on her 1994 CD *Bedtime Stories*. In 1985, when Feld asked Hancock "if he felt any legal or moral concern surrounding his *hindewhu* copy on *Headhunters*," and whether he felt that musicians "could side-step the music industry and copyright conventions to directly remunerate the sources of their inspiration," Hancock replied that blacks were brothers and all had suffered equally from oppression, so Feld's question was not relevant.[26]

If this issue is relevant, then it behooves us to ask whether anthropology's alternating rationales, of scientific authority or artistic authenticity, both tend to blind us to the practical exigencies of everyday life among marginalized peoples and to give rise to the illusion that our preoccupation with the latest intellectual fashions and discursive styles trumps all other concerns. Since the composers I have mentioned, like most anthropologists, are products of bourgeois upbringings, how is it possible for them to resolve the contradiction between the values of the class to which they belong and the concerns of the classes or cultures from which they draw their raw material? Does making anthropology more literary help overcome this contradiction or exacerbate it? As for those whose origins are working class or third world, how can they overcome the guilt at having abandoned the people and places that formed them? In her compelling study and memoir of family and class in postindustrial Chicago, Christine Walley condenses this experience into her changing relationship with her father. "In the inner places of my psyche, I . . . wondered whether somehow [in becoming a middle-class university teacher and intellectual] I had betrayed him by choosing to lead a life he could not follow."[27]

A couple of years ago, on a return visit to my own country of origin, I looked up some old friends who had been living on a remote commune for over thirty years. I was immediately struck by how much of their energy and attention was absorbed by the tasks of day-to-day survival—fishing, gardening, cooking, repairing things that were broken. In the subdued light of their living room, it was easy to see them as pioneers. It wasn't only the surroundings that reinforced this impression—the wood-burning stove, the ironware, the tins of homemade bread, the bucket of local honey, the organic fruit from the commune orchard. It was their very appearance: their serviceable clothing from Kathmandu or Swanndri, their lack of cosmetic pretension, their ability to make do with basic amenities, their rough-and-ready language. You discussed fitting a wider diameter pipe to a stove, improvising a chimney cowl from a scrap of hammered tin, or replacing a worn wheel bearing on a truck with the same intensity and ingenuity with which a group of Harvard professors might debate the ethics of intervention in a foreign state. If you rarely touched on or inquired into the life of another mind, or a school of thought, or the nature of experience, it was not because these things were irrelevant; rather, time did not permit such departures from the mundane and the never-ending struggle to make ends meet. As for social life, relationships were mediated more by doing things together than by sharing intimacies. All this strongly reminded me of my experiences of living in West African villages, and it brought home to me the difficulties of being an intellectual in societies or situations where the life of the mind is supererogatory if not absurd.

Much of what we know as middle-class existence depends on having the sufficient means to get the mundane tasks of life performed for us by a tradesman or a machine, and of being cushioned from the primary work of production. Having bought time in the form of leisure, we can afford to cultivate manners (rather than crops), dwell upon our own thoughts and emotions (rather than occupy ourselves with the demands of extended family), and contemplate nature as an aesthetic object (rather than as a resource whose exploitation exhausts us). Because we possess a surplus of time and money, we are free to devote our energies to décor, fashions, fine foods, and fads, none of which are, strictly speaking, necessary for our physical survival.[28] We create worlds centered on ourselves. In rituals of shopping, showing off, distracting ourselves, or taking costly holidays to "get away from it all," we magically conjure illusions of autonomy and of being "special." For the African migrants in Europe with whom I had worked, this pattern of immediate sensory gratification and personalized consumption stood in stark contrast with the traditional African emphasis on accepting hardship and awaiting one's due—a contrast between narcissism and stoicism. Indeed, the bourgeois cultivation of inwardness and "intravidu-alism"[29] implies a set of symbolic contrasts for separating self from society, drawing invidious distinctions between the civilized middle classes and peasants, primitives, and underlings. The migrant's preoccupations with economizing—in what one spends money on, what one consumes, what one says, and what one does—reflect the value placed on conviviality as a measure of the worth of one's words and deeds. What one possesses accrues value in being given away or loses value in being kept solely for oneself. Gluttony and logorrhoea are both modes of self-gratifying overconsumption, and they have no social value. Language should be used to express rather than impress, to connect people rather than create hierarchies. Everything is measured against the standard of social rather than merely personal fulfillment.

I have often asked myself whether my philosophy of writing reflects these African values, and whether my years of living in one of the poorest societies in the world have made me more than ordinarily aware of the need to economize and minimalize, both in practical and literary matters. Perhaps this is why I have argued for a view of writing as techné rather than epistemé—a "tool for conviviality,"[30] a means of bridging the gulf that lies between oneself and others, subsuming the singular in the plural.[31]

My conversations with African migrants continue to remind me of this historical tension between societies in which people struggle for bare life and societies in which people's desires and preoccupations "surpass the material reproduction of existence."[32] In its fetishized concepts, its specialist jargons, its loquacity and intellectual excess, the academy exemplifies this "affirmative culture" of the bourgeoisie, and I sometimes imagine the conventional academic essay as an overfurnished baroque drawing room—designed to impress, but hermetically sealed off from the brute realities of the outside world.[33] Nevertheless, I do not want to exaggerate the differences between these worlds, making one the measure of the real and mocking the other for its artificiality and folly. Neither of these worlds guarantees complete well-being. And while the cult of inwardness and the "dissociation of sensibilities"[34] that accompanied the rise of the urban bourgeoisie in eighteenth-century Europe did not preclude the possibility of community or nostalgia for the agrarian past, so-called primitive ontologies have never precluded the possibility of self-realization, reason, and critique. What is common to all cultures is the quest for life. Though intellectuals tend to emphasize the "meaning" of life as a fundamental existential imperative, "meaning" is only one form that life assumes in the human imagination and is no more or less significant than mobility, love, family solidarity, health, wealth, energy, or union with the divine—all of which figure as paths for attaining well-being.

A Dream of Sewa

On my last night in Santa Fe I woke in the small hours of the morning from a disturbing dream. In this dream, a Kuranko friend, now living in London, appeared in a dark doorway in an unfamiliar and desolate city. He was emaciated to the point of being cadaverous, and he seemed to have suffered a series of beatings that had destroyed his handsome features and left an expression of pained bewilderment on his face. I was given to understand that he was in thrall or bondage to a slaveowner. Without a second thought, or any exchange of words, I took Sewa's hand and began negotiating the deserted yet menacing streets, working our way to freedom.

I shared this dream with Todd Ochoa, whose memorable phrase "Each one of us is the resurrection of the dead" I had jotted down in my notebook two days ago. Todd said it was "a Zombie dream." It uncannily recalled the pain and brutality of slavery, particularly in seventeenth- and eighteenth-century Haiti, where Africans were starved and worked to death on the French sugar plantations. Only in death could one escape, and death was imagined as a return to a verdant and Edenic Africa (*Lan Guinée*). But a slave could die and yet not complete the journey back to Africa—and be doomed to eternal life in the cane fields as a zombie. I had intervened, Todd said, to rescue Sewa from this thralldom to eternal servitude.

I also shared my dream with my wife, Francine, who was a Jungian therapist. "What aspects of yourself are represented in the dream?" she asked. And I wondered then if an old issue had surfaced in me during my days and nights in Santa Fe, of exploiting my ethnographic sources for my own professional gain, of betraying my Kuranko friends in writing about them in ways they would not understand or approve, and that every anthropologist risks becoming a slaveowner, working his subjects to death in order to augment his or her own life.

How can our writing refuse this complicity in the death of the subject, and become a form of natality, recovering life in the face of death? Is there a transcendent subject, defined aesthetically or epistemologically, that justifies the eclipse of the individual subject, whose "death notices" appeared at the very moment that postmodernism burst upon the scene? And might not that subject be the existential imperative to live as though one's life were one's own, even though it is shaped by external circumstances and always implicates others, sometimes unfolding in affluence and sometimes in dire poverty, and finding expression in words as well as deeds?

Notes

1. "Its material had been collected by the composer during his tours to the counties of Maros-Torda (Mures), Bihar (Bihor), Torda-Aranyos (Turda) and Torontal in 1910 and 1912. Romanian folk music offered Bartók a number of elements that were attractive, not found in Hungarian folk music and, moreover, stimulating to his further renewal of twentieth-century art music. Above all, the Romanian instrumental folk music was much richer than that of Hungary, and involved such instruments as one or two violins, violin and guitar, peasant flute or bagpipes. . . . Bartók hardly ever preserved the tempos of the original tunes, but made fast dances even faster and the slow ones even slower, thereby giving an individual character to each one." Gillies, *Bartók Companion*, chapter 11, referring to the 1915 piano version, the author Janos Karpati.

2. Husserl, *Crisis of European Sciences and Transcendental Phenomenology*, 119–20, 297–99.

3. Husserl's most explicit acknowledgment of the relation between the philosophical and political dimensions of "the crisis" is in an open letter to the Prague Congress of 1934. Carr, "Translator's Note," xxvii.

4. Berger, *Keeping a Rendezvous*, 216–17.

5. Derrida, *Margins of Philosophy*, x–xxix.

6. Derrida, "This Strange Institution Called Literature," 73.

7. Arendt, *Human Condition*, 277–79.

8. Jackson, *Barawa, and the Ways Birds Fly in the Sky*.

9. Jackson, *Accidental Anthropologist*, 244.

10. This was particularly true of my earliest poetry books: *Latitudes of Exile: Poems 1965–1975* (Dunedin: McIndoe, 1976), which won the Commonwealth Poetry Prize in 1976, and *Wall* (Dunedin: McIndoe, 1980), which won the New Zealand Book Award for Poetry in 1981.

11. Arendt, *Human Condition*, 178.

12. James, *Essays in Radical Empiricism*, 10. See also Dewey, *Experience and Nature*, 8–9. Both writers echo Hegel, *Phenomenology of Spirit*, 55.

13. Marcel, *Being and Having*, 100.

14. Kofman, "Beyond Aporia," 10.

15. Kofman, "Beyond Aporia," 12.

16. Montaigne, *Essays*, 394.

17. Goethe, *Elective Affinities*, 53.

18. Keats, *Letters of John Keats*, 193.

19. Jackson, *Other Shore*, 65–71.

20. Perkins (Tarr, *As Ever Yours*, 25) slightly misquotes Virgil's *Aeneid: et vera incessu patuit dea*, "and the goddess was revealed in her step," referring to Venus revealing herself before Aeneas.

21. Berg, *Maxwell Perkins*, 386.

22. Tarr, *As Ever Yours*, 232.

23. Zahan, *Religion, Spirituality, and Thought of Traditional Africa*, 117–18.

24. Luria, *Making of Mind*, 174.

25. For a critique of the origins of the concept of culture in twentieth-century anthropology, see Jackson, *Lifeworlds*, 52–54.

26. Feld, "Pygmy POP," 5–6.

27. Walley, *Exit Zero*, 161.

28. Elias, *Civilizing Process*; Frykman and Löfgren, *Culture Builders*, 126–53.

29. Lasch-Quinn, "From Inwardness to Intravidualism."

30. Illich, *Tools for Conviviality*.

31. Jackson, *Other Shore*, ix.

32. Marcuse, "Affirmative Character of Culture," 120.

33. Brown, *Bourgeois Interior*.

34. T. S. Eliot argued that while metaphysical poets like John Donne sought to unify sensations and ideas, feelings and thoughts, the early seventeenth century saw these modalities of experience become increasingly separated, creating an increasing division between ratiocination and emotionality, and giving rise to genres of writing that defined their identities in mutually exclusive terms.

4

WALKING AND WRITING

ANAND PANDIAN

Michael Jackson walks out into the desert one morning in New Mexico. It's a cloudless day, the sun still rising from the mountains in the distance. Jackson is walking, and yet he is somehow stuck, brooding, caught up in a moment of impasse. In his work, the scholarly and the poetic keep forking from each other, tailing competing demands for fidelity and invention. Jackson finds himself somewhere between these two paths, unsure of where or how exactly to move onward from here. This choice, however, is not one to make on his own. A ringdove coos, flinging him elsewhere: to the south of France; to his once-ailing wife, Pauline; to a Harvard University classroom and an aging composer's unrequited love affair; to the realization that faithfulness and betrayal always shadow each other in life. On the trail, with this encounter, a path opens up for an essay, a line of thought for the anthropologist to follow.

"You must walk like a camel," Henry David Thoreau wrote, "said to be the only beast which ruminates when walking." Thoreau recommended walking as a way of thinking out of doors, of investing the mind with "the tan and callus of experience."[1] Jackson, as it happens, lives not far from Walden Pond, and I've had the chance myself to tag along those storied shores beside him. But the affinity between Thoreau's words and Jackson's essay goes much deeper than this. Look at how his composition winds from instance to instance, slowly working out a problem as it moves along a course much easier to follow than foretell. Is there not something peripatetic about this writing, its form?

The essay is best understood, Charles Forsdick suggests, "as the perambulation of an idea."[2] From Montaigne to Rousseau and countless others since, the essay has been pursued as a narrative mode of divagation, a way of thinking through the vagaries of sensory impression and worldly encounter. A diagrammatic sensibility would find the essay frustrating, for, as Theodor Adorno observed, such writing bears truth only "in its progress, which drives it beyond itself." The essay is a form composed of fragments, discrete pieces that betray nothing of a lucid structure on their own. All the same, as Adorno insists, the essay gains coherence through movement—"the elements crystallize as a configuration through their motion."[3]

Consider, for example, the way that this essay moves, how it takes an idea for a walk. Jackson begins with a problem: the difficulty, in ethnographic writing, "to do justice to life." He lays out this problem as a matter of deep and ambivalent commitments, verging on quandaries of knowledge, ethics, and aesthetic technique. Then the problem begins to pass through a series of scenes, subtly inflecting their various shades and textures: betrayal for Janáček, Bartók, Kuranko, phenomenology; the enduring spell of Buñuel, that desert walk, aporia, and Janáček's affair; troubles posed by a radio show, an epistolary romance, Mande adages, existential confusion; visions of a good life for Pan-African musicians, Antipodean communes, migrants to Europe, bourgeois anthropologists; a friendship expressed as dream, zombie flashback, Jungian archetype, and undying provocation. The essay makes departures that keep circling back to somewhere near their point of flight. And yet these circles are not closed. There is a destination beyond the impasse, an insight that emerges at a place impossible to forecast from the initial coordinates.

Jackson's work has long sought ways of being faithful to the inconstancy of experience, to the tendency of living beings and their circumstances to assume strange and unexpected forms, like the djinn and other shapeshifters one often encounters in Kuranko folktales. This tendency lends a palpable feeling of danger to writing and other such acts of expression. "One writes to relate," Jackson muses here, "but one is terrified that a careless word or clumsy gesture will destroy the bridge before a single step has been taken across it." What to do in the face of such peril? "How can our writing," as Jackson asks, "become a form of natality, recovering life in the face of death?" The answer to this question, it seems, lies in the vicissitudes of the essay itself, the form of writing that he pursues, a writing that treads carefully with experience, attuning itself, as it goes along, to both the promise and the risk of what happens. Life exceeds the "sclerotic tendency" of thought to confine and entomb its happenings. As a perambulation with words, the essay seeks an alliance with these forces of life, exploring the value of their openness.

Taking a walk, as we know, can be good for the often-torturous task of writing. Amitava Kumar recently put the activity among his "ten rules of writing"—"Walk for ten minutes. Or better yet, go running. If you do not exercise regularly, you will not write regularly. Or not for long."[4] The essay, however, seems to concern itself with a different relation between walking and writing, beyond the question of how to arrive at the bottom of a page replete with text. The essayist, the walker in writing, is given over to the rhythms of this movement, trusting that a worthy destination will emerge in time. And this writing, in the very mode of its passage, shows us how to traverse that familiar and stubborn line between fidelity and invention. With care and a bit of cunning, it would seem, we might just be able to step ever so lightly over it.

Notes

1. Thoreau, "Walking," 601.
2. Forsdick, "*De la plume comme des pieds*," 46.
3. Adorno, "Essay as Form," 13.
4. Kumar, *Lunch with a Bigot*, 122.

Anthropoetry

ADRIE KUSSEROW

LOST BOY
For Gabriel Panther Ayuen

Panther sits inside his apartment,
heat cranked up to 80, curtains closed,
a pile of chicken boiling on the stove,
slides another Kung Fu movie into the VCR,
settles back into the smelly,
swaybacked couch, a Budweiser between his legs.
He giggles.
In half an hour he'll ride his bike
to Walmart, round stray shopping carts
from the cracked grey lot,
crashing them back into their steel corrals.

At first they dropped by all the time,
the church ladies, the anthropologists,
the students, the local reporter.
They all left elated, having found something real,
like yoga and organic food.

The first Thanksgiving, three families booked him.
Leaning hungrily across
the long white table,
they nibbled at his stories,
his lean noble life.

Over and over he told them about lions,
crocodiles, eating mud and urine.

He remembers joining
a black river of boys,
their edges swelling and thinning
as they wound their way
over the tight-lipped soil, sun stuck to their backs.
He remembers dust mushrooming up
around a sack of cornmeal as it thudded
and slumped over, like a fat woman crying in the sand.

And the Americans came alive, with a sad,
compassionate glow, a kind of sunset inside them.

When he got off the plane
the church ladies took him to a store,
bought him fresh sneakers
soft and white as wedding cake.
The next day he walked through whole aisles of dog food.
Two years later, November again,
he's dropped out of high school—he can't take
the kids staring, the tiny numbers and letters
he can't keep straight,
the basketball team he didn't make
despite his famous height.

Now he looks like a too-tall gangster,
all gold-chained and baggy-trousered.
The church ladies give him hushed looks:
we regret to inform you, the path you've taken is not what we had hoped for.

He's channel surfing,
listening to Bob Marley on his walkman,
his long legs awkwardly pushed out
to each side, the way giraffes
split their stilts
to drink water.

Africa's moved inside him now,
all cramped and bored, sleeping a lot.

He cracks another beer
starts to float,
the reggae flooding the vast blue-black continent
of his body draped like a panther
over the sides of the sofa.

His cousin calls, she needs more money,
her son has malaria. She can't afford school fees anymore.
His uncle gets on the phone to remind him to study hard,
come back and build a new Sudan.

Later he stumbles into the bathroom
to brush his teeth, inside him
groggy Africa flinches at the neon light,
paces, then settles in the corner
of its den, paws pushing into the walls
of his ribs with a dull pain.

The next morning he wakes,
stubborn bits of Africa still shoved up against his ribs,
refusing to roll over, into the middle
of himself where he can't feel them anymore,
into some open place
where he ends
and America finally begins.

Poetry is a tool I use to get into the very multidimensional middle of where I need to be as an anthropologist. It allows me to be firmly in the moment, in motion, in process, in the very thick of things, at the heart of Indra's net. Most of the poems in this essay are about my experiences with refugees from South Sudan whom I have worked with over the past ten years, in Uganda, South Sudan, or Vermont. My ethnographic poems, especially about refugees, have to be able to accommodate the hybrid consciousness of the displaced as they live through the global friction and violence of cultures existing inside of each other, as well as the power differential between the refugee and myself.

Far from documenting a neat life, a poem, in its very nomadic vagrancy and line length, rhythm and unsettling metaphor, can depict the borderlands, the liminal places of confusion of a refugee, the internal tug of war. A poem is also nomadic in its ability to move the subject from room to room, city to town, birthday to funeral, each with its changing Goffmanesque dramas and social roles, the echoes of which all exist in one human and resonate with each other.

Perhaps this poem allows us to ask the following questions. How might poems, through the use of metaphor and simile and the movement from recent past, present, and future, depict the multiple and jockeying selves that exist within any human? And are there certain subcultures anthropologists study—those who cross borders, split identities, experience a push and pull between tradition and acculturation—that especially need the temporal flexibility of poetry?

Ethnographic poetry allows us to move the character situationally, like Goffman might, from one drama to the next, where the refugee is expected to play various roles. The Lost Boys also have a very performative element to their public persona, insofar as a good "African" performance can mean the acquisition of choice perks from the wealthy host family or church congregation like a used car, an underground part-time job, a better apartment. In this way it seems that poetry allows an exploration of the full range of roles humans are expected to play.

WAR METAPHYSICS FOR A SUDANESE GIRL
For Aciek Arok Deng

I leave the camp, unable to breathe,

me Freud girl, after her interior,
she "Lost Girl," after my purse,

her face:
dark as eggplant,
her gaze:
unpinnable, untraceable,
floating, open, defying the gravity
I was told keeps pain in place.

Maybe trauma doesn't harden,
packed tight as sediment at the bottom of her psyche,
dry and cracked as the desert she crossed,
maybe memory doesn't stalk her
with its bulging eyes.

Once inside the body, does war move up or down?
Maybe the body pisses it out,
maybe it dissipates, like sweat and fog
under the heat of yet another colonial God?

In America, we say Tell us your story, Lost Girl
you'll feel lighter,
it's the memories you must expel,
the bumpy ones, the tortures, the rapes, the burnt huts.

So Aciek brings forth all the war she can muster,
and the doctors lay it on a table, like a stillbirth,
and pick through the sharpest details
bombs, glass, machetes
and because she wants to please them
she coughs up more and more,
dutifully emptying the sticky war
like any grateful Lost Girl in America should
when faced with a flock of white coats.
This is how it goes at the Trauma Center:
all day the hot poultice of talk therapy,
coaxing out the infection,
at night, her host family trying not to gawk,
their veins pumping neon fascination,
deep in the suburbs, her life flavoring dull *muzungu* lives,
spicing up supper, really,
each Lost Girl a bouillon cube of horror.

Most of us engaged in discussions around literary ethnography have
asked the question: in being fanatically loyal to linear, literal facts, exact
locations, direct quotes, surveys and chronologies, and a confident, intellectual tone, what realities and insights into human life do we leave out?

What do we risk losing without deeper, multidimensional, and more subtle portraits of social realities? Thick description requires all of one's aesthetic antennae to be fully alert, so that the anthropologist not only can enhance, but also can bring meanings to the "literal facts." Hence, ethnographic poetry is not just about accurately describing an experience, but using the insight of its acutely nuanced language and artistic aesthetic to bring a wider array of meanings to these facts than conventional wisdom offers. I also hope each of these ethnographic poems in this essay points toward what might be left out of anthropology if we don't engage in a more poetic literary ethnography that grapples with issues of inequality and social suffering.

I initially considered writing this poem as a more formal paper for a conference about New England survivors of torture and trauma, but then I found that the required language and length of a traditional academic article diluted and dulled the truly jarring impact and tension of this ethnographic encounter. Some of its images also try and convey to the reader the full violence of Western assumptions about healing as they are worked through the bodies of refugees. Aciek was taken as a sexual slave in Sudan during the civil war. I was hoping to interview her, get her to "open up," so to speak, but she was locked tight. For some refugees, the pop psychological process of expelling the pain through talk therapy was invasive and traumatic in and of itself. I needed language, images, and line breaks that could jar the reader, questioning lines that could instill doubt, and finally incredulity at the naiveté of a well-run trauma center, smug in its assumptions of health and healing. This poem also acknowledges the power differential between a Sudanese Lost Girl and the ethnographer, hinting at the ways in which this unequal relation might bring about the very silence of the girl.

THE UNRAVELING STRANGENESS

You are losing it, they say,
     paranoid delusions of soldiers breaking into your house,

hiding your car from the police,
     clutching the hot vein of your cell phone

as you drive your mother in her conical straw hat
     across the bumpy Vermont fields,

staring out from her yolky Alzheimer's haze
        as the car lurches over the mud and leaves.

No one wants to challenge your story,
        you who never should have left Bhutan,

your loneliness first swelling
        high above Atlantic City

where you built your makeshift apocalyptic nest
        pulling in the cheapest Gods that flew around,

storm after storm in that neon grim city.
        Now your fingers bruise your rosary with mad devotion.

No one can weave as fiercely as you
        in your tattered white bathrobe,

grey roots frosting your scalp,
        peering out from the curtains

like a spider sensing its web pricked,
        wrapping each social worker

in the pure white gauze of your stories
        as they look at you with the tenderness

reserved for an infant or a dog
        and speak to you of boundaries,

calling you back to the steamy jungles of your birth
        where you ran and ran through the night

and woke to a python wrapped around a tree
        your father hacking its head off, prying

its 17 foot long body off the trunk.
        It took so long for it to die,

uncoil enough so you could feast on the eggs
        lined up like potatoes in its womb.

Let go of the steering wheel, just a little.
        Who is to say what suffocates, what heals,

coaxing yourself home each night,
>out from the ragged edges of this life you were given,

without asking, without knowing,
>the billions of explanations and justifications

you fitfully braid and fuse, tangle and knot,
>the sticky plots that hold them in place

as you're hurled through space,
>landing with a thump,

into the great American refugee hive to begin
>this frantic human work, perpetual manic revival,

stretching your way through the half-light
>of this vast unraveling strangeness.

Anthropologists attempt to understand lives of humans who themselves are often confused, liminal and in flux. Poetry, in its freedom from a fixed place in time, can also convey the strangeness of adapting to a new culture. And yet, amid this unraveling strangeness, the refugee is not simply passive, acted upon; she is weaving stories that will lull the social worker and refusing certain treatments by locking herself inside the house. Though she suffers, she is cunning. This can be conveyed from stanza to stanza as opposed to the weight of a locked-in "topic"—humans have agency, and a shrewd sense of survival one day and yet the next might feel the dizziness and "passivity" of the unwinding journey of the American refugee landscape.

Poetry allows me to use unsettling images here to bring about the qualities of confusion, the jarring quality of crossing cultures and the inevitable lifeboat of a cheap religion, to keep one afloat. Here the ethnographer, usually occupying an authoritative voice, is somewhat lost herself, as she somewhat desperately asks the questions at the end, "Who is to say what is the best way to heal?" Refugee resettlement is inherently messy and cannot be wrapped up in a pretty package. So too the ethnographic poem can resist the temptation of painting reality in a kind of perfect and familiar symmetry.

BUS STATION, KAMPALA, UGANDA
For Will, *age 3*

We are lost.

Holding you tight,
the drunks pawing me
as I weave through the stalls
sticky with beer and urine
looking for a way to get us out.
Grey buses wheeze over the colossal potholes,
barnacles of street kids
clinging to their sides.

I don't know if you know it,
but we are winding through alleys
where dogs bleed from their butts,
a freshly pummeled woman
lies like pounded meat in the gutter,
reeling from the punches for requesting a condom,

or if you hear the gurgle that is blood in her cheek
as she slumps into a puddle
while the drunken crowd jeers.

Meanwhile, back at the Lake Victoria hotel,
the hibiscus lashes its red
tongue into the cool night,
wealthy *muzungus* spread their stiff white napkins
starched and white as calla lilies.

Hush, sweet boy,
swollen broken nests of these slums,
I can hardly breathe
but for the rotting and the birthing.
For now, cooing, clueless, you can hardly see the difference
between the squashed condom
the man threw at her in disgust and the crushed
lily flattened by the *muzungu's* high heel,

between the bleeding, the bleeding from everywhere there is an opening
and the languid arch of the red hibiscus
sprawled against the night.

An ethnographic poem can point toward the ethical questions that inevitably arise within the anthropologist about issues of power, whiteness,
and social inequality in the field. What does it feel like to be in the middle
of the ethical barbed wire of power differentials in the ethnographic encounter? These issues are something that can overwhelm and take away
the very breath of anthropologists as they engage in fieldwork, as opposed
to thinking about them clinically and objectively after returning from the
field.

I feel quite strongly that anthropologists who study war and refugees
have an ethical responsibility not to numb, but to move the reader. A
poem can be a "bouillon cube of horror" and, in that sense, give the reader
the needed punch and sting that must be conveyed. It seems unethical to
dilute the horrors of poverty and AIDS in a slum bus station only through
literature reviews, homage to the academy, footnotes, and excess ver-
biage. In teaching, I use my ethnographic poems to move students into
currents of feeling that will hopefully lead them toward some kind of action or state of discomfort. In this way, poetry can recast the legitimacy of
anthropological research toward one of expected action or feeling on the
part of the reader.

How should the anthropologist respond to the suffering of others and
the power relations of ethnography? How do we write to a wider audience in
gripping, charged, and yet still comprehensible ways, if we want the public
to viscerally engage with issues of social inequality? Does the ethnographic
poet dare to consider whether such poetry would be understandable or
usable by the disempowered it describes? And would my poems be understandable to the Lost Boys themselves?

SKULL TREES, SOUTH SUDAN
For Atem Deng

Arok Deng, hiding from the Arabs in the branches of a tree,
two weeks surviving on leaves,
legs numb, mouth dry.
When the mosquitoes swarmed

and the bodies settled limp as petals under the trees,
he shinnied down, scooping out a mud pit with his hands
sliding into it like a snake,
his whole body covered except his mouth.
Perhaps others were near him,
lying in gloves of mud, sucking bits of air through the swamp holes,
mosquitoes biting their lips,
but he dared not look.

What did he know of the rest of South Sudan, pockmarked with bombs,
skull trees with their necklaces of bones,
packs of bony Lost Boys
roving like hyenas towards Ethiopia,
tongues, big as toads, swelling in their mouths,

the sky pouring its relentless bombs of fire. Of course they were
tempted to lie down for a moment,

under the lone tree, with its barely shade,
to rest just a little while before moving on,

the days passing slyly, hallucinations
floating like kites above them

until the blanched bones lay scattered in a ring around the tree,
tiny ribs, skulls, hip bones—a tea set overturned,
as the hot winds whistled through them
as they would anything, really,

and the sky, finally exhausted,
moving on.

Poetry allows for a kind of ethnographic fabric to be woven from both the ethnographer and the voice, memory, imagination, hopes, and desires of their subjects, a dreamy movement in time and space. The people anthropologists try to understand do not come to us in bulk form, as past or present; they carry their pasts and the cultures they are bristling against or gobbling up with them, as well as their hopes for the future, right into the present moment. This condensing of multiple lived realities can be achieved in a poem in a way less cumbersome than in an article, which might demand the author stick with only one theme, a geographical place, a selection from past, present, or future.

Atem Deng, like many Lost Boys who have reconnected with a parent they thought dead, now holds inside him the story of his father's survival as well as the memory of his own past brutal trek toward Kaukuma. Though never dwelled upon verbally, danger also hangs inside him, like shadows and bones under the lone tree, through a profound geographical and bodily memory instead of statistical fact or the more romanticized media depictions of the Lost Boys.

MILK
(Sudanese Refugee Camp, Northwest Uganda)

I.
Our drivers gun insanely over the dusty, red roads,
        lurching from pothole to pothole.
                Caravan of slick, adrenalized vans,

tattooed with symbols of western aid,
        Will on my lap, trying to nurse between bumps,
                my hands a helmet to his bobbing skull.

A three-legged goat hobbles to the side,
        and though we imagine we are a huge interruption,
                women balancing jericans on their heads
                face our wake of dust and rage

as they would any other gust of wind—

Water, sun, NGO.

We arrive covered in orange dust, coughing,
        fleet of SUVs parked under the trees,
                engines cooling, Star Trekian cockpits flashing,

alarms beeping and squawking as we zip-lock them up
        and leave them black-windowed, self-contained as UFOs.

Behind the gate, we stumble through the boiling, shoulder-deep sun,
    Will and I trying to play soccer
        as a trickle of Sudanese kids cross the road

hanging against the fence, watching the chubby *muzungu* boy
    I've toted around Africa like a pot of gold.
        Three years old, he knows they're watching, so he does a
        little dance,
            his Spider Man shoes lighting up as they hit the dust.

II.
Part African bush, part Wild West,
    we're based in Arua, grungy, dusty frontiertown,
        giant dieseled trucks barrel through, spreading their
        wake of adrenalin,
            obese sacks of grain lying like walruses inside.

    I chase Will from malarial puddle to puddle,
        white blouse frilled like a gaudy gladiola,
            lavish concern for my chubby son
                suddenly rococo, absurd.

III.
7 foot giants of the SPLA,[1] huddle together, drinking,
    talking Dinka politics, repatriation, the New Sudan,
        wives lanky as giraffes set food on the table
        and move slowly away.

In candlelight the men's forehead scars gleam,
    I flutter, acting more deferential than I'm used to,
        slowly I'm learning Sudanese grammar:

men are the verbs, women, the conjunctions that link them together.

In the thick of rain we walk home,
    Ugandans huddled under their makeshift bird cages,
        Will now pointing to the basic vocabulary of this road:

dead snake, prickly bush, squealing pig, peeing child.
      Three drunk men sit under a shack,
            scrape the whiteness off us as we walk by.

Though I don't want to hear it,
      though I love Africa,
it starts up anyway, the milky mother cells of my body high-fiving,
my mind quietly repeating the story of my son's lucky birth,
      his rich American inheritance.

IV.
My husband drops into bed, dragging a thick cloak of requests.
      All day, I've labored behind him, toting our clueless *muzungu*,
            watching him, dogged Dutchman in his rubber clogs

climbing the soggy hills of Kampala, despite the noonday heat,
      a posse of hopeful Lost Boys following him,
            he, afraid of nothing, really, not even death,
me afraid of everything really, most of all his death.

In the distance, trucks rev up to cross the bush
      where Sudanese families perched like kites caught in trees,
            wait for the next shipment.
But it's night now,
      the three of us inside the cloud chamber of our mosquito net,
            the two of them breathing, safe.

Will's nursing again, though he doesn't need to,
      swelling like a tick
            and though I don't want to love
the sweet mists of our tiny tent home,
the lush wetlands of our lives,
            its thick rope bridges and gentle Ugandan hills,

the fat claw of my heart rises up,
      fertile, lucky, random
            pulsing and hissing its victory song.

    How can ethnographic poetry flush out the multiple subjectivities harbored in any one subjectivity as we navigate the landscapes of the Other? In the poem "Milk" I wanted to stay mainly with the subjectivity of the anthropologist, which involves an acute and awkward sense of how she must appear to the Ugandans and Sudanese refugees in Arua as well as the voice of herself as mother. More and more, families have become part and parcel of the experience of anthropological fieldwork. Ethnographic poetry allows me to introduce the ethnographer's self as not single but multiple, in an immediate way, through the images of a mother, fresh from birth, still nursing despite the lurching car.

All of these poems were written after the actual fieldwork was done, when I went back to scenes, ideas, and images that I had jotted down in field notes. Poetry always demands a place of intense quiet as I revisit the scenes, emotions, concepts, encounters, and images I remember. I have never written a poem in the middle of fieldwork, as that seems to complicate the ethnographic challenge of being fully present. Writing these poems allows me to dig further into the field experience for new insights. Beginning a poem, I usually have some idea of what I want to convey, but the act of writing always brings up many layers of feeling, insights, confusions, reflections, and reactions that were occurring in any "one" given ethnographic moment.

There are moments when I am more consciously "crafting" such poems, weaving strands together to build a larger picture, or deciding on line and stanza breaks. But often I try to get out of the way of the poems themselves, sitting in a sort of fierce meditation on that one packed ethnographic moment and letting the metaphors and similes come through me, as they might for a child. This transference of experience into metaphor and simile involves a stepping aside, as I "allow" the images to come through consciousness until the exact one does justice to that moment's nuances, dimensions, and subtleties. Only then can I move on.

MUD
(Vermont/South Sudan)

The pond black and bulging,
    twigs, branches poking from the water
like the stiff feet of, dare I say, fallen soldiers.

I drag whole limbs onto shore,
    globs of frog eggs surface like transparent brains,

Ana cupping the dimpled jelly,
    the dogs licking it like caviar.
Entranced, she squeezes it,
    while Will plunks his toes into a fleet of tadpoles,
cold mud sucking his foot into its mouth.

I tell myself it's not violence
    but overeager love,
this lust with which they squeeze the living.

Meanwhile, the rains just started in Juba, South Sudan,
    making travel near impossible.
Still my husband pushes a saggy jeep for eight hours
    through four feet of mud, a Sudanese boy
lying unconscious in the back seat.
    The jeep rocking and lurching
on the only road cleared of mines
    as my husband tries to inch it forward, this, his own labor of love,
like birth, like sex, something always tears,
    his foot jammed with a thorn as he heaves and sinks
his toenail tearing off, until even he gives up
    and forces them to turn back,
still 40 miles from Aliab, the whole village waiting,
    caught in an outbreak of cholera,
its one river littered with rusty ammunition,
    trucks large as elephants lying on their sides.

When Abraham, their Lost Boy, came home after 18 years
    the elders sacrificed a white cow.
Jump over it, into peace, they cried
    while the women tipped their thin necks back,
their whips of ululation uncoiling in the heat.

A day later, I find a frog shrunken in the corner of the bathroom
    but still breathing. I race it to the pond,
children running confused behind me,
    watch it sink, stunned, still dried and wrinkled,
like Abraham, now more American than Sudanese,
    sitting wide-eyed and stiff amidst the wailing and singing.

At dusk, the peepers scream themselves into existence,
   Ana and Will, draped in raincoats
run across the field.

When I catch up, Ana is horrified—
two male frogs griplocked onto a female,
   her flesh bulging between the swollen buds of their fingers.

And it occurs to me, how I came to be married to this man,
   I followed him from country to country,
gripped him hard as the frogs—
   Still he did not pry me off, as I have tried to do
with his overeager love, for this gangly country of Sudan.
   Who knows what will be torn next,
   as he moves blindly, but well-intentioned,
      amidst the irresistible mud.

I fell in love with writing poetry because it helped me bring to the forefront of consciousness a whole landscape of deep emotion, unspoken inequalities, and conceptual complexity I wasn't seeing or feeling in conventional writing. It also allowed me to take on a different tone of voice, a more vulnerable and more empathic one, than that of the confident, rational distant observer who is merely reporting the facts from a supposedly level field. Many of my poems have intentionally viscous titles ("Mud," "Milk," "Yolk") as a refusal of such spurious distance from the world. My poems are poems of discomfort, attempting to unhinge the reader, make the reader uncomfortable with the jarring inequalities that exist both in the world and in the fieldwork encounter.

Anthropologists know that when cultures rub against each other, it is not always a polite and orderly affair; something usually tears, breaks, or bleeds in the process. We romanticize and use each other in embarrassing ways. I fell in love with fieldwork because it demanded that the anthropologist wade deep into the mud of humans, where we get stuck, stick, slip, and tear. A place we leave tracks and giant potholes. The poem "Mud" touches upon the viscous quality of contact with a new culture other than one's own—the tenacity of its grip, such that stepping in can change both the ethnographer and the Other to the point of being almost unrecognizable by one's own kind.

OPENING DAY, MUKAYA
(New Sudan Secondary School for Girls)

All day we wait
     for the moist gills of night to open,
         croak and squawk of frogs, lizards,
bats soaring over the tent
     land with a splash in the mango tree,
         clutching and sucking the glorious fruit.

We have arrived again
     through the screeching heat of day,
         sun stripping the fields violently like a bed.

Planet of Mars, planet of fire and war.

Even grief, escaping the sun's manic inquisition,
     waits to swell.
For three nights the eerie death drumming for a toddler
     pummels our tent like rain.

Like missionaries staring from the toy plane
     swallowing the vast expanse of Sudan
         we are dropped onto the earth,

and begin the drive, whole jaws of road gaping open,
     van rebirthing through mud hole after hole.

Chiefs arrive for the ceremony in their Salvation Army clothes,
     battered cowboy hats. Not the tall stalks of fierce Dinka,
         but old men tamed by war, rising up on their wobbly canes
             in this nursing home post-war Sudan has become.

For six hours we sit through their sedating oration,
     wives lassoing us back from sleep
         with their fierce whips of ululation.

Women squat, poke at the coals,
     feathers stuck to their hands, hair,
         white chickens thrown like pom poms in the dirt.

And we don't know how they take it, the stirring and tending
      of their daily cauldrons of meat and blood,
          the war still raw inside them.

We say our goodbyes to the new school girls lying
      under their mosquito nets like captive brides,
          rows of bunkbeds, this their new life,

of education, three meals a day, the word has spread,
      as far as Wau and Aweil, girls from around the county
          on the backs of motorcycles

skirts tucked up, tin luggage on their heads,
      military convoys winding their way
          around the gutted mines,

filled with female cargo bumping, jostling, giggling,
      this their opening day, fierce reckoning,
          spilling their futures across the pockmarked soil
             like milk, fire, rain.

    This poem describes a place whose reality can only be described through metaphor and simile. South Sudan is a place where very few anthropologists have been able to do research because of civil war. It is pockmarked with fire and war, more akin to another planet than another country. For any anthropologist it is a conceptual and physical stretch, and I still struggle with finding a language that can hold it. This poem attempts to convey the epic geographic and political postwar landscape of South Sudan, as well as to record the ethnographer's part in this moment in history: the end of war and the beginning of girls' education in one of the most male-dominated cultures on earth.

    Sometimes guilt accompanies writing these poems. I returned from Juba, South Sudan, five days before the attempted political coup in 2013. I was haunted by subsequent articles and emails from friends, colleagues, and global media on the fallout from this attempt and continued fighting—the truckloads of bodies and stories of Sudanese refugees fleeing another possible civil war, the arrested journalists and many girls trapped inside the slums with no connections to get them out.

    To fly home via the US Embassy and write about these lives while they continue to suffer seems completely unfair. It is their voices that should be writing about their own experience of war in South Sudan. This is why I resist the "I" of the ethnographer as a wholly objective eye, but rather as one who records her "version" of South Sudan and makes her often muddled, vulnerable, and confused presence known. Making my emotions part of the poem is less a solipsistic indulgence than an act of honesty—a testament to the fact that my voice necessarily differs from theirs.

Notes

In using the title "Anthropoetry," I am following Renato Rosaldo's term *antropoesia* (in Spanish) for verse informed by ethnographic sensibility, a poetry deeply situated in the social and cultural world. In his "Notes on Poetry and Anthropology," Rosaldo speaks of the work of poetry. Poetry "brings things closer, or into focus, or makes them palpable. It slows the action, the course of events, to real depth of feeling and to explore its character. It is a place to dwell and savor more than a space for quick assessment. Poetic exploration resembles ethnographic inquiry in that insight emerges from specifics more than from generalizations. In neither case do concrete particulars illustrate an already formulated theory" (*Day of Shelley's Death*, 105). Like Rosaldo, in anthropoetry, I try to engage in forms of inquiry "where I am surprised by the unexpected. Antropoesia is a process of discovery more than a confirmation of the already known. If one knows precisely where a poem is going before beginning to write there is no point in going further. The same can be said of thick description in ethnography where theory is to be discovered in the details. The details inspire theory rather than illustrate already formulated theory" (106). Like the ethnographer, the antropoeta's goal is not to clarify, to distill into the well defined, but to stay with the complex and to use the very act of writing poetry to sit within the density of thick description long enough to "bring home to the reader the uneven and contradictory shape of that moment . . . to convey a yes and a no, to hold opposing forces together, making both present" (107).

1. The SPLA is the Sudan People's Liberation Army.

6

POETRY, UNCERTAINTY, AND OPACITY

MICHAEL JACKSON

In the course of one of our discussions in Santa Fe, Stefania Pandolfo observed that "some of us write poetry and fiction on the side of ethnography" while others "only write ethnography, and for them the ethnography is charged with everything, including ideas." In response, I noted that everything we do is "on the side" of something or someone else. The multifaceted, ever-changing character of life leads us to deploy different techniques, personae, and languages to engage with these different facets of being. Thus, we turn to images or to concepts, poetry or prose, depending on the situation we are trying to grasp or do justice to.

This oscillation between poetry and prose, or fiction and ethnography, can be compared to Heisenberg's uncertainty principle. Crudely put, uncertainty or indeterminacy in quantum physics reflects the fact that our *instruments* for grasping the nature of subatomic phenomena partially determine what we see. Some methods suggest that subatomic phenomena are particular; others that they are wavelike. In other words, the means of observation constitutes the reality of what is observed. For George Devereux, this insight is crucial to understanding the nature of ethnographic method—in which the instrument of observation is a human being, with unique predispositions and anxieties, and the observed are not objects but other subjects, with predispositions and anxieties of their own. Our understanding is born, therefore, of the interactions between observer and observed. This broaches the ethical question as to what *interests* determine any choice of a theoretical framework or writing style.

Adrie Kusserow makes a somewhat similar point when she speaks of the deliberate opacity or muddiness of her poems—of moving "blindly, but well-intentioned, amidst the irresistible mud" of a Vermont pond.[1] Anthropologists sometimes turn to literature, she says, to unsettle that which social science has considered settled and to make good what science has left unexplored and unspoken. And she speaks of her "ethnographic poems" as gestures toward these penumbral domains. Engaging her own subjectivity with the subjectivities of South Sudan refugees in Uganda, she works against the "spurious distancing" of ethnographer and other, and the reduction of persons to homogeneous cultural identities or historical circumstances. "Far from documenting a near life, a poem, in its very nomadic vagrancy and line length, rhythm and unsettling metaphor, can depict the borderlands, the liminal places of confusion of a refugee, the internal tug of war." But for Adrie, an ethical commitment overrides all these aesthetic and epistemological issues—a commitment to provide the means of life and livelihood to those whom war has robbed of even a bare life.

In a recent *Publishers Weekly* review of Adrie's book *Refuge*, the reviewer wrote scornfully of her "conceit" that "the suffering of Kenya begets Uganda, / begets my husband, / begets me, begets Ana, begets her brother."[2] For the reviewer, there is something amiss in Adrie's linking of Sudan's civil war with her life in Vermont, as when the image of a crow picking at compost conjures an image of war as a constant pecking on "the earth's beleaguered back." These worlds are incommensurable, the reviewer argues, and Adrie's poetic comparison diminishes the suffering in the Sudan to which she ostensibly seeks to bear witness. Though there is always a risk of voyeurism in ethnographic work (a risk Adrie is keenly aware of when she asks, "Would my poems be understandable to the Lost Boys themselves?"), the question of whether we do justice to those we write about can never be answered directly. In this vein, Adrie answers her own question by pointing out that her poems might be understood, not by *these* boys, now, but by some other boys in the future. One might include in this potential audience the members of the "Literary Anthropology" seminar in Santa Fe, listening to Adrie recite her poems, moved by her breathtaking imagery.

> The days passing slyly, hallucinations
> Floating like kites above them
>
> Until the blanched bones lay scattered in a ring around the tree,
> Tiny ribs, skulls, hip bones—a tea set overturned . . . [3]

It is not, therefore, a question of direct reciprocity—of gathering data from or drawing inspiration from someone, then repaying the favor as one might discharge a debt, or of meeting some absolute moral standard for how we should respond to the suffering of others. It is a question of acknowledging the unpredictable and surprising ways in which a gift received comes back to the giver, or how a gift given in good faith may yet do harm, the road to hell paved with good intentions. One has only to think of the CIA's covert use of Georges Condominas's published fieldwork[4] among the Mnong of Indochina (that led to the carpet-bombing of villages in which the French ethnographer had lived and worked), or the uses to which ethnographic works have been put by indigenous rights activists (uses that the original ethnographers could not have foreseen), to be reminded that we can never know or completely determine the outcome of our actions. Even Adrie's decision to return the royalties and profits from the sale of her book to the refugees may have surprising consequences, to be recounted in future poems.

Though we cannot know with any certainty the consequences of our words and deeds, we can, perhaps, remind ourselves of Marcel Mauss's observation in *The Gift*:

> A wise precept has run right through human evolution [that] we would be as well to adopt . . . as a principle of action. We should come out of ourselves and regard the duty of giving as a liberty, for in it there lies no risk. A fine Maori proverb runs:
>
> > *Ko maru kai atu*
> > *Ko maru kai mai*
> > *Ka ngohe.*
>
> "Give as much as you receive and all is for the best."[5]

Notes

1. Kusserow, *Refuge*, 23.
2. Review of *Refuge*, *Publishers Weekly*, March 18, 2013.
3. Kusserow, *Refuge*, 13.
4. Condominas, *Nous avons mangé la forêt*.
5. Mauss, *Gift*, 69.

7

Ta ʿbīr: Ethnography of the Imaginal

STEFANIA PANDOLFO

Through all beings spreads the one space:
the world's inner space. Silently fly the birds
all through us. O I who want to grow,
I look outside, and it is in me that the tree grows
—R. M. RILKE, August 1914

The text that follows, and that was discussed in an earlier version at the workshop that led to this book, is part of my long-term ethnographic work on the experience of madness in Morocco and on the forms of life and expression that are woven in its surroundings—inside and outside of the psychiatric institution, as well as in the world of Islamic healing.[1] The story I present here stands aside, however, and poses for me the question of the literary or, as I will also call it, the Imaginal, in its relation to trauma, and in the way this summons the practice of ethnography. I take the literary not simply as a matter of genre (in the sense, for instance, of a literary genre of ethnographic writing that would pay attention to the poetics of description and evocation) but, receptive to Maurice Blanchot's intimation in *The Space of Literature*, as the uncanny site of a "passage," a passage to another side of the real, which can only be seized in the unreal forms of myth, where the subject recedes and the world comes to the fore in the impersonality of what Blanchot calls the "imaginary space."

Such a *passage*, I argue, following my interlocutors' Arabic conceptual vocabulary—and the terms of an Islamic tradition of the Imaginal where the image is a modality of presence, and cosmic existence is identical to imagination (*khayyal*)[2]—is the cipher of the relation between loss and expression, between this world and the other. The insistent terms are 'ibra and ta'bīr (from the same semantic root in Arabic): 'ibra "a passage or bridge across incommensurable places, spaces, languages, or times, as well as the incommensurability of the spaces; a moral example, a lesson to be drawn from things past, events, portentous signs, or histories; the passages of migration, translation, or conversion, and the crossing of death"; ta'bīr, "expression and figuration, giving form, imaginalization."[3]

Such a "passage" directly concerns for me the practice of ethnographic writing, as a double responsibility to the real in the sense of both the "document" and its "transfiguration."

It is Blanchot who reflects most radically on writing as a "passage," a "metamorphosis," a "conversion," or a passing to another side, the Other Side (l'autre côté), as he calls it, where consciousness is delivered to the Outside, where the subject ceases to say "I," or where the one who says "I" is another (and yet not another person); where language ceases to want to "grasp" and "represent" the world, where images cease to serve representation, and mastery is surrendered; where objects are no longer held at a safe distance, but the distance of things holds us, and life and death are no longer opposed.[4] Writing in the margin of Rilke's poetry, Blanchot names this region of the passage l'espace intérieur du monde, "the world's inner space": "He [Rilke] names it Weltinnenraum, the world's inner space, which is no less things' intimacy than ours, and the free communication from one to the other, the strong, unrestrained freedom where the pure force of the undetermined is affirmed."[5] Animals and plants have an advantage over us, Blanchot writes, channeling Rilke, because they are capable of entering the world without having to be at the center. They just "are," and in that capacity they partake of the world from all sides. But for us humans, at least in Rilke's view, consciousness comes with the inability to access the Other Side, that is to say, to enter reality from all sides. "With all its eyes the creature sees the Open. Our eyes only are as if turned away."[6] Blanchot completes Rilke's thought: "To accede the other side, would be to transform our way of having access."[7]

Literature, for Blanchot, is the site of that transformation. It is the region of a backward glance, Orpheus's turning his gaze back from the world of objects and toward the region of death, which destines him to the loss of his beloved and commits him to the Other Side. It is there that the orphic song originates. In Blanchot's rewriting of Rilke's Orpheus, it is not

Orpheus's impatience that loses Eurydice to the invisible world, but his going directly to her, his not "reversing" his gaze. Losing her as a possession amounts to encountering her in the Open. His gesture is the cipher of another mode of relation beyond relation, one that strives to reach beyond "grasping," beyond possession and mastery, beyond greed and accounting, in a movement of dying that is also an opening to the infinity of relation: "in imaginary space (*espace imaginaire*) things are *transformed* into that which cannot be grasped."

"In the world things are transformed into objects in order to be grasped, utilized, made more certain in the distinct rigor of their limits and the affirmation of a homogeneous and divisible space. But in imaginary space things are *transformed* into that which cannot be grasped. Out of use, beyond wear, they are not in our possession but are the movement of dispossession, which releases us both from them and from ourselves. They are not certain but are joined to the intimacy of the risk where neither they nor we are sheltered anymore."[8]

Because, as Blanchot explains in a remarkable appendix by the telling title "Two Versions of the Imaginary," "to live an event as an image is not to remain uninvolved . . . the way that the esthetic theory of the image and the serene ideal of classical art propose. But neither is it to take part freely and decisively. It is to be taken,[9] to pass from the region of the real where we hold ourselves at a distance from things the better to order and use them into that other region where the distance holds us."[10]

An encounter with a woman I call Samia led me from the everyday reality of an ethnography of dispossession and mental illness in the wards of a psychiatric hospital and in the neighborhoods of a Moroccan city, to being summoned to the Outside in the imaginal world of the mural frescos that Ilyas, her companion, painted in the surrounding of illness, and where his experience was transfigured in the density of an image. For much of his adult life, Ilyas had been subjected to the intermittent spells of a mental illness. He had a predilection for painting since childhood, when he used to draw pictures in the school of the rural town where he was born, and had developed that art later in life through his activity as a traditional wood engraver and decorator. But even though the strokes of the brush on the walls of his apartment carried a trace of traditional iconographic motifs, the pictures that he "threw" (as he put it) on the walls in the grips of his "state" had a radically different quality. They were witnesses to his "disappearance," and to the emergence of an impersonal other in his place, a presence in which "I" did not recognize itself. The central image—an enormous snake painted, or "imaginalized," on the interior wall of his two-room dwelling—occupied the front stage of what had been their home, at once an expression and materialization of being-at-risk, and an eschatological summoning.

This writing started in the shadow of that image and that summoning, and in the form of a conversation with Ilyas and Samia, in a room populated with mural paintings and canvas, an interior that was also "the inner space of the world," where the Outside folded into the most intimate, the personal into the impersonal. In that space, and in the aftermath of their respective illnesses, Ilyas and Samia reflected on the nature and the "lesson" of that "passage," which for Ilyas was apprehended in the Islamic ethical and theological vocabulary of "passage" and "admonishment" (al-ʿibra), and in terms of the symbolic operation of figuration and expression (taʿbīr) in the perilous region where the self subsides, and the soul is exposed to abandonment and divine trial. All this happened without memory, for the "he" who could speak now was another. Yet the passage (ʿibra) and the figure (taʿbīr) were the terms of an ethical mode of relation, the operation of bridging incommensurable places and states, in the vision of one's own disappearance.

Over the years of our conversations, and in the course of multiple attempts at writing and apprehending the visual and spiritual logic of the paintings and what they could teach us of a mode of relationship with illness, I repeatedly asked myself what kind of writing would be adequate to the scene of Ilyas's "ravishment" and to the ethical question of registering an experience of madness. On the one hand, this required surrendering the instrumental dimension of the work, the oeuvre, as Blanchot called it, and allowing the ethnography, and the ethnographer, to be seized by the image, by the event, by the path, projected onto the Outside, traversed as it were by a silent flight of birds ("Silently fly the birds all through us"). On the other hand, the responsibility of tracing differing or alternative vocabularies and possibilities of the imagination, madness, and the soul, in the winding path of Ilyas's and Samia's lives and through a conceptual engagement with the Islamic metaphysics of the imagination as a central analytic resource, is itself an opening to the Outside, an undoing of the work.

The Serpent

To live an event as an image is not to see an image of this event, nor is it to attribute to the event the gratuitous character of the imaginary. The event really takes
place—and yet does it "really" take place? The occurrence seizes us, as the image
would seize us, that is, it releases us, from it and from ourselves. It keeps us outside. It makes of this outside a presence where "I" does not recognize "itself."
—M. BLANCHOT, *The Space of Literature*, my translation

To get to Ilyas's place one has to walk through densely populated streets
that in the afternoon become so crowded that it is arduous to make one's
way, a long descent amid street markets and vendors. Toward the end of
the hill, as the street dead-ends into a ravine overlooking the valley below,
is the beginning of his immediate neighborhood. Side streets are numbered, as in a lotissement that was never completed, shapes and spatial
arrangements bearing the trace of the shantytown that this once was and

has in part remained. A metal door among others opens onto narrow stairs leading the visitor to the third floor, on the roof, where Ilyas's apartment is located. The first time I walked up those stairs I was warned by a sign to the visitor: written in French, in capital letters and red paint, it said, "ILYAS DANGER."

Inside the apartment, on the back wall of the sleeping area, an immense fresco protrudes from the wall, staging a gigantic snake, in dark blue, black, and teal colors. The snake has horns, like a dragon; has scales, like a snake or a fish; and brandishes a sword; it is adjoined by an Arabic inscription, an injunction and a warning, which reads "la ghāliba illa allah" (No one is victorious except God). Other prominent iconographic elements include three crosses drawn in the style of a Christian crucifixion, a disconnected arm holding a key with chains, the recurrent motif of an eye, and surrounding water and waves—the sea.

The fresco occupies the entire surface of the wall, and in the empty room it dominates the scene from every angle. Surging from the depth of another scene, it visually claims the space of the home. Under the gaze of the painting, of the snake, the house ceases to be a habitation for the living. We, the occasional visitors, are called in, delivered to the scene of the painting, literally in its grip. The feeling is that of being surrounded, included or abducted in a scene, which is not of this world and is however here, not elsewhere, in the midst of our world. Foreground and background are blurred, and the serpent pushes out of the wall, spilling into the space of ordinary life. The scene is not for our eyes; yet we are here in its midst.

Only when he is ill does Ilyas paint the shapes that take form in what he calls his "unaware" imaginings. And these "forms" or "shapes" (ashkāl) are "expressive" (ta ʿbīri), or "symbolic" (ramzī), he says: they don't correspond to the forms existing in the external world but carry the shapes of a mythical world, inhabited by monsters and nonhuman creatures, a theater of violent struggles and scenes of torture.

To an eye attuned to Islamic ethical and eschatological themes, and reinforced by the inscription invoking the sovereignty of God, the snake fresco is evocative of the Quranic scene of the "torment of the grave" (ʿadhāb al-qabr). This is the event of the soul of the person's being subjected to trials and questioning by the angels in the immediate aftermath of death, and to bodily torments from which no one will be spared. In classical narratives, such as those of Tirmidhi and al-Ghazali, torments are visualized in the form of scorpions and snakes. It is a scene of great emotional intensity, reiterated in the eschatological tones of homiletic literature, in moral storytelling, and today vividly present for many in the affective texture of everyday life through contemporary forms of pious exhortations, printed pamphlets, and in the visual media.[11] And yet Ilyas was hesitant when I inquired about the possible kinship of the snake on the wall with the bestiary of the torment of the grave.

To qualify his own hesitation, Ilyas explained that the two images were discrepant, and visibly so in some iconographic traits: the snake of the torment of the grave was usually drawn in the shape of a cobra, while his own snake was "changed" or "altered" (mbeddel): it had horns, like a dragon or a dinosaur. As if to emphasize its foreignness, he characterized it with a French word: incroyable. Unbelievable and impossible, Ilyas's snake is not fully part of a shared eschatological cosmos; its emergence undoes, shatters the coherence of the cosmos, disconnects the faithful, and sets him adrift from the community of trust in which he can belong. It is that ontological sense of being adrift, that being shuttered, exiled from a community of sense, which is displayed by the snake on the wall. Something in it makes its apparition untranslatable, impossible to share within a given discourse, be that an eschatological narrative. Its emergence is the event of a danger that is announced at the entrance of the home: "ILYAS DANGER."

And yet the serpent on the wall is also adjacent to the Quranic vision of the grave. Ilyas articulates this point much later, as we looked at a photograph of the painting, which by then had long been erased from the wall. "The snake is the illness of a person, thu'bān hwwa l-marḍ dyal shakhs. And the illness too is 'adhāb, a torment, a trial. So much pain and torture a human being is made to endure, by the Illness!" And he went on to say that at the time of his illness he had not been able to sleep for months, moving restlessly, anxiously, aimlessly. When he finally returned home he was crushed; the torment was overwhelming. Then the painting materialized. He "threw" it on the wall outside of consciousness, and the gaze of the image became a sanctuary for him. In the shade of the serpent he could finally sleep.

When we first met, Ilyas was forty-one, emerging from a psychotic illness that had lasted for more than two years. He had lived the previous months in despondent seclusion, at one with the walls of his home and the paintings on those walls. Now he was slowly returning to the world of relationships. Samia was herself afflicted by a condition that reduced her to apathy, at times giving way to a delusional state. In her late twenties, she was tormented by physical pain, especially in her joints, and by an unbearable weight on her chest that at times suffocated and prevented her from getting up in the morning. Ilyas and Samia had been married four years: at the birth of their daughter, who was now three, they had fallen ill, each in their way, and drifted into madness. For Ilyas it was the third time; he had been ill in the past, in a similar and an even more acute way. For Samia it was the first time; it was also her first encounter with Ilyas's psychosis.

Their perceptions of illness were different from one another, as were their experiences of being ill. Samia saw her illness as the sedimentation of the story of her life; she considered the psychic crisis, paradoxically, to be both a release and a coming of age. She explained, "The illness made me aware; it is as if there was a (psychic) knot in me, and it was blasted open," bringing relief (w 'anī l-mrḍ; bḥal ila kent fiya waḥd l- 'aqda u tfarga 't). She had chosen a charged term: w 'anī: al-wa 'ī is awareness, consciousness, and hence responsibility, in the sense of awakening, also in an ethical-religious sense. In a vocabulary common to many spiritual narratives of transformation-via-illness, from al-Ghazali's twelfth-century autobiographical account of his illness and spiritual crisis[12] to the innumerable vernacular Moroccan popular hagiographies, Samia suggested that the illness had been a (spiritual) crisis that had caused her to see and thus grow. After her illness she had started to pray. She meant that she had become a Muslim with invested awareness, but also that for most of her life she had been unaware, frozen to early childhood by the disabling pain of abandonment, and illness had transformed her into an adult, in a struggle that remained ongoing.

For Ilyas, madness could not be integrated or made intelligible in a narrative form or a life story: it was a being seized and being undone, delivered into an Outside where the "I" ceases to exist. Its recollection was at best an avowal of a chasm and a lapse. The serpent on the wall was the memory,

the imprint, of such undoing and being seized. Yet the forms (ashkāl) of the pictorial composition—what he also described as ʿibara or ramz, "expressions," "symbols," or "ciphers"—opened for Ilyas a space that could become the stage of a confrontation in which his very existence was at stake. In our conversation he conceptualized such an emergence of form as the operation of taʿbīr, the carving of an interval and a bridge. I will come back to this crucial point.

Several other wall paintings, in smaller size, punctuated the walls. The shape of a woman-fish, ʿarusat-l-baḥr, "the sea-bride," or mermaid, in blue and gold, was enclosed within a painted frame, an aquarium perhaps. It had scales, like the snake, and at the place where the head should be there is instead a white spot, a bit of unpainted wall. It is the place (Samia explained later) where a picture had been scratched off the wall. An uncanny meeting of the mythical and the biographical. A Maghribi and Middle Eastern mythical image of watery metamorphoses, sexual desire, temptation, pleasure, and demonic intercourse, the mermaid is recurrent on the walls in a multiplicity of forms and versions. It holds the key to a dimension of the snake that partakes of its traumatic insistence, and its painful, deathly, and ecstatic corporeality.

On the front door of the house, turned toward the outside and addressing the visitor, there was another painting: one that along with the fresco of the snake would become important in our conversation as well as in the unfolding of their relationship—the bond that ties Samia and Ilyas. The door painting shows a tree with two human personages, visually unmarked in their gender, that are reminiscent of the Quranic story of Adam and Ḥawwa (Eve) and their expulsion from the Garden. "It's the two of us," Samia told me the first time we walked through the door. Painted in red, black, different shades of green, and energetic strokes of color, and as if emerging from a thick bed of vegetation, the tree is heavy with fruits hanging from its branches. A roughly sketched human figure stretches an arm upward to pick a piece of fruit that lies outside its reach. Another figure, with its back turned to the other, stands on the opposite side of the tree, offering an empty hand to the viewer. Outstretching one's hand, Ilyas says, is the gesture of the beggar. Later on, Ilyas explained the circumstances in which the painting had come into being. He was trapped in his illness, he said, unable to provide for Samia and for the necessities of their life. The painting shows Samia hungry and unable to reach, and himself, his back turned, empty-handed. He calls this image shajarat al-ḥayat, "the tree of life."

When I ask him—and I will ask him many times over the course of the years we have been talking, through his different states and in different phases of his life, from 2005 to the present—Ilyas insists that there is no direct relation between his attraction to painting and his mental illness. He never stops painting: it is what he paints that undergoes a mutation. When he is not ill, he paints "ordinary things": realistic scenes, landscapes, or traditional geometric motifs. He shows me a painting hidden in a corner of the room and removed from sight, piled with other works he had made prior to his illness.

Those paintings on the wall, he says, "are pictures that contain a ḥalā, a state" (luḥat lly fihum ḥalā). They are made in an altered (ecstatic, or pathological) state. Ḥalā, literally condition or state, is the common nonmedical term for a psychopathological state; it is used in the context of mental illness as well as the cures of the spirits, where it designates the event of possession. Ḥalā also means "state" in the sense of trance, and the related term ḥāl designates a nonpathological altered state in Sufi-inspired practices. Ilyas's use of the term evokes this entire semantic configuration.

Luḥa lli fiha ḥalā, "a picture that contains a ḥalā," has for Ilyas the status of a concept. Over the years of our conversation I came to realize that a "picture that contains a state" designated for Ilyas a particular kind of efficacious image, one that can become an operator of transformation. It is an image that stores the affect of a "state" (the encoded memory of loss and self-annihilation) and that at the same time constitutes an imaginal barrier. It opens an "interval" that is also a "bridge" or a "passage" to another modality of being and to the possibility of witnessing a divine address. This has resonance within an Islamic tradition of the image that is directly implied by Ilyas's choice of terms. The efficacious character of his images, and more generally of the operation that he calls taʿbīr, can be related to the ontological intercession of images in the space of the limit that Ibn ʿArabi (twelfth century) had called barzakh: an "imaginal" border that joins by separating, such as an isthmus or a bridge, and that is the site of a passage for bodies and spirits; a partition, a screen, between two modalities of being; an imaginal barrier, connecting-yet-separating, at once being and nonbeing, spiritual and corporeal, widening and delimiting, this world and the other; the site where the impossible can manifest itself in concrete form.

Ilyas's repertory of figures associated with the illness, as well as his own analysis of the nature and work of the images in the "paintings that contain a ḥalā" (through the concepts of ashkāl, taʿbīr, and ramz) bear some resemblance to the kinds of visual forms Aby Warburg called bipolar images or dynamograms:[13] forms charged with contradictory and nonpolarized energies, which bridge without resolving incommensurable times, states, and qualities. Bipolar images are potent visual forms in which opposites remain copresent—concept and passion, life and death, building and destruction, movement and paralysis—in visual assemblages or in a ritual theater. Stylized figures and "affective signs" are the active operators of transformation and of the unconscious transmission of social memory. As Warburg himself experienced with the psychotic illness that afflicted him for the later part of his life, such images and signs are powerful forms that "emerge" in the dissolution of the subject and from the ruins of representation and culture, in the "contortions" of delusional experience.[14]

For Warburg one such form was the serpent. It was a serpent he first encountered in the ritual life of the Hopi Indians and that later became for him the insistent trait and ambivalent intercessor of existence and healing, in a struggle that Warburg dubbed "the dialectic of the Monster." What was the nature of obliteration, survival, and regeneration? What was the relation of catastrophe to emergence, to the insistence of a trace, and to the work of a social memory, transmission, and creation? What was the historical and ethical lesson of images, and of the "interval," the "distance," "intercession," and "passage" introduced by the iconological mode of thought?

The capacity to inhabit and grasp this double movement was for Warburg the presupposition of any possible cure. It is a cure that acknowledges and engages with a dimension of the incurable, and that is not just healing for an individual, but for a collectivity, and even the "civilization" of which the person, the symptom, the artist, and the historian are witnesses. In Agamben's words (writing about Warburg), they are "extremely sensitive seismographs responding to distant earthquakes, or . . . ' "necromancers' who consciously evoke the specters threatening them."[15]

Ilyas is one such seismographer. The ethnographer must be too, in allowing her voice, and her words, to be transmuted.

One afternoon in 2005, while completing the whitewashing of his home and getting ready to brush over the two personages and the tree, Ilyas asked me whether I would like to have the door he had painted them on, so that I could keep and care for it at my place. By then we had had many conversations about these images, his visions, his ḥalā, and his paintings. He was ambivalent about destroying the door—it "stored" the cipher of his relationship and life with Samia—but he knew that he could not start living again in a space populated by these witnesses to the world of his illness, traces of a burning exposure. He needed a new door. I proposed to buy it, but he said that such paintings (paintings that contain a ḥalā, encode the intensity of a "state") could not be sold. We arranged for a small three-wheeler truck to transport the door to my place, where it still is today, "on consignment," or, as one says in Arabic, as an *amana* (something entrusted to a temporary caretaker). That is also the mode in which I am writing today.

Each time, after an illness episode, Ilyas covers up his frescos with a coat of whitewash. Once he emerges from the ḥalā, he says, he cannot bear the sight of these images. This is why they must be withdrawn from the realm of the visible. We are looking at these images in a narrow interim, just prior to their disappearance. It is getting dark. I take photos of the paintings and Ilyas lights a candle for me to see where to orient the camera, for in the apartment there is no electricity. Samia asks questions based on her intimate familiarity with the images, which are so important in the story of their life together. Ilyas is explaining. Samia interrupts, to provide a context or fill a gap in his words.

The way Ilyas narrates the painting now is different from when, in his words, he "puts down, throws his state, his being, his illness, in the picture" (kanḥattu f-ṣūra, "I throw it in the picture"). Now he can recognize the shapes (ashkāl), the figures (ʿibara), and what they express—their ciphers (ramz)— but in the mode of a textual reading, and in terms of a "symbolic" lexicon of figures (the serpent, the sea, the cross, the sea creatures) that accompany Ilyas and Samia in their lives and are drawn, in part, from a collective theological and mythological repertory. Ilyas emphasizes the gap; for him there is a radical discontinuity between the person who is speaking today and the one who drew on the wall. Even though, at one level, he remembers the act of painting, at another he has no recollection or knowledge of it.

He no longer knows, he says, what the experience of the painting actually was for him when he painted it. He smiles—and his mercurial smile betrays a glimpse of what might have been. He emphasizes the rift, the inadequacy of his account. He was not the same person then; he painted "without awareness," driven by a powerful urge, and the shapes or forms emerged ready-made, from an inner upheaval. There was no intention of composing a meaningful picture. He just "put down" the shapes on the wall or the canvas, and in fact he wasn't even there agentively in that sense: the shapes emerged on their own. He says "nḥatthum f-luḥa": "I put them down in the painting," as one unloads a heavy charge. He was not there to compose the painting, it came out already composed, "like something that was already there, present," he said. He smiled: "Bla shuʿur ḥetta hua keykhaddem" (Unconscious creation is effective as well).

There was a whole world in there, live, powerful forces, in those colors and shapes. Again he smiles. Have they really withdrawn? But he jokes, the serpent, now "ḥaddu l-ḥayt daba," "it is confined to the wall now! . . . And in a few days, when I'm done white-washing, it will disappear altogether! . . . I no longer have the snake here . . ." ("mabqash ʿandi lfaʿ hna!," pointing to his head).

But, yes, the paintings are "his," in the sense in which "his" life is a collection of a multiplicity of states and chapters, and in some of those, under the pressure of a pain he no longer remembers (a torment encoded in the snake on the wall), he turns into another "consciousness" or another mode of existence, which from the standpoint of what he calls an "ordinary person" (insan ʿadi), and of himself in his ordinary state, can only be described as unconsciousness and delusion. Such is what from the outside, and in its aftermath, Ilyas describes as his illness. At no point in our conversation does he present his experience as anything other than (mental) illness; in the aftermath of his episode at least, he does not see himself as a mystic, a majdūb or inspired visionary (from jadba, trance), or a person haunted by the jinns (majnūn).

Ilyas makes a clear analytic distinction between his ḥalā and what he calls "ordinary" existence (ḥayat ʿadya). In his ordinary life, when he is not ill, he is better adjusted to the practical requirements of the world but has no access to the experiences and heightened visionary awareness of his states—states in which, however, he is no longer present as the same person. The different styles of his paintings, when he is ʿadī (ordinary) and when he instead paints in a ḥalā, attest to the discontinuity of his experience, as also does his inability to reach, in his "ordinary" mode, the aesthetic pathos and formal complexity of his paintings of "states." Yet neither he nor Samia, Ilyas says, can ever really be considered "ordinary persons" (insan ʿady). They have what he calls a ḥassa, "a sensibility," ḥassa nafsiyya, a special psychic/spiritual attitude, a way of being, that is not ordinary and that makes them permeable and sensitive to the world. It is Samia's "sensibility," Ilyas says, that enables her to relate to his paintings. This sensibility and vulnerability is something that artists share with the mad (l-ḥmaq), he elaborates, assigning both to an exilic position, given to an Outside, out of the bounds of the ʿada, the practical norms of customary life that bind a collectivity together.

The artist, l-fannān, may seem to people like a mad person: mumkin kayban ll nnas bḥal shi ḥmaq. An ordinary person will not look (at a painting) and understand it. He will not be able to grasp its forms and the emotions expressed [insan ʿadi, maghadish yshuf u yfhem]. An ordinary person will not value and respect the artwork [ben ʿadem ʿadī maghadish y ʿatah qima]. Instead, the painting is an expression, a coming to form, by the artist [hua key ʿabbar biha]. The artist has thoughts, ideas [afkār], and his thoughts are those lines [khuṭāt], those curves, those colors; they contain thinking and meaning [ʿandhum afkār u ʿandhum ma ʿni]. In the past, and even more than now, ordinary, normal people didn't attribute any value [qima] to works in the plastic arts [luḥat shkiliyin].

What Ilyas calls a shape (shkel: classical Arabic shakl, pl. ashkāl) is the site of a coming to presence of something withdrawn from existence, something that assumes sensory form by being "imaginalized." According to Ibn al-ʿArabi, imagination takes form from sensory perception to then disclose suprasensory meanings (ma ʿnā) through these sensory forms.

Understanding Ilyas's explication of the figural logic of the paintings calls for a different philosophy of the image, capable of grasping the image's fundamental relationship with Being. Only from this angle is it possible to apprehend and appreciate how for Ilyas the painting of the serpent can become the transformative stage of a "real" confrontation where the coordinates of the subject's position in the world can be reordered in a passage through madness.

Visual Meaning and Imagination of the Real

Ilyas begins to interpret the painting:[16]

If we want to explicate the painting [l-luḥa], there is the Serpent [thu ʿaban, lfa ʾ], it is the torment of life [humūm l-ḥayat]: life when it is hard, when it is painful, is like a Serpent. It is poisonous. As for the sword [ṣif], the Sword is the force that conquers [ghaleb] all things: next to the sword he wrote in Arabic [speaking about the painter in the third person], Lā ghaliba illa allah, "No one is victorious except God," because God, praise and glory on him, only God is sovereign on all things. And [this means that] all that happens in the life of the creatures, of human beings [insān], all human beings suffer and endure, their successes and their failures, it happens with the permission of God. However much a person wants or likes something, what happens is because God allows it to happen. And over there [pointing to the right side of the painting] there is a key, it is the shape of imprisonment [sklel sujun], the form of a human being imprisoned in life [serūt, bḥal shkel masjūn, shi insān masjūn fi l-ḥayāt]; because the life of a person without ʿamal, without works [ethical and material works, activity that pleases God], without aim and without fulfillment, is the life of a person in prison. This much is expressed/visualized in the painting [dak shi lli fiha diel taʿbīr].

For Ilyas, four figures recapitulate the scene: the serpent, which is the torment of life; the sword, an image of the divine power that conquers, punishes, and saves (but also, Ilyas will say, the sword is jihad, "struggle," and ḥarb, "war," with the illness and with the hardship of our times [jihad wa l-ḥarb maʿ l-mrḍ wa l-waqt]); the writing (kitaba, kteb ʿlih) that proclaims God's sovereignty over all things and reminds humans of their vulnerability; and the key and the chains that depict the prison of life. The figures, once again, are not symbols in the conventional sense of representations that stand for other things, whether objects or concepts. Their nature is imaginal: they are at once a screen and a bridge to what they make visible. Such is the force of the taʿbīr.

The emphasis is on the torment of the self in the grips of destruction and madness, a state of things that, Ilyas suggests, is the outcome of a specifically historical condition, that of a society built on dispossession and where human beings are abandoned to wander and waste away (ḍāʿa) without an aim, without work (l-ʿamal) or fulfillment. "Empty-handed," as in the painting of the tree. The snake, the illness, is not just an existential condition and a theological dilemma: it also is that very historical prison. Theodicy, the theological question of human suffering, and mental illness itself take on a political significance. Most of all the writing is crucial: Lā ghaliba illa allah, "No one is victorious except God," has the status of a divine utterance, the injunction of a heteronomous law. In the scene of the illness—the illness as a struggle of the soul in which the self/soul and its very existence are at stake, exposed to the double risk of madness and damnation—the injunction of the divine writing has illocutionary force.

Ilyas explains the relation between the figures (ashkāl) and what they make visible through the concept of ramz (sign, cipher, symbol, or emblem, pointing to a secret at the core of a symbolic relationship, something that will remain hidden, call it a "signature") and in terms of the operation of ta'bīr, and refers to the painting as ṣūra, "image," and often also as luḥa, the "tablet" on which something becomes visible. In the classical tradition of the image, tasawwur is the imprint of a form—from al-ṣūra, image and form, and al-musawwira, the formative faculty. The "formative faculty" or retentive imagination is related but not identical to the imagination (takhayyul, from khayāl, imagination). Ta'bīr on the other hand is a noun from the verbal form 'abara, which means to cross over, to traverse, between two shores of a river, an ocean, from one mode of existence to another; to interpret a dream, to illustrate; to be taught a lesson, to admonish, to give an example. 'Ibara means expression, concrete manifestation, sign, passage, and interpretation.[17]

"Do you see the serpent actually appearing in front of your eyes?" I ask.

"It is a ramz, it is not real/true [haqiqi]," Ilyas replies. (Real/true here in the colloquial sense of something concrete, with a material reality, in the external world.)

He pauses, and then qualifies his statement: "The snake allows me to visualize, to express [deba l-hensh kan'abbar bih, hua ta'bīrī]; its nature is ta'bīrī ["expressive," or "figural"]. It has horns, like something terrifying, and flames and smoke in the mouth, like a dragon."

Ilyas says, "Kan'abbar fi l-luḥa," "I express, give form, in the painting, to what moves inside me." Kan'abbar, "I express": this term, from the vernacular vocabulary of poets, speaks of the immediacy and pathos of expression as an epiphany of form. The related noun ta'bīr, so important in Ilyas's vocabulary, can be translated as expression, in the sense of an example that makes something manifest, but something that can only be expressed by way of a bridge or a crossing, and as such marks an inadequacy, a disjunctive encounter of the visible and the invisible. "Dak shi lly fiha dyel ta'bīr," "this is the ta'bīr in the painting."

Ilyas's recourse to the concept of ta'bīr is interesting because of the double-edged nature of its semantic constellation, which can convey the immediacy of expression even as it gestures to the indirect nature of allegory and the ethical dimension of the "lesson." The related noun al-'ibra (plural 'ibār) carries the sense of a sign as an admonition, example, or lesson: the "example" that is the image of the serpent and that becomes an "admonition" for those who can see it.[18]

Understanding what Ilyas means by ramz and ta'bīr requires considering the place of expression, manifestation, and form within an Islamic conception of the image and its relation to the soul (*nafs*, *ruḥ*), in both medical and metaphysical terms: a tradition in which images are not representations but concrete events, "subtle" realities with a density of their own. Ilyas does not refer explicitly to these notions in a scholarly sense, but his way of reckoning his pictorial practice in the space of illness in effect does.

The snake is not an apparition or perceptual hallucination (that was my psychiatric question to Ilyas) but it is also, at the same time, not simply a metaphor of the illness; it imaginalizes the illness of being, and as such it becomes the stage of a direct confrontation whereby Ilyas's existence is at stake. Dense with eschatological themes, the painting stages a struggle with harm, with the serpent, with forces in the self/soul and in the world that are materialized in the symptoms that hurl Ilyas into a ḥalā. On that stage of life and death there is a literal wrestling with history, Ilyas's singular history, but also a collective history of oppression and violence. In the scene of that struggle, *in the painting*, the sovereignty of God is rendered visible as at once an unattainable limit, a command, and an appeal.

Melancholia and Transformation

As Samia listens and asks questions during Ilyas's explication of the mural of the snake, I realize that the wall paintings in the apartment, the very paintings that had taken over their home and had forced her to move out, are paradoxically also hers. Not because they are the product of a shared delusion, a folie à deux, but because they had become the ground of an encounter in the region of the Outside. In telling about the paintings she could articulate the enigma of her life.

In our conversations Samia spoke of her vulnerability, of the wound that kept reviving itself, carrying the trace of former losses, of the abandonment that had scarred her early life. Each time the wound reopened, her world was shattered. Everything changed around her; she felt the world collapsing on her and crushing her under an unbearable weight (bḥal ila kulshi keythat-tam 'aliya). She felt a weight on her chest that no medicine for the lungs could relieve, and her tongue became so heavy that speaking required an immense and overwhelming effort. Her perception of her surroundings was altered, she became mistrustful and hostile, and, sometimes, when her energy came back, she erupted, ranting in an incontrollable fury. "My state/illness [ḥalā] is such, when I lose someone I am attached to, I transform, I become another." Ilyas had cared for her as no one had before. He was an "intercessor" of her coming into the world; he shielded her from the devastating force of her memory.

ʿArfti shahl mrḍt f-Ilyas? "Do you know how sick I got over Ilyas?" She went on to tell me of her engagement to him, their marriage, their relationship, and then his illness. When they got married, she felt that she entered childhood for the first time because of the affection and care (ḥanan) that he had for her. She told of how he would bring her presents when she was pregnant, and of how, once when she had a craving for grapes and there were none in the market, he painted for her a picture of a basket full of grapes. And she told of the emptiness (faragh) she felt when he withdrew after she had their child (she didn't know about his illness then), when he started going out at night and wouldn't come back until daybreak. She spoke of his family and the way they kept the secret of his illness. When he started transforming they told her to hide her gold, her good plates; she didn't understand why. Then she understood. He had turned into that snake on the wall. But by then she was herself gone.

Samia describes the snake as a wahsh, a monster or a beast, a dreadful apparition that is a concrete manifestation of Ilyas's madness. Ilyas listens and does not disagree. Samia is a witness to the lapses of his life.

Yet as I look at the snake I see a figure at once pained and gentle, a wounded creature, whose features recall some of the other drawings on the walls, hybrid feminine images of maritime inspiration, with their flexing fish bodies and skin covered by scales. There is abandonment in the shapes, a lack of energy, and a sense of life shrinking that evokes a melancholic beauty. "The eye in the picture gazes at life all around," Ilyas says. The composition winds and curls as if protecting that gaze within. It is the gaze of things, the gaze of death looking back at us humans from all sides.[19]

The arm that holds the key appears as if brandishing a weapon. And there are the two little arms: the arm that holds the sword but cannot strike, and the arm that strives to grab the key but cannot reach—echo of another arm, on the front door of the house, which strives to grab a fruit but cannot reach. Arms that cannot reach, cannot strike: it is a scene of disablement.

But there is more: the second arm can be seen in a reflexive movement of striking the snake. And, in fact, precisely where the arm is attached to the body of the snake there is a wound, and the mark of bleeding. The snake torturer is also being tortured. We can see, with the intercession of Warburg's reflections on the serpent ritual as a theater of being, that Ilyas's snake is a "bipolar" image, staging a never-resolved theater of destruction and healing. The snake is also the self, the soul (al-nafs, al-ruḥ) in agony under attack, exposed, wounded, tortured, and yet enjoying. It is an image at once of pain and of pleasure, which bears a certain resemblance to the mermaids and their enticing gaze of demonic beings. The painting "shows" or "imaginal-izes" the self-in-despair in the position of the damned.

The same inability to reach salvation, the same sense of dispossession and impairment, is found in the painting of the tree, on the door of the house. Of that picture Ilyas says that we should pay attention to the two human figures. He had painted this picture during the time when Samia's brothers and family were accusing him of not providing for her, of being inactive and worthless. He is the figure on the left: "my hand is empty" (yddy faragh). She is the figure to the right, who attempts to grab an apple from the tree but cannot reach.

Samia says she is moved by this interpretation, about the apple and the empty hand. She asks him why he hasn't told her earlier; this would have explained so many things.

Ilyas says that he couldn't have told her; it was too shameful, too hurtful.

Samia says it wouldn't have been hurtful; what was hurtful was his silence, his absences, and the fact he spoke with his brothers about her, but not directly to her.

Around the paintings, their "delicate task of repair."[20]

Notes

Epigraph: "À travers tous les êtres passe l'unique espace: / espace intérieur du monde. Silencieusement volent les oiseaux / tout à travers nous. O moi qui veux croître, / je regarde au dehors et c'est en moi que l'arbre croît." Cited by Blanchot, L'espace littéraire, 174; English translation by Ann Smock, Space of Literature, 136.

1. Pandolfo, Knot of the Soul.
2. Chittick, Sufi Path to Knowledge, 116ff.
3. Mahdi, Ibn Khaldun's Philosophy of History, 63–73.
4. Blanchot, L'espace littéraire.

5. Blanchot, *L'espace littéraire*, 135.

6. " 'De tous ses yeux la créature voit l'Ouvert. Nos yeux seuls sont comme renversés.' Acceder à l'autre côté, ce serait donc transformer notre manière d'avoir accès." Blanchot, *L'espace littéraire*, 135. Translation modified.

7. Blanchot, *L'espace littéraire*, 133.

8. Blanchot, *L'espace littéraire*, 98.

9. The French here says, "C'est s'y laisser prendre," literally, "let oneself be seized" or "taken." The allowing oneself, as an active surrender to the image, has an ethical dimension that is not rendered in the translation "taken."

10. Blanchot, "The Two Versions of the Imaginary," in *The Space of Literature*, 254–68.

11. Quran 6:93, 8:52, 9:102. See also Smith and Haddad, *Islamic Understanding of Death and Resurrection*, 43ff.

12. Al-Ghazali, *Al-munqidh min al-ḍalāl*.

13. Warburg, *Diaries*, cited in Agamben, "Warburg and the Nameless Science."

14. In *L'image survivante*, Georges Didi-Huberman discusses a number of drawings and diary entries produced by Warburg during his psychotic illness, while in Binwanger's Swiss psychiatric clinic. In some of these drawings, forms are produced, or return, in what he calls the "contorsions" of delusional experience. Such genesis of form in madness is also explored by Lacan in his first writings on psychosis and paranoia, particularly a short text on "schizographies," in *La psychose paranoiaque* (1932).

15. Agamben, "Warburg and the Nameless Science," 94.

16. I borrow the term "visual meaning" from Hamdouni Alami, *Origin of Visual Culture in the Islamic World*.

17. *Arabic-English Dictionary: The Hans Wehr Dictionary of Modern Written Arabic*, ed. J. Milton Cowan (Urbana, IL: Spoken Language Services, 1979).

18. On this question of the ʿibra as an example or admonition, see *The Arabian Nights* (and the story/life as example), and the writing of the story in the corner of the eye; cf. Kilito, *L'oeil et l'aiguille*, and Colla, "Ladies and the Eye."

19. See Lacan, "Of the Gaze as Petit Objet A," in *Four Fundamental Concepts of Psychoanalysis*. The eye/ʿayn is an important motif in Maghribi vernacular iconography: ʿayn, source, origin, letter of the alphabet, predatory violence of and protection against the gaze—of the ʿayn/evil eye. For a discussion of the ʿayn/eye/source in Morocco, see my *Impasse of the Angels*, as well as Khatibi, *La blessure du nom propre*, and, of course, a multitude of Arabic magical texts, as well as an Islamic pietistic literature that addresses the healing of illnesses caused by sihr (sorcery) and the ʿayn, the (evil) Eye.

20. This phrase is from Das, *Life and Words*, 15.

8

WRITING THROUGH INTERCESSORS

STUART McLEAN

The Chilean poet Raúl Zurita tells us that the dead return to speak when we speak, see when we see, feel when we feel.[1] But is it only the dead? Beyond the named and individuated dead, commemorated in obituaries and on memorials and gravestones, beyond even the dead conceived of as a vast, undifferentiated backdrop to the existence of the living (what Todd Ramón Ochoa elsewhere refers to as the "ambient dead"), the language of poetry also provides a conduit for an impersonal, inhuman life of matter that both preexists us and carries us beyond ourselves.[2] Is it perhaps through this simultaneous presencing of the dead and of an other-than-human materiality (and temporality) that poetry—and art more generally—is able to open the present to the possibility of alternative futures? Such futures should not be thought of as the product of human agency alone but rather as demanding an acknowledgment of and an artful engagement with powers and presences extending beyond the human realm, extending indeed beyond the conventional distinctions we are accustomed to draw between the human and the nonhuman, the animate and the inanimate. Yet if literature and art direct us toward a zone of desubjectification, of the dissolution of the "I," how is this to be articulated and made manifest? What stories, what images are capable of traversing the space or time between the eclipse of meaning and subjectivity and a recognizable human, cultural, and historical world? Michel Serres writes of the ubiquity and universality of messengers putting worlds in communication. He draws a line from the Greek Hermes, winged-sandaled messenger of the Olympian gods, through the angels of Christian and Islamic tradition to today's jet aircraft traversing the globe, and the international travelers they carry, along with the importuning emissaries of homelessness, hunger, and poverty these travelers will encounter on leaving the airport—angels of steel on the one hand and of flesh and blood on the other. Then there are the less obviously substantial messengers, some of them humanly generated, like signals sent out across the airwaves, and some not, like tides, ocean currents, meteorological fluxes, and weather systems on the move. A world of messengers.[3]

Stefania uses the term *intercessors*. Don't we as anthropologists always write through intercessors, whether in the persons of our informants or, less tangibly, in the form of stories, images, atmospheres? And don't we always court the risk of betraying them or being betrayed by them, a risk that is, arguably, as much endemic to the practice of writing as to the project of anthropology, however conceived? Ilyas and Samia are intercessors, figures who allow us to move between, on the one hand, the stories of their mental illness, the paintings through which it finds expression, and the realities of early twenty-first-century Morocco that furnish the context for their lives and, on the other, a space that resists articulation in such terms. For Ilyas in particular images too are intercessors, the images of his paintings produced in a psychopathological state of ḥalā, images in which the mythical and the biographical meet and reciprocally transform one another, allowing him to achieve an otherwise impossible proximity to his own madness and thus to reorder his existence and resume his life in the world.

Where then do the images in Ilyas's paintings come from? Ilyas describes them as coming from another world, a world of monsters and nonhuman creatures. Yet they draw upon an identifiable repertoire of cultural significations. The snake in particular evokes the Quranic scene of ʿadhāb al-qabr ("torment of the grave"), the trials and questioning to which the soul of the deceased is subject after death. At the same time the snake disrupts the coherence of the eschatological imagery upon which it draws, both through idiosyncratic additions like horns and through its more general demeanor of vulnerability. It is thus expressive of Ilyas's own feeling of severance from a community of sense-making, the experience of the eclipse of subjectivity that is also, potentially, the prelude to its curative restoration. Issuing from the depths of another scene, the image of the snake at once partakes of and exceeds cultural legibility, just as its materialization on the wall renders strange and unfamiliar the everyday realities of Ilyas's apartment and the surrounding neighborhood.

The image as intercessor traverses the zone of *barzakh*—understood in Islamic eschatology as a border, bridge, or isthmus that simultaneously connects and divides body and spirit, being and nonbeing, this world and the other, where the impossible and unrepresentable can become manifest. Other intercessors are present in the text too, including Aby Warburg's account, informed by his own experiences of mental illness, of "bipolar images," in which seeming opposites remain simultaneously present and, equally important, the theorization in certain varieties of Islamic thought of images not as representations but as "events" endowed with their own density and reality. The latter are evoked not as "cultural context" or data requiring analysis and explanation, but as interlocutors, capable of engendering new possibilities of thought. At the same time, the writing itself performs an intercessory back-and-forth movement between the descriptive detail that anthropologists so often pride themselves on rendering and the otherworldly "sendings" that disrupt any taken-for-granted sense of an ethnographic real. Perhaps indeed it is through cultivating such a plurality of intermediaries that anthropological writing is best able simultaneously to limn the contours of an identifiable and knowable social world and to evoke the presence within it of that which forever resists the attempt to know and explain. Perhaps this is why anthropology has always been, among other things, a "literary" art.

Notes

1. Zurita, *Dreams for Kurosawa*.
2. Ochoa, "Versions of the Dead," 482. Ochoa's description echoes Elias Canetti's account of the "invisible crowd" of the dead as among the most ancient and universal of human imaginings. Canetti, *Crowds and Power*, 47.
3. Serres, *Angels*.

Desire in Cinema

ANAND PANDIAN

The scriptgirl and the stuntman, the actor and the actress, the propman and the makeup artist, even the director and that raven-haired stranger in the hotel lobby . . . "What is this movie business where everyone sleeps with everyone?" asks the production manager's wife, always watching over her husband from the edge of the set with a deadly pair of knitting needles in hand—"your movie world, I despise it!" The director, played by François Truffaut himself in this film, Day for Night, glides in and out of scenes like this one with a box on his arm and a plug in his ear, a slender black cord dangling between them. They say that it's a hearing aid, this metallic instrument, for ears blown out by the gunfire of a recent war. To me, though, this small device looks like something else, some other kind of mechanism, some way of tuning in to the pulse of that world, its continuous murmur, the intensity of its desire.

Dusk is already falling when we pull into the parking lot and I point out the actress and the taxi driver says that she's the reason for his divorce, that Tamil director, sitting now on one of the plush lawns of the MGM Beach Resort, picking at a plate of French fries as his crew remakes a guest cottage into a nuptial boudoir, still waiting for the satiny sheets stuck on a lorry somewhere in Chennai, thinking about what was printed in the papers just this morning, more news of his impending divorce, about what his wife had said when she left him, that he wasn't stable, wasn't reliable, "how could I be stable?" he turns to ask me, "I can't be stable, I have to live somebody else, otherwise I can't make my films," telling me to imagine some film-maker, any filmmaker, "two weddings, four weddings, three weddings, countless affairs, because you're not yourself, you can't be yourself, you

can't have a steady life," his words beginning to tumble now in a rush of
recollections, "you've been a gangster, you've been a king, you've been a
slum guy, you've been a decent guy, I've been that girl, this girl, in a given
film I play some seventy, sixty, fifty, forty characters, and this is my ninth
movie, so nine times fifty, you can calculate how many characters I've
played," he says, "you can see why all filmmakers are mad, some people talk
to trees, they have to let it out somewhere," and as I listen, I begin to wonder, what is it that they have to let out, all these men that he has in mind,
expression, emission, is it the spunk of genius or something else for this
director, Selvaraghavan, for whom, as he says, filmmaking is literally or-
gasm, multiple orgasms, more intense than a hundred orgasms, this man
whose films are so flagrantly sexual, like *Thulluvadho Ilamai* (Youth, how it
leaps), his first, a coming-of-age story crammed with brothels, porn, and
amorous predilections of all kinds, one man winking suggestively at a trio
of boys, a girl alone running her hand down, down the length of her own
dress, the forest tryst she has with her schoolboy friend, "so that's how
much you're itching for it?" her confidante chides, a line that set the
Thambi's Theatre crowd around me screaming and hollering a decade ago
in rural Cumbum, the hall packed with young men and no women for what
was said about the pornographic tones of the film, nominally directed by
Selva's father but a story really put, Selva says, into his own tender hands of
twenty-one years, "hell," he says, "every night I used to come back and cry,"
too many people awaiting instructions, too little control over the technicians, until suddenly, "something happened on one of those days," suddenly there was "somebody else yelling inside me," someone else bursting
out, "someone bold and arrogant, he just goes in, 'I want this shot, do it,

push! no, I want it that way!' he screams," some presence you might describe as a person but is really more like a thing, something not to judge whether good or bad, something not to caution or censure for its injury or harm, "coming like a rush, you just do it, you just become it," he says, it, this it, let's call this "it" something, *desire*, "for it is a matter of flows, of stocks, of breaks in and fluctuations of flows,"[1] something to undo its subject, something to exceed its object, something that wants only to make things and break things, "after a point, nothing else exists for me, I don't care much about anything else," Selva says, knowing only too well what they say about him, that he's mad, that he's arrogant and eccentric, "an awful person nobody can call a good husband or a good son," and yet so many of them seem to adore his films, looking past—maybe riveted by—whatever they find distasteful or repellent in these stories of coupling and decoupling, union and divorce, sex and death, films that seem somehow to tap, even machine, the rush of feeling that Selva describes, like what happened a few years back at the Sangam Theatre in Chennai, the opening day of his sixth film, *Ayirathil Oruvan* (One in a thousand), all 887 seats sold out for the 11:15 a.m. show, a thunderous crowd of young men mostly, roaring and whistling for that song that came an hour into the film, *un mela asai than*, "yeah, it's desire for you," whose desire, my desire, your desire, their desire, those guys in the hall or that guy on the screen or that rowdy pair of girls flanking and mounting him that voice never said, singing into being a desire that belonged to no one in particular but was everywhere at once, a desire that settled delighted on the spectacle of that threesome but seeped as well into everything else, the desert, the thirst, the booze gold and meat, an encompassing landscape of delirious want, "delirium is cosmic," says Gilles Deleuze, "this is the great secret of delirium, we become delirious with the whole world,"[2] as with the aftermath of that drunken revel onscreen, as that desire passed more fully into madness, as the film descended into caverns spattered with blood and human flesh, haunted by the depraved heirs and followers of a Chola prince exiled to that island eight centuries back, as the ruckus in the theater subsided, as it grew into a palpable feeling of unease, as all of us fell into a silent longing for daybreak, for sunlight, for punctuation—for something other than another fucking comma, please!—for a release that wouldn't come, the film dawdling still in that night of pillage, rape, and gunfire, then dipping into an abrupt and startling blackness, "is it over?" puzzled voices calling out in the theater, sober and uncertain, still awash in that fate, in that "cultivation of desire,"[3] that production of desire, that erotics of affliction and delectation, desire like a machine winding up and sputtering out, the cinema as a "desiring-machine,"[4] a collective production, all those elements of conjuncture and disjuncture, unleashing pulses and fluxes of various kinds, passing through an audience and the world, undoing their integrity and the solidity of that world, desire bordering on delirium, as with so many of Selvaraghavan's films, like this one too, now under way at the MGM Beach Resort, a film without a name, or at least a name that has stayed with it for very long, "Shri Films Production No. 1" is what the clapboard reads for a shooting schedule that began in a basement studio just a few days back, a film, it seems, that had started up all at once, Selva still writing the script in the corners of that house, casting additional roles between each take, for "everywhere else," as his art director says, "the sun rises in the morning and sets at night, but not here, things here, they suddenly happen, all at once," something wry and sardonic about what he says and how he laughs but a commotion all the same that the director had wanted, "we're throwing out everything we've learned," he told me, speaking of French New Wave cinema, "trying to do something new," his heroine reading between takes from Truffaut's The Films in My Life, his cameraman Ramji improvising long and uninterrupted shots with a handheld camera trembling with the tension of what was happening, a shoot, in fact, unlike anything else I'd seen before, more private, more intense, Selva and Ramji always huddled close to the video screen in a swirl of smoke, offering no more than a murmur of assent to an okay take, mostly calling instead for more of this, less of that, one, two, five, nine, fourteen, the take count building relentlessly for this director who acts out each scene himself, who projects with his own face and body what he wants from his players, like the argument they staged around the dining room of that house in T. Nagar, "he doesn't even deserve to look in my fucking face, are you fucking mad?" that young woman screaming, "I'll arrange the marriage only if you like him, what am I gonna do, grab you by the neck and shove you at him?" her father belting back, Selva telling the father that he should feel the fury in his bones, telling the daughter that she had to lose herself completely, the director gesticulating wildly with his own clenched fists, letting out a raw growl of rage—zhzhzhzhrrr!—that left him parched and needing water and muttering something to himself about losing energy, the father admitting that he was exhausted himself, "she's banging the table saying 'Fuck!' and automatically, you get pumped up, it flows, you have to feed off that energy," and the more he spoke, the more the shoot began to feel like an economy of energetics, some system of flows, blocks, transfers, and relays, "plus-minus and you have current flowing through the shot," Selva, once a mechanical engineer, told me, "nobody wants to see plus-plus or minus-minus," like Sergei Eisenstein, I said to him, "conflict as the fundamental principle for the existence of every art-work,"[5] but Selva said he hasn't heard of Eisenstein, only Einstein, and so we got to talking about other things, like what they would do here, at this resort, for another scene in the film, the art director now inside the guest cottage, painting a wall with swirls of blue for an episode of misfired seduction, a scene, Selva says, that will "propel the entire first half of the film," plus-minus, minus-plus, "people are never gonna believe that these two will live together," their desires pulling to opposing poles, the actor stripped down already into his boxer shorts and clambering eagerly into bed with a glass of champagne as the actress steps wearily out of the bathroom and fixes him with a look that passes from horror to disgust to despair to rage, "so you think two people having sex is some kind of game, I know nothing about you, to have sex with someone I know nothing about, what, do you think of me as a prostitute or something?" she screams, "I can hardly stand, my whole body hurts, there's so much else you could have asked me, 'dear, you haven't eaten since this morning, can I get you something to eat . . . you look tired, why don't you sleep . . . you said you had a headache, how is it now . . . can I cut you some fruit,' not one damn bit of this, instead, 'come, lie down with me,' you say, tearing off your clothes just like that, and you call yourself a man?" and as the director leads the two of them through the scene, living out each of these characters himself, I can see what he means about an impossible stability, for there he goes, first with earnest glee on that rumpled bed, then with bug-eyed rage in a corner of the room, leaping, in a matter of seconds or even less, from one place into the other, one mood and then the other, one character into another, a subject undone by these predicates, these "successions of catatonic states and periods of extreme haste, of suspensions and shootings, coexistences of variable speeds, blocs of becoming, leaps across voids,"[6] desire much more than a personal feeling to fulfill, the director much less than the operator of this machine, the director, in fact, as someone operated himself, someone directed, bisected and dissected by all those relays, blockages, and flows, by the canister of film that needs to be changed, by the pocket phone that suddenly rings, by the glycerin nagging at the heroine's eyes, interruptions warping and confounding whatever lies unspoken between the director and the actress, his wanting that she wants what he wants, his wanting that he wants what she wants, "see, any woman, standing and standing from the morning, standing for four hours, you're dead tired, you can't go on, you come in and he's sitting there, at least he could have spoken to you for five minutes, 'how are you, okay, sit down,' but nothing, just 'come, come, come,' you're totally frustrated," Selva tells her, exasperation beaming from his face, but she is somehow missing from the mirror of his gaze, and so they try another take, and then another and another, and this is how it goes, night after night, as this small scene of desire sputters into life, the director wanting more from her than from anyone else in that crowded cottage, most especially the actor, his brother, a beloved star and a fixture in Selva's films who just shrugs off what is expected of him here ("he tells me what he wants and I can easily Xerox it"), preparing for each bare-chested shot with a few quick pushups while the tension mounts between the director and the actress, "hit him nicely," he's insisting, "don't fake it, I need an emotional outbreak, it should come like a storm," but it's not until the next morning that the brewing storm lands, the director just past shouting when I walk in the door, the actor buried under the bedclothes while the director and actress argue beside the bed, she, sighing, "I wouldn't do that myself, but if this is what you want, I'll do it for you," he, muttering "I can't shoot like this," someone handing her a tissue for her reddening eyes, the actor imploring the director not to cancel the shoot, each of them locked for most of the day within their dressing-room strongholds, finally coming out to work into that night, but only that one night, not the next night, or the one that follows, or even the night after that, for there is rain more rain and even more rain in Chennai, drowning out their plans for another scene, and by the time the rain lets up the actor is gone, the director's back to editing another project, and the actress who knows as they've hardly let me speak to her for more than a minute at a time, more than a year going by before I read, in the papers, that she's walked out of the project at last, and that Selva is directing another film now, *Mayakkam Enna* (Why the tumult), a new film that will bear, less like a scar than a sluice, all the force of this movie that barely happened, all the rage, the disdain, the nearly imperceptible twitching of want, all this feeling borne onward into yet another world, yet another trial, "desire," writes Deleuze, "never needs interpreting, it is it which experiments,"[7] or, as Selva says, "it's like jumping into the sea, you have to keep swimming, it's too late now to swim back."[8]

Notes

This chapter was originally published in *Reel World* from Duke University Press. Copyright © 2015, Anand Pandian.

1. Deleuze and Guattari, *Anti-Oedipus*, 105.

2. *Gilles Deleuze from A to Z*, with Claire Parnet, directed by Pierre-André Boutang, DVD (Cambridge, MA: Semiotext[e] Foreign Agents, 2012).

3. Ali, "Anxieties of Attachment," 106.

4. Deleuze and Guattari, *Anti-Oedipus*, 1–50.

5. Eisenstein, "Dialectical Approach to Film Form," 46.

6. Deleuze and Parnet, "Dead Psychoanalysis," 95.

7. Deleuze and Parnet, "Dead Psychoanalysis," 95.

8. Among experimental works of fiction helpful in working out the form of this chapter, I owe the greatest debt to Bohumil Hrabal's one-sentence novella originally published in Czech, *Dancing Lessons for the Advanced in Age*.

10

FLOWS AND INTERRUPTIONS, OR,
SO MUCH FOR FULL STOPS

STUART McLEAN

It is at work everywhere, functioning smoothly at times, at other times in fits and
starts. It breathes, it heats, it eats. It shits and fucks. What a mistake to ever call
it the id. Everywhere it is machines—real ones, not figurative ones: machines
driving other machines, machines being driven by other machines, with all the
necessary couplings and connections.
—GILLES DELEUZE AND FÉLIX GUATTARI, Anti-Oedipus: Capitalism and
   Schizophrenia

Because he wasn't stable, he wasn't reliable . . .

Selva says his wife left him because he wasn't able to be "stable" or "reliable"—it's not surprising he can't, he says, as he has to be so many other
people, all the time—all the characters who feature in his films—the gang-
sters, the kings, the slum dwellers, the men and women . . .

But perhaps no one and nothing is ever really stable and reliable, least of
all film and writing, least of all desire . . .

Pier Paolo Pasolini, himself both a filmmaker and a poet, refers to the
"cinema of poetry," involving the dissolution of distinctions between what
is presented as seen "objectively" by the camera and what is seen from the
subjective vantage point of a particular character, a mode that he likens to
the narrative style of free indirect discourse, in which third-person narration
blends successively with the idioms and sensibilities of individual protagonists, so that as spectators we can never be sure from where (or when) we
are looking . . . [1]

In Selva's case it is not least the director himself who exchanges view-
points with the characters in his films, acting out their passions on set for the

benefit of the actors who are to play them, becoming each of them in turn in his own body—a father trying to arrange a marriage for his daughter, the daughter screaming at him that the bridegroom he's chosen "doesn't even deserve to look in my fucking face . . ."—exhorting the actors to lose themselves, to be consumed and carried along by the passions that take hold of their characters, feeling the fury in their bones . . .

Anand's writing carries this perspectival shifting to yet another level—immersing us in the stories and settings of Selva's films (brothels, failed seductions, bloodthirsty orgies in subterranean caverns), then bringing us back to the set, the actors, the film crew, then away again into reflections on Deleuze, Truffaut, Eisenstein . . .

It's a matter of doing rather than self-conscious citationality—neither Selva nor any of his crew has heard of Eisenstein, who declared that conflict was the fundamental principle of every artwork—but they enact Eisenstein's insight without ever having heard his name . . .

Fits and starts, relays, blockages, flows . . .

A former mechanical engineer, Selva understands the energetics of currents and flows—not plus-plus or minus-minus but plus-minus and then "you have the current flowing through the shot" . . .

According to Selva, filmmaking is orgasmic—multiply orgasmic—each of these serial sexual climaxes amounting to a dissolution of self, a merging with other characters, other bodies, other scenes . . .

It was through such a loss of self that Selva realized his own vocation as a film director. Aged just twenty-one and working on a film nominally directed by his father, he found himself overwhelmed, often reduced to tears by all the people on set waiting to be told what to do, by the technicians who refused to be told, until, suddenly, there was "somebody else yelling inside me," somebody giving orders, saying I want this shot, that shot, a somebody who was not so much a person as a "thing" . . .

Desire here bespeaks not lack or insufficiency but superabundance, an overflow too copious to be confined within a single subjectivity, a single voice, a single sentence; desire is impersonal and the writing of desire becomes the medium of depersonalization, desubjectification, the shedding of identity in favor of serial metamorphoses . . .

To be caught up in this is to relinquish the security of an authorial vantage point external to the work (whether it be film, text, or any other medium) and to enter instead into a continuous, two-way mimetic interchange with characters, objects, scenes, to plunge headlong into the material and temporal flux that subtends the differential fashioning of selves and worlds . . .

Deleuze called it "cosmic" delirium—"we become delirious with the whole world"—a delirium that recognizes no definitive boundaries, allows of no full stops, no matter how much we, like the audience watching Selva's film *Ayirathil Oruvan*, might crave them, longing for punctuation, for something other than "another fucking comma, please" . . .

Pasolini's reflections would later influence Deleuze's writings on the post–World War II cinema of the "time image," in which the shattering of the sensory motor schema underpinning habituated perceptions of space and time allowed for the emergence of an image of time as such, no longer subordinated to movement but akin rather to Bergson's duration, not linear chronology but the coexistence of pasts and presents, a time of becoming, in which the actuality of the present was carried continuously beyond itself in the direction of the new, the unforeseen . . . [2]

In Anand's writing, pasts and presents no less than documentary and fiction as conventionally defined interpenetrate and reciprocally transform one another—a recollection of Truffaut's film *Day for Night* (1973), a conversation with a taxi driver, waiting to interview Selva at the MGM Beach Resort, memories of watching Selva's film *Thulluvadho Ilamai* a decade previously in a theater in rural Cumbum, the film's female protagonist running a hand suggestively down the length of her dress, the all-male audience screaming and hollering—nor are all of the voices and presences conjured here human—some are meteorological, like the rain that, over successive nights, impedes further work on the shoot, rain and more rain, night after night, until the lead actor has walked out and Selva is back to editing another project and the shoot is on hold, indefinitely . . .

It becomes impossible to tell whose desire we are following here—the director's? the audience's? the ethnographer's?—the reader is carried along by a continuous sentence morphing and shifting across adjacent subclauses between perspectives and times and places, blurring distinctions between the stories the films tell (and the mythic and historical antecedents on which they sometimes draw) and the world(s) inhabited by filmmakers, audiences, and ethnographers (and those who read them); histories and localities are drawn into a flux of becoming in which there is no clearly differentiated past, present, or future, fact or fiction, here or elsewhere, as though to follow the movement of desire were to be carried beyond not only the reassuring fictions of identity but also the parceling out of semantic units that sentence breaks seek to effect, as though the force of desire threatened to overrun both the boundaries of bodies and subjectivities and the ordering operations of grammar and syntax . . .

Finally we arrive at a long-deferred full stop—appended to another statement by Selva about the necessity of self-abandonment—another unintentional echo (but no less an echo for being unintentional?), this time of the advice offered to Joseph Conrad's character Lord Jim ("The way is to the destructive element submit yourself, and with the exertions of your hands and feet in the water make the deep, deep sea keep you up"),[3] the effect being less that of a conclusion than of an abrupt and somewhat arbitrary cutting off of a flow, signaling perhaps the futility of all efforts to punctuate desire, which flows on always, like a subterranean river traversing the words of Selva and his characters' words (which are not always readily distinguishable), Anand's words, and the words that I write in response to them and to the other voices (living and dead, human and nonhuman) in which they partake—so much for full stops . . .

Notes

1. Pasolini, " 'Cinema of Poetry.' "
2. Deleuze, *Cinema 2*, 148–49.
3. Conrad, *Lord Jim*, 125.

11

Denial: A Visit in Four Ethnographic Fictions

TOBIAS HECHT

Whereas one can recoil from being called a communist or accept it grate-fully, those accused of being denialists never celebrate themselves as such. In the absence of card-carrying denialists, we are returned to arguments over the factual. Does HIV cause AIDS? Is there evidence that certain herbs restore the immune system? And we are also reminded, as Didier Fassin has suggested, that denialism is "an ideological position whereby one [is said to] systematically [react] by refusing reality and truth."[1] Yet if "denialism" always takes the form of an accusation and involves arguments about the factual, it also requires an imagination that is not always a simple struggle over facts. Even in the first years of the twenty-first century in South Africa, when the country's president was refusing to clarify whether he believed that HIV caused AIDS, the statistic that hundreds of people were dying each day[2] across the country from the syndrome was not widely debated. What was taken as the basic facts about AIDS at medical conferences in New York, Geneva, or Sydney was no different from what was believed by most doctors in South Africa—especially those who had far more clinical practice with the syndrome than their colleagues almost anywhere in the world. Yet living with this fact of omnipresent death involves the imagination in many senses.

The passages included here are set in Cape Town at a time when South Africa's toll from AIDS had already well surpassed the number of dead in the Rwandan genocide. All are set in 2002 and 2003, when over a quarter of women attending antenatal clinics across the country were testing posi-tive for HIV.[3] The Actuarial Society of South Africa estimated there were a total of 388,000 AIDS deaths in 2003. The uncanny thing is that tourism was picking up, and cafés with Mediterranean-inspired names were sprouting up across the city. This was a heady time for the real estate market. Prices soared, foreign purchasers abounded, and houses in what had once been the city's slave quarter were renovated and sold for a lot of money. Still, many white people were leaving, and others, call them the rand-locked, only wished they could. In the background, even the most complacent, even those who had never had it better, had a sense that an epidemic was lurking and spreading like the blindness of José Saramago's eponymous novel.

Fiction that emerges through ethnographic observation and engagement is suggested here as a means of engaging with the generative apparatus of everyday understandings of what it means to live in a country where life expectancy for humans has plunged while domestic animals, at least in certain neighborhoods, are eating so well. With denial, Freud suggested, we protect ourselves from the pain occasioned by an unpleasant fact—say, the memory of abuse or the specter of death. Whereas denial draws our attention to what we do not wish to see or feel, the alternative is that inward pleasures would be scarce in a world without this possibility. The thought that hundreds of thousands of children are at this very moment wasting away from kwashiorkor is incompatible with good coffee or even a few minutes of window-shopping. How can we enjoy a Brahms clarinet sonata when a woman is being raped in a prison, somewhere—as one surely is—or an elderly person is dying alone? What we prefer to deny is coincident with erotic poetry and the bouquet of an Australian Pinot Noir. Denial is by turns protective and corrosive, inevitable and unforgivable, human and inhumane. It is a failing, it would seem, that permits us some leeway in which to live without the full benefit or devastation of perception.

While denial implies not seeing what overwhelming evidence tells us is there, denialism is different for it implies not only failing to see what by consensus is visible but also seeing something that consensus tells us is not there. Like a historical novel that weaves invention in and out of a generally accepted articulation of the past, denialism requires taking elements of what we nearly all take to be reality and infusing or replacing them with a parallel narrative. Unlike the workaday sleight of denial, which at its most innocuous is a benign inattention or even healthy accommodation, denialism requires an alternative narrative: not only was it not genocide, it was something else. In the case of Rwanda, the Clinton administration did not go that far. They were concerned only with the implications for foreign policy of using the precise word "genocide" to describe the speed with which the bodies were falling. They never suggested an alternative explanation. Denial and denialism, though the latter requires the former, are no more alike than blindness and a feverish imagination.

And denial rarely grows into denialism. At the time when Jews were disappearing from Poland, their Catholic compatriots might have denied that anything was amiss; but today no one can say the Holocaust did not occur without saying what did. Those years passed. Something, of course, did occur during that time. There was a war. Millions died. While denial can be the course of least resistance, denialism requires careful thinking.

While many South Africans were struggling courageously in civil society in 2002 and 2003 to confront the AIDS epidemic, taking on the full weight of stigma, bearing HIV-Positive T-shirts, challenging government health policies, several thousand were dying each week, many without comment. Many of the sick claimed they were ill with anything but AIDS, families grieved for loved ones who died of maladies they had never contracted, and some politicians suggested that AIDS was not a problem at all. Certain politicians went further. In a letter to world leaders, former President Mbeki suggested that the immune-deficiency problems in South Africa may not be responsible for his country's AIDS epidemic; rather it might be poverty, malnourishment, and poor health in general. The then Minister of Health, Manto Tshabalala-Msimang, not only echoed the president's refusal to confirm that HIV causes AIDS but also argued that in lieu of antiretroviral medications—which she regarded as toxic—beet roots, garlic, lemon, olive oil, and other items available in ordinary supermarkets were so efficient at boosting the immune system that they could restore the health even of those near death. On the other hand, there was enormous pressure from inside and outside South Africa to distribute antiretroviral medications through the government health services, and South African medical professionals widely rejected the notion that AIDS was being caused by something other than HIV and that Western medicine was doing more harm than good.

The writing from which the excerpts emerge is the result of a multisited ethnography of the AIDS epidemic in Cape Town that includes extensive work at an informal settlement where 25 percent of pregnant women were testing positive for HIV and also visits to a tuberculosis clinic, hospitals, a pet shop where fresh pasta with rosemary and basil was prepared for dogs, and the city of Khayelitsha (where there were two dozen toilets for half a million people, tens of thousands of whom were dying of a syndrome that causes incessant diarrhea). But the ethnographic roots of this work grew out of ordinary conversations about what people saw and didn't see, how they lived with the secret of their own impending death, what they thought would happen to their children.

Holocaust literature took decades to emerge, and I doubt it will be possible to make sense in the short run of an epidemic that has claimed a genocidal quantity of lives, a good number of which owing to what a few individuals said they were not seeing. Denialists do not rely on the mediocrity and insouciance of denial. They may even be students of what most people take as reality; they simply do not limit themselves to it. They see a larger picture and argue it into existence.

Though based on ethnographic research, these excerpts emerged from a sense that fiction engages with an imaginary that has a tendency to overflow the bounds of more traditional forms of ethnographic writing; neither denial nor denialism can be apprehended fully without recourse to the generative apparatus that they themselves make use of and depend on. But, to be certain, like Jorge Edwards's *Persona non grata* ([1973] 2015), a work based on the novelist's experience as a diplomat in Cuba, these pieces could be read in different ways, even as memoir. They are narrative-based interpretations of social life where the details emerged through observations and interviews undertaken in a familiar ethnographic manner. The settings and dialogs reflect how they were observed and experienced. Yet while ethnography can interpret what is viewed from a psychological perspective, it falls short in delving into the consciousness of others. This is a speculative anthropology, one that aims to blend what can be seen from the outside with what can be imagined about it, also from the outside. Denial and denialism, discrete as they are, concern the imagination, and these pieces are a willed approximation to imagination, to different ways of living with HIV and dying of AIDS.

1. Upon Arrival

Cape Town, Bree Street, ten steps past the Heritage Hotel, on his way to hail a cab and what the astonished visitor noticed first about the blade against his stomach was the reddish hue of the boy's thumb so tight along the upper flat side of the metal that it looked like a small tomato under pressure, close to bursting. Then the voice jagged with puberty that announced, "I have something for you."

Something for me . . . he puzzled. An echoed voice, a ruddy thumb, an unsteady hand but all told dozens of little fingers, the eager nervous digits of boys—four, five, six of them—rifling his pockets, yanking at the bag slung across his shoulder, grasping at his arms. Safety in numbers, danger in numbers. Numbers that recast our perception of calamity. Like the photograph he'd once seen for a famine relief campaign: the mother's gaze lost somewhere before or beyond the viewer while the daughter (belly distended, legs rachitic, hair sparse) was entreaty itself. Together, the mother and daughter awakened the urge to shelter and protect. But there was a subtext of desire (the contours of the mother's breasts adumbrated beneath the tatters of a blouse, the child's knowing eyes in contrast to her thumb lost in the last refuge of her mouth). But reveal the mother with her entire brood—the whole half dozen of them—amid countless families of the same genus (parched, stunted people indifferent to the flies jittering near or even across their eyes) and we might say, What can we do anyway? *or* Didn't this happen last year in another country? Or the line that says it all: Why do they have so many children? The more overwhelming the calamity, the easier it is to turn a blind eye or point an accusing finger. Train the gaze on the mother, on the child, on the parched earth, on innocence or supplication but never on the reaches of human cruelty: the politician's motorcade, the billions spent on night cream or liposuction, the fine print of a structural adjustment package. With time racing at a snail's pace, every detail was amplified but the larger picture remained distant, inaccessible, the knife just that side of his liver. Fingers yanked at his back pocket, tearing the cloth. Suddenly his wallet was gone. His right front pocket was weightless as well, without the cell phone. The missing wallet didn't contain more than the equivalent of fifty dollars and a credit card. There is a fearlessness in children that is different from the fearlessness you sometimes encounter in adults. Adults can suppress fear, even overcome it, but sometimes children lack it altogether. The boy holding the knife against his flesh had nothing to overcome.

The bag slid down the visitor's arm, but he caught it and held it tightly. For reasons that, even with the wisdom of hindsight, he couldn't understand, he pulled away from the knife, grabbed for his bag, and, with the full force of unreality, shouted *Fire!* A visceral "fire!" that startled even him, a "fire!" from down near his liver. That's what a friend had told him she'd learned in a self-defense class: "Don't yell 'police!' No one wants to get involved. Yell 'fire!' if you want to get people's attention."

Suddenly his arms were free, the bag, the one thing he couldn't lose, was secure in his grasp and the clutch of children were marbles dropped on a granite floor, scattering, tumulting through the confusion but, as it turned out, not on account of anything he had said or done. Because, when it came right down to it, a single word of protest shouted into the vastness of a city street and a brusque movement away from the knife's edge notwithstanding, he was just there, startled like a white man from somewhere else. The boys were running from someone but it wasn't from him. It was the stick-wielding body-builder with a sun-bleached bounce of hair and his accomplice: good Samaritans or goons who appeared as if from nowhere to come to his rescue or, more likely, to do what they were hired to do by nearby merchants: to steady this runaway world. It is they who had spooked the boys and made them flee into what, for their pursuers, was the indistinction of a lot of African faces. All of them—all except one—had gotten away.

The unlucky boy, airborne, raised by the scruff of the neck, flailed his limbs like an upturned beetle. A knife fell to the ground, either the knife that a moment ago was against the visitor's belly or else a different one. He had no idea who was who, which knife was which, if this was the boy who said he had something for him or if this was another boy with a knife and a breaking, frightened voice. The boy's green sports jersey was several sizes too large for his Lilliputian body. The visitor took it all in: the people staring at the spectacle of the boy in the air, the white man effortlessly suspending him.

He had never been in a city where nature presided over everything forged by men. Between the buildings flanking each side of Bree Street, he could see a piece of Table Mountain, partially shrouded in mist, rising above the upper edges of the city. It was as if the mountain were looking down upon the city, watching babies learn to crawl, couples embrace, acts of cruelty and kindness. We have earthquakes and tsunamis to remind us that nature is indomitable and exempt from exact prediction. This mountain, with more varieties of plants than the entire United Kingdom, as he'd read, seemed to have the same effect. All around were those things that had taken shape, stood, and crumbled under the larrup of white farmers, tradesmen, adventurers, petty administrators, rogues. Everything that had become so much rubble had risen again. The stucco-fronted brick houses with their flat roofs and cornices and ample *stoeps* had given way to Victorian latticework and this, in turn, to cyclone fences around squat structures of aluminum, brick, and tar. The mountain older than any of it, older than the *Iliad*, the Bible, even the Himalayas. The mountain was the beacon that called one to this Janus-faced land, at once the Cape of Good Hope and the Cape of Storms, beckoning and betraying, embracing and engulfing.

"Can't you see he's a child?" the visitor shouted. "Don't hurt him!"

"Hurt him?" the man holding the boy in the air demanded to know. "We're going to kill him!"

"No *baas*!" the child screamed. It was a cold day but his brow was glistening and his eyes were flitting everywhere. The other man, the white one, Goliath you could call him, his elbow scraped and slightly bloodied from the scuffle, brandished a big metal pole.

"No!" the child pleaded. I did nothing! "No, *bass*! No!" he pleaded. "It was dat one!" he said, pointing imprecisely at the group of African onlookers, a few of whom might have just mugged the visitor, or might not have. The men turned in that direction but they were satisfied with having caught one of them.

Goliath bellowed, "It was you and some others, I saw everything. Where are you from? Zim? Let's see your papers?"

"From Durban, bass."

"*Ngubani igama lakho? Uphumaphi?*"

The boy didn't seem to understand. He screamed something in broken English.

"*eThekwini?*" the man insisted.

More silence.

"You're not from Durban, you're not even South African. Where are you from, Mozambique?"

"What are you doing?" the visitor interrupted the man.

Goliath opened a smoked glass door, and the other tormentor and the boy, airborne still, disappeared behind it.

"Why doesn't someone call the police?" the visitor mumbled into the crowd or to himself.

The onlookers shifted their weight and some of them milled about, but no one was phoning anyone. After a few moments, Goliath stuck his head out from the other side of the smoked glass door, with a cell phone in hand. "Is this yours?"

It was. He walked over to take it.

"It was in his underwear," Goliath informed him and the swelling ranks of white onlookers on the uphill side of the street.

"Why don't you call the police?" the visitor said before the door was shut again.

Goliath held it open for a moment, thinking it over. "Will you lay charges?"

The image that came to mind was that of a child in a holding cell of grown men, the sort who relish boys with breaking voices.

2. In Translation

Life seemed to be escaping through the cracks in the benches, out the drafty windows, between the misty recesses displayed on the X-ray illuminator. All of the patients had TB, and almost all had HIV. Their bodies were not fighting off the infections. As more patients came through the small office, the more ordinary their desolation became, the more corporeal their looming deaths. There was discussion about a big pill and a little pill.

At one point there was a man sitting across from the doctor. He must have been a beautiful child and his teeth were big and white. He wore jeans and a sports shirt. The doctor asked him if he had been to see Vuyani.

"Yes, I am so happy to know about my life," he answered, in his best version of the white doctor's language, the light glinting off his forehead. And he looked as if the satisfaction had welled up inside of him. Only he had just told the doctor yes, yes, Vuyani gave him the results of the test done Friday and, yes, he had been told that the virus was in his blood.

No one else in the room understood why he was happy. "So you tested positive for HIV?" the doctor said, looking up from the papers strewn across her desk, squinting, a pen aloft in her right hand. But then the puzzle across her lips eased. "It is better to know, isn't it?" With which she looked down at her desk again and wrote something on a form.

"It is better," the man smiled back.

She jotted another something on a sheet of white paper and then something on the form, which was green. As the visitor learned, the green form must be signed by a doctor if the patient is to receive a disability grant. The grant was because he had TB.

"I want you to take one of these big pills each day, and I'll give you a very small one. That one will help to keep you strong. How many weeks have you been coming for TB treatment?"

"It seems like five."

"Five?"

"Yes."

"So, continue to come for your treatment."

"And the beer?"

"Excuse me?" she said.

"I can drink beer?"

"The beer is another matter," she replied tersely. "You'll have to take one of each of these pills every day. Do not miss a day. If you miss a day, it will make the fighting in your blood weaker."

She paused for a moment. "You can drink beer but do not drink so much that you get drunk. That will make you weak." The man seemed satisfied with the answer, and when he rose from his chair with nothing in his movements or in his demeanor to hint at what was in his blood or in his future, his sheen was of happiness itself.

At night the visitor listened to the fury of the rain and remembered the patients at the clinic. He found he could not distinguish many of them clearly. It may be, he thought, the wind lashing at the window, that when you look death in the face so many times in the course of a morning, you eventually find yourself before a single indistinct calamity where the eyes of one become set in the inscrutable sockets of another. So it is difficult to remember exactly what was said and by whom, and which mother had the thinning hair or the red islands on her neck. By the end of the morning, eleven of the thirteen patients, without counting the infants, had turned out to have the virus in their blood. The infants—two, or was it three of them? . . . he wondered—were also HIV positive. What is worse than death is to stare it in the face and know that between now and then there is not a second remotely worth living. Most of them had that look in their eyes, a dull inattention to life. Though they may seek the counsel of the ancestors, pray to the Christian god, heed the words of the soothsayer, or weigh the merits of the big pill versus the little pill, they all seemed to fear that none of this would make a difference.

"What did that man mean when he said that he was so happy about his life?" he wondered. He was beaming. He had thought about it during the consultation but only for a moment. Now he couldn't stop thinking about it. He had just told the doctor that on Friday he learned he was HIV positive. And in a country where medication is available only to rich people . . . why would the news make him so happy?

There was silence in his mind and then he hazarded, maybe the man heard the word "positive" and thought it was a good thing, being HIV positive. He might have thought that being positive meant he had nothing to worry about.

Suddenly he understood. Or did he? The patient had been speaking a version of the white doctor's language, the visitor's language. Now the man was up there on the teeming hillside where the shacks might slide down if the rains continue for long enough, the man, drinking beer, radiant or shattered, like a translation without a certain original.

3. The Bucket

Before ushering him in, Nomsa placed the blue plastic bucket outside. She held the baby in one arm and motioned the visitor toward the inside of the cockeyed slant where she and the baby lived and her mother had died. He ducked as he came through the doorway and when he was inside, it seemed to him as if time and space were out of true. Put the tumbledown shack on wheels and onto the roads of Southern California and it would be no bigger than a Suburban. The infant, for her part, was smaller than what it means to be rooted in this world. Jesus hung askew in the picture above one of the beds.

With her eyes, Nomsa told him to take a seat in one of the two matching armchairs with their clear plastic covers that didn't seem to fit with anything else in the shack. The chairs were what the house might be like if things had been going better. Sitting, he made a mental list of everything he saw: an aluminum pot, a kerosene burner, a makeshift cabinet, some clothing in a slumping box, two single beds, and the portrait of the savior.

One of the beds was Nomsa's. The other must have belonged to her mother, who gave in at an age when other women might be setting eyes on their firstborn. Three generations in less than four decades. But now just two left and the baby wheezing what for all he knew was the very strain of TB that accompanied the premature grandmother to her skeletal, hairless, shattered end. A picture: the grandmother had had her hair straightened and wore a blue jacket, pearl earrings, and a golden cross. Her lips were full and her cheeks round. The chairs had been hers, no doubt.

Before his eyes was an intimate madness and a collective one. To watch your mother lose her hair, her flesh, her sight, her mind, in a world that couldn't be twelve meters square. . . . But while the shack was something squeezed into unlikely proportions, its hue and cry echoed across a violent sweep where each shack was an island adrift: dozens, hundreds, thousands of them, shacks of hunger and drunkenness, prayer, studies, fury, and the sparkle and disappointment of children. A country with nuclear-powered submarines and in this city hidden from the white city, they resolved the most basic problem of human existence in plastic buckets. Anyone who stops to think knows that the poor eliminate just as the rich do, but that thought can be held at bay. It is a sort of Freudian repression, denying what is patently undeniable, what is universal, what no political, cultural, or economic argument could refute. And there was Nomsa's bucket placed outside, a gesture to the visitor. There were only a couple dozen houses with toilets in this city of half a million.

Back when Nomsa's mother was strong enough to walk to the public toilet, a day with diarrhea might have involved twelve trips, he imagined. A dozen trips, a dozen rands: 7 percent of Nomsa's monthly income. He wondered how much it would cost if a lawyer from Orange County had to pay 7 percent of his monthly salary to cover the trips he made to the bathroom in a single day.

He took Nomsa's picture, first just her and then her with the baby, and then a number of pictures of the baby. The eyes of the infant were listless, world-weary.

He knew there was nothing to eat in the house and he wanted to leave the woman with something, but he didn't know how that would be interpreted. When her attention was turned somewhere else, he pulled a bill from his wallet and left it under a small cushion on one of the plastic-covered armchairs, as if it had fallen there.

As the afternoon wore on, he met other children. As he photographed this child or that one, a group of them playing at this or another game, his mind was equally where he was and where he had been. From an elevated walkway he looked out over the shacks, one after another, as if looking made it possible to comprehend the colorless color of rippled zinc, the bedlam of muddy pathways between the shacks and, far off in the distance, as ever, the mountain.

When the light grew dim and the minibus taxis spilled maids and cooks, mechanics and clerks—the lucky ones who have jobs—the visitor set back for where he had come from, to the white city, close to the white mountain. Those people had done it better than the Brazilians, the Filipinos, the Egyptians. The rich everywhere else wanted the poor out of sight, but no one had managed to do it as completely as had been achieved here.

The sun had set but the sky was luminous, an orange encounter of sea spray and diesel particles over Table Mountain.

4. Vice Itself

After a few minutes a white man emerged carrying a video in one hand, extended his free hand, and with an American accent from somewhere spoke, "Welcome to Forest Pines." Forest Pines was an orphanage for children left behind after the epidemic had swept through the generation of their parents.

The visitor made a gesture of affirmation.

"Phillip Aimes. It's a pleasure to have you here. What brings you to South Africa?"

When that bit was over, the man was saying, "That's what I'm here for, to help people get to know this place that God helped us to build. God doesn't do everything for us. He knows that it is good for us to search for our own way. I imagine you would like to know what God has taught us about working with AIDS orphans?" The visitor had seen a lot of them, the proselytizers. They had knocked on his door over the years. His mother would send them away, but a few times when he was home alone and had let them in and they, wide-eyed, had laid out what was heaven and what was hell and which was a road to where. They didn't have eyes for anything that wasn't damnation or rapture. He would listen to them and wonder what it would be like to face a Holocaust with the feeble legs of an agnostic and wish that he had that hard certainty to help carry him through or make sense of his eventual perishing. But he remained there, observing, on the fence, with no way of understanding death or explaining why men raped boys or why millions starved or died of simple diseases.

"I have learned that the Lord lifteth up the meek but man must do his part too," Phillip Aimes continued. "We cannot wait for Jesus to do everything for us; we must live as his servants. Jesus wants to help the orphans in Africa. Jesus has the means to lift them up. But he is giving us the chance to show that we can help him in his work."

His accent came as if freeze-dried from somewhere in the middle of the country, far from the oceans, somewhere in the vast sweep east of the Rockies, west of the Mississippi, north of Texas, from somewhere in there, all surrounded by pig farms and the sway of cornstalks, full of good folks with a soft manner and a hateful certainty.

"God lets us know these things in our prayers. We pray for guidance, so we will know who to help. In this case it was God telling us that these orphans needed to be helped, because they were truly helpless, without the care of their families or people."

Phillip Aimes had a few tense hairs poking out from one of his nostrils and together they were the most expressive part of him. "Children who have no mother or father. Or no mother and daddy's off drinking in some forgotten corner of the country. I think everyone understands what orphans are, especially the children themselves.

"These are children in need," he continued, "children who've been left behind. But we see them as children of God even though they may not know the Bible from a tulip when they arrive. They find themselves in an environment where they can thrive, far from the drinking and sexual shenanigans of their parents . . ."

The visitor gave him a certain look.

"We don't know the parents, because they're dead or, like I told you, they're off in some shebeen gettin' soused. But we know this environment, we've been here long enough to understand how they live. The children are innocent, they aren't responsible for the lifestyle of others around them. . . . We believe AIDS orphans are not only those children whose parents have died of AIDS but children who are suffering because they live in a society riddled with AIDS and with vice."

"Vice . . . ," the visitor echoed, just loud enough to be heard. It wasn't a word he heard very often. It had always seemed to him that while vices, or vises, like the carpenter's tool, hold us, that we hold them too, we cultivate them. He didn't have such a low opinion of vices and had never met an interesting person who didn't have one.

"Yes, with vice." The hairs in Phillip Aimes's nose were still for a moment, resolute. "It's everywhere. Vice is all around us. You should see the townships on a Saturday afternoon. The men are all blotto and the women are too. You can't tell the houses from the brothels, and the children see this. AIDS is a part of all that: it's the expression of a lifestyle."

"A lifestyle?"

"Yes, you could almost say that AIDS is a form of living. Most people don't know this, but that's what it is, that's what we know, as believers. It's consistent with the other things people are doing, it's part of their general behavior. What is different about the children, and why we want to rescue them, is that they're innocent. They can be saved; they take to the Bible like ducks to water. They have a natural inclination for salvation."

The visitor nodded.

"No one is beyond salvation, but in a lot of cases the families only keep on going down the same slippery slope to damnation. The children here each have two volunteers looking after them. They don't have to be a man and a woman, like a father and a mother, but often they are. The volunteers teach them their school subjects, the Bible, supervise them when they are playing, talk with them. We think the children need guidance. 'The integrity of the upright shall guide them. But the perverseness of transgressors shall destroy them,' Proverbs 11.3. The volunteers are here for the children twenty-four hours a day. The kids eat with us in the mess hall, we play together and we pray together.

"What we offer is a loving home, shelter, food, protection and a road to Jesus. We think that's a lot."

"Do the children visit their families?" the visitor asked.

"If the families ask for it, or the children ask for it, but we don't encourage it. The devil is tempting."

"And what if a child wants to be next to his mother when she dies?"

"When she dies of AIDS?"

"Yes."

"We think that could be very harmful for the children."

A silence.

"It brings them too close to the forces that led their mothers to get AIDS in the first place."

Things were moving behind Aimes's eyes and he squinted slightly.

"I'm going to get you a pamphlet about this. . . . Carol!" he called. "Carol!" But no Carol came forth so he exhaled a breath of annoyance and went to find the good word himself, each imperious step leaving a momentary imprint in the carpet till the pile slowly rose again and became indistinguishable from the broad savanna of synthetic fiber. Alone, the visitor looked around and his eyes traveled from the room to the children outside. They were playing in a big plastic house. And Phillip Aimes was a man of astonished hatred. The visitor turned to the plastic ficus at his side. It was a realistic lifelessness, as if a living plant had been dipped in a fine coat of plastic. He'd read in the paper that some German fellow had done that with human cadavers from Vietnam and other places where golf isn't played very much, to send them around the world on display. The ficus couldn't be nourished, it couldn't grow: it was just there, indolent like received wisdom.

Notes

1. Fassin, *When Bodies Remember*, 115.

2. According to actuarial statistics, approximately one thousand were dying daily. That estimate is higher than what South Africa's Medical Research Council reported at the time. For a quick overview of AIDS statistics in South Africa, references to databases, and different ways of counting, see "HIV and AIDS in South Africa," AVERT, last reviewed May 1, 2015, http://www.avert.org/south-africa-hiv-aids-statistics.htm.

3. The precise figures for those years are 26.5 and 27.9 percent, respectively. The rates subsequently rose to about 30 percent—nearly 40 percent in kwaZuluNatal—by 2010. See "HIV and AIDS in South Africa."

12

ETHNOGRAPHY AND FICTION

ANAND PANDIAN

Tobias Hecht's stories take you places you wish you hadn't gone, tumbling a reader into prickly, confounding, and at times enraging scenes. The curbside rescue of a hapless traveler, tilting vertiginously into the prospect of a child being raped. Blue plastic buckets instead of toilets for a citizenry dying slowly, painfully, of dehydration but defended by nuclear submarines. The man who beams at the "positive" news of an HIV diagnosis, or the cheery sangfroid of a missionary caretaker who seems to make a business of children as yet spared by this worst of epidemics. You think at first that these stories couldn't be true, but then you lose your bearings in their intricate weave of hope and depravity, and your convictions begin to feel hollow. Even the mountain overlooking this wracked city, it seems, can scarcely remain impassive and unmoved, "watching babies learn to crawl, couples embrace, acts of cruelty and kindness."

We are in the presence of things that seem unreal yet remain unmistakably there—like the unknown signs of a deadly illness on the move, like the baroque ways in which its symptoms have been explained away, like the rationalizations that shrug off evidence of mounting death. Hecht grapples with a social reality that owes a great deal to the "generative apparatus" of fiction, to layer upon layer of narrative and imagination that pervade whatever sense can be made of what is happening. This is a world thickly populated by what Bruno Latour calls "beings of fiction," not illusory or false, strictly speaking, but instead "fabricated, consistent, real" presences in their own right, acting on and through the world despite their imaginative origins, "taken up again by subjectivities that would not exist themselves if these beings had not given them to us."[1]

Clifford Geertz convinced us some time ago that ethnography depends upon the powers of fiction, *fictio*, from the Latin *fingere*, to make, mold, form, and shape. What Hecht's stories bring into focus is the relationship between the fictions that anthropologists make and the fictions that their interlocutors must live with. Take what happens immediately in the first of these stories, "Upon Arrival." The protagonist, an anthropologist, finds a knife at his belly and the mystery of an aggressive phrase, "I have something for you." These words call to mind, for him, a flash of calamitous images. But there is already a dramatic flair to the encounter for the young assailant too, who speaks as if a character in a film he's just watched. Without even realizing it, the anthropologist seizes on the drama of the situation, calling out "Fire!" upon which the clustered children become like so many "marbles dropping on a granite floor." There is no fire, nor are they marbles, but these distinctions hardly matter. What the language conveys is a force of movement, a means of passage, borne by the pulse of stories through a world.

Hecht was working already in this manner with *After Life*, a haunting novel set in Recife, Brazil. In fact, it was precisely his confrontation with a reality indistinguishable from artifice, as he has reported, that led his own writing there to turn toward a fictional mode. One of the two central characters in that book was patterned on Bruna Verissimo—Bruna "Most True"—a street child who had lived into adulthood as a transgender prostitute. For over a decade, Hecht recorded the stories of her travails with an ethnographic biography in mind, only to realize that "though everything Bruna was telling me was plausible, a substantial amount happened to be untrue." How best to engage with those like Bruna, deep in the pursuit of a fabricated existence? "The only way to do justice to her life, it seemed to me, was to yield to her inventions."[2]

Under such circumstances, in other words, the ethnographic observer cannot simply fall back upon the familiar burden to frame and explain the stories of others, as Didier Fassin has suggested we do in a recent meditation on the boundary between ethnography and fiction.[3] Instead, works of ethnographic fiction take us further inward rather than outward, into some semblance of the thoughts and perspectives of their characters. But then as well, through the dizzying flight of topological inversion that fiction always depends upon, the recesses of this inside open into the expanse of an unseen outside, and we emerge in a space where we didn't expect to be—not the world as it is, as we ought to understand it, but another world instead, a possible world, "a world that could be as it is told."[4] Ultimately, in other words, what happens through the telling of such tales is an intensification of what is real, as if fiction were merely the ordinary seen in relief.

To some this may seem a frivolous pursuit, most especially given the gravity of what we encounter in these glimpses of "Elysium Burning." The stakes of this work upon the givenness of the real, however, cannot be more serious. Denialism makes for toxic fictions indeed—witness the countless painful deaths that limn those years in South Africa, or the suffering yet to come on account of climate change denialism today. But Hecht shows us too how fiction can serve as a resource for life in perilous circumstances. I think of what he had written of Bruna Verissimo, that "she probably owed her very survival to the ability to imagine,"[5] or how he etches the state of that patient at the HIV clinic here, "radiant or shattered, like a translation without a certain original." These stories tell us something crucial about what anthropology can do in the face of such struggles: to represent these difficulties as faithfully as possible but also to respond to the demands they make for new kinds of facts or truths, truths that we and others could actually live with. "We possess art," as Friedrich Nietzsche once suggested, "lest we perish of the truth."[6]

Notes

1. Latour, *Inquiry into Modes of Existence*, 238, 242.
2. Hecht, *After Life*, 5, 6.
3. "If the fictional imagination lies in the power to invent a world with its characters, the ethnographic imagination implies the power to make sense of the world that subjects create by relating it to larger structures and events," Fassin writes in "True Lives, Real Lives," 53.
4. Hecht, *After Life*, 8.
5. Hecht, *After Life*, 5.
6. Nietzsche, *Will to Power*, 435.

13

SEA

STUART McLEAN

The work of writing and reading and thinking is the tending of the otherwise.
—MYUNG MI KIM, interview, 2007

Let Ross, House of Ross, rejoice with the Great Flabber Dabber flat clapping fish with hands.
—CHRISTOPHER SMART, *Jubilate Agno*, 1759–63

SEA

I
I could never be an aardvark because

Moved inside as the weather worsened

II
The world has

Always been

As it is now

The residue is thrown

In some place

Where no one goes

III
Its cool and fast spread of sunken ships

And all the stories buried in
the main

IV

Silence, which is not one of us broken dream a few moments later,
"Gentlemen," said a calm and penetrating voice, "I'm French, English,
German, and Latin, and I worked so well. Therefore can you respond to
the interview, but I want to know you first."

V

I know that I can eat flesh and bones at the bottom of the sea

VI

It begins in the middle
            All the drowned sailors
                              There is a huge amount of
                                      allusion

VII

          We have heard before
               Of
Amulets
       Soothsaying
              The food-ordeal
                       Snake-charms
                              Gospel charms

VIII

The multiplicity of every person's possible identifications
The best wave resources in Europe
Its hints of earlier and other creation
Scrape them down, marl, parcel, and serve them

IX

Tae Guthaland he's geen awa',
Tae muckle pagan loons tae slay

X

Raised by giants
Lost track of the upper world
A change had come over us

XI

The walrus stabbed him in the head with its tusks and the swordfish
    swam off

XII

Sovereignty transmission
After-traces of two deaths
Ethnographic comments
Will continue non-stop

XIII

They first appeared in the North Sea:
Contact persons, sea erosion,
Colors, materials
As well as food (fishing, etc.)

XIV

To maintain its presence
In the core of the breed jam

XV

My goal interwoven stories
That explore
The living and the dead

                                        Including the environment
                                        And animals

And doing it badly

XVI

Everybody smelt the same

XVII

Uplifted masses
Contained
Minerals

Jellyfish swarm,
Worms evolved
And starfish

Complexly curving tongues

XVIII

The Sea Mither did not, however, reside permanently in the watery element, indeed she was not allowed to do so. For in this, as in most of the Northern traditionary myths, the dualistic idea is strong. She had a powerful and black-hearted rival, with whom she maintained periodic warfare. His name was Teran, which in Orkney dialect means furious anger.

XIX

Too many of them

        Shellfish toxins

                When the wind

                        Was the last of it

XX

Islands are
Places apart
Where Europe is absent
Wrote Auden

                    Islands are
                    From before or
                    For after humankind
                    Wrote Deleuze

XXI

Islands are

Until the sea

               Covers them

                            Again

XXII

Hell of a fright would maybe use three broken up and it was like clams on
that piece of ground maybe over each other and then at ninety degrees the
Norwegian officers concentrated down into a meat stock like a banana
without damaging the flesh

XXIII

                        Made easy

        We're trying so hard not to laugh

My convulsive ocean

XXIV

A fifth of Europe's coastline is being eaten away by the sea and increasingly
frequent storms and floods, the European Commission has found.

XXV

Pearls and razors

        Urging inhumanly through
        The spectral moonlight

                    All 74 ships were scuttled

XXVI
For GMB

Same scattered darkness
Haddocks loom seapink
Purifying crag sciptorium

        Storm-shaken nuns
        Shadows dancer
        Between somewhere

Axemen twilight
Westward touch
Through blessings soiling

                              Skull licks stonemason
                              Here's worms and horse
                              Lured askew singing screen

Disputed brother
Fire-dance
Snowflake gray-eyed

              Random highness
              Twisted midnight
              Then smile edges

                              Three muted shifting
                              Boys barrel praise
                              To oyster

              Boatbuilder laughter
       Broken answer
              Solstice crystal
                       Guests hunger
                                    Many trudged
                                       thought
Bare like golden fish

XXVII

Almost every marine plant and animal brine goes more bitter petroleum is
the result of fundamental earth processes paleozoic the living and dying

Of creatures at once completely changed those first voyagers everflowing
stream of time pumped through subsea pipelines to the

Terminals at Sullom Voe and Flotta

                       And now worshipped heathen fiends

XXVIII

Whales speak Japanese

                Our island nation

       The pursuing jelly

                        Our great sweet mother

Within her live snakes and ghosts

XXIX

Pirates or demons

                      Fictional truancy quotation non-definition

All the fantastic stories about

                Wires and infernal machines

A twisted, un-catalogued, unsuspected life

XXX

Strong winds are forecast

Shipping Forecast—Issued: 1625 UTC Tue 16 Oct

Wind
Northwest becoming cyclonic later, 5 to 7, becoming variable 4 for a time.

Sea State
Moderate or rough.

Weather
Occasional rain.

Visibility
Good, occasionally moderate.

XXXI

He kept twiddling his thumbs and making up poetry all the time

XXXII

The dead husks of that same life

Conflates   provisional   unbodies

The ooze-born goddess

Beckoned

XXXIII

Thorfinn was waiting at Deerness
A thin membrane separates

XXXIV

You weren't allowed to say "pig," you weren't allowed to say "rabbits," you weren't allowed to say "minister"

XXXV

Our test sites and facilities

No other noise
To please them all

Deep in the water

XXXVI

And it was this larger class of seals that were called "selkie folk" because they had the power of assuming human form

XXXVII

And all these surfaces are equally deep and superficial

XXXVIII

Beautiful singers
Some of them were careless
You shot them and they fell into the sea

XXXIX

Elisabeth says it's good to feel out of your depth
It was part of the territory

But I think it was me

XL

The funneling effect of the local coastline and seabed
We can imagine the battles

The results of their previous

metamorphoses

XLI

The mask remained especially popular for the appearance of spirits and
apparitions from the depths

XLII

And underwater volcanoes
Made of dead

XLIII

And Svalbard's seed-vault
Made of dead

XLIV

And Lady Gaga's sunglasses
Made of dead

XLV

And the rings of Saturn
Made of dead

XLVI

And the Great Wall of China
Made of dead

XLVII

And Occupy Wall Street
Made of dead

XLVIII

And all the living and the dead
Made of dead

XLIX

Deadalive languages
Beforeafter
Word stuff
Sea stuff

The ghouls are always coming

L

Conjecture six horses
Although now with difficulty
Vomits the prophet
Sand dunes and rooftops
And little fishes flow in

LI

Captain Nemo is a reference to Captain Nemo. Google does not know my
grandmother under the sea

LII

Gardens of colored seaweeds, halls of crystal, lit by the phosphorescence
of the sea, curtained with the ever changing colors of the Northern Lights

The identity of "Europe" has always been uncertain and imprecise

LIII

The king's last words (before he sank into the depths)
His back toward the fishy smelling sea:
"Grotesque brachiate efflorescences"—

Exposed waters offshore will have the greatest energy

LIV

Eyeburst
Liquifiction of universe

      Veers in all directions at once
      Aquatime

            "I" birthed
            Into a billion scatter-animals

All godless

LV

The dust of ground pearls sprinkled
On the mermaids' tails

The whale was pumped up

            with compressed air to keep it afloat

LVI

In among the islands another boat you couldn't stand upright going
through the tropics depends on different times of the year weren't supposed
to kill pure machine oil information increased then go straight back out
and do it again the

LVII

But this does
Not authorize us
To posit the aquatic element
As symbolic of the womb
Or maternal environment

A letter from your doctor
On a regular basis
Is not
A work of art

LVIII

In 1431 a fish was caught in the kingdom of Poland that was as long and
broad as a living bishop and decorated with mitre, staff, white chasuble,
stole, maniple, shoes, hems, gloves and all other requisites that correspond
to the dignity of a bishop. Further, this fish had a head, eyes, forehead,
nose, mouth, cheeks, shoulders, arms, hands and feet and all other limbs
exactly like a grown man or bishop. In front and behind his chasuble
was raised to the knees, but to the touch he felt like a cold living fish. He
allowed all kinds of people, and especially the bishops of that country, to
touch him.

LIX

The devilish cacophony of the wind
Making diagonally toward the stern
There was no point in being homesick

LX

I wasted all my wealth

on these wanton fools

LXI

They say there was once a girl
At the bottom of the sea
Sometimes with antlers

LXII

The rushing water, the
Screams of tormented
Men, the spectacle was
Overpowering and enchanting

LXIII

A girl who didn't want to marry

                              Fumbled for the emergency signal
                              lamps

Now she lives at the bottom of the sea

And there they found Halfdan Long
Leg

LXIV

Only an ordinary
starlit night

"What caused those explosions, Engineer Commander?"
Sigurd's mother was a sorceress

LXV

They say she married a dog
Had a litter of furry puppies

Then he left
To sink a British ship

In a British naval harbor

LXVI

Skin hanging in shreds
Giving essential orders
The old familiar sound of breakers

Not many people know an Earl when he's dressed as a fisherman

LXVII

Dazed, in pitch-darkness
The starboard portholes submerged
No one would carry
the raven banner

LXVIII

A boy who was abused on account of his long ears ran away and became a
hare

LXIX

Betrayed in advance

        The sound of the wind

                On the hydropoles

        Is not permanent
        Giving water
        A common voice

                In Europe

LXX

Einar had his ribs cut from the spine with a sword and the lungs pulled out through the slits in his back. He dedicated the victim to Odin as a victory offering, then made this verse:

LXXI

A great and benign being, who gave vitality to every living creature

LXXII

The last and most remarkable empire builder of modern times

LXXIII

        So her father took her out in his boat
And pushed her into the water

LXXIV

"Make way for Lord Kitchener!"

LXXV

Midsummer's Day—sunshine and calm
Gave Tree Beard to the Trolls
He was dead before that

LXXVI

Stones awaken in the night to drink
The girl struggles

LXXVII

To Byzantium
                    Through a sheave-hole in the rail
Make sure that all the lighthouses
                                        Fed wolves at Tarbert Ness

LXXVIII

She tries to climb back in the boat

So her father takes his knife

And cuts the top joints from her fingers

LXXIX

"Hang on, Stripey!"
                                        The ship lurched
And not a scrap was ever found of Hareck

LXXX

Severed stumps turn stump-animals,
Mer-mammals
Sprout flippers and swim away

LXXXI

Now he's history
But she's folklore

LXXXII

Changed as those who take to the water change
Answering to all the purposes of protoplasm
Our duty is to the dead

LXXXIII

My children
                                    My digital progeny
To give or withhold
                            Otherwise than as in the scriptures

LXXXIV

Chaos of wreckage

    Lighting the beacon on North Ronaldsay

        Staying in Novgorod over winter

           Sometimes with antlers

LXXXV

           Something out of the ordinary had
           happened
                An orange pillar of glittering
                flame
      And then the Earl was pierced through with a spear

LXXXVI

  Now she's a planet
Or not quite a planet
    A "trans-Neptunian object"
2003 VB12 "Sedna"
    Orbiting the sun every 11,400 years
The oldest and coldest not-quite-planet in the solar system

    At least for now

LXXXVII

An element of considerable importance in this narrative is foam

LXXXVIII

Themes of ruin, decay, and time
Through the lubber hole
Arctic furs
Ships from the Baltic

LXXXIX

    The dark blue
    Bodies piled
    Black on deck

XC

Kali and his shipmates

Drinking in Bergen

XCI

Nothing but darkness
And an abyss of waters

Seventy percent of *you* is water

XCII

And what about him?
Field Marshal Horatio Herbert Kitchener
Secretary of State for War
En route to Russia on a secret diplomatic mission
Sunk by a German mine

Or was he? (The body was never found)

XCIII

I wonder if he's down there still
With his walrus moustache
Seachanged

Bobbing along
Singing a song

On the bottom of the beautiful briny sea

I think I like him better that way

XCIV

BBC Radio Orkney

March 8, 2013

BARRIERS UPDATE: The barriers are OPEN.

XCV

A golden helmet on his head, a sword at his waist, clutching a cigarette
   lighter,
With prodigious, bulging eyes that never closed—
"Where on earth have you come from?" I said
                              Unrivalled—but all this is a digression

XCVI

Nonsense classification
Just   might   change   the
knowledge

                                          I think

XCVII

And there on the sand
Blasphemous fish frogs of the nameless design
Hopping along
Croaking a song
Where the sea is the land's edge also

XCVIII

Storytellers used to describe
Tides never stop

Other people in your body
To channel this demand for difference

What other context
Might have kept these verses alive?

XCIX

Carrion rivers
               Down to a sunless

C

They say he still wears clothes but he'll take to the water soon

"SEA" represents my first venture into poetry for many years. It combines "original" writing (whatever that means in this context) with collaged fragments of other texts, most of them relating to my ongoing research on art, storytelling, and perceptions of long-term environmental change in the Orkney Islands, off the northernmost tip of Scotland. Some of these are historical sources.[1] Some are oral histories or folktales.[2] Some are works by other writers like T. S. Eliot, James Joyce, Clarice Lispector, H. P. Lovecraft, Alice Notley, and the Orcadian poet and novelist George Mackay Brown (the GMB referred to in Section XXVI).[3] Others make connections to more distant places like the Canadian Arctic, to which many Orcadians emigrated as employees of the Hudson Bay Company and that provides the setting too for the Inuit legend of Sedna, rebellious daughter and latterly mistress of the sea mammals on which Inuit hunters long depended for their survival.[4]

Orkney is a setting densely marked by the presence of the dead in the form of Neolithic burial sites, traces of the era of Viking settlement (when the islands were part of the kingdom of Norway), and memorials to the fallen of World Wars I and II (when the islands served as a major British naval base), along with the oil, composed from the compacted, geothermally heated remains of long-extinct, prehistoric marine organisms, that is now pumped so profitably from beneath the North Sea to a terminal on the southern island of Flotta.[5] At the same time, the islands of Orkney and its northerly neighbor Shetland are themselves being slowly eroded by the sea that beats against their shores and that will eventually cause them to disappear beneath the waters from which they first emerged. It was my overwhelming sense of the presence of the dead over successive visits to Orkney that prompted me to turn to poetry. Ezra Pound once defined literature as "language charged with meaning to the utmost possible degree," but poetry also reminds us continuously of the materiality of language as a medium, of the sounds, rhythms, and shapes of words.[6] For both of these reasons, poetry struck me as an idiom that might register these multifarious dead as a tangible presence, an idiom through which the dead might speak. Some of the dead who return here are identifiable historical figures like Earl Sigurd of Orkney, killed at the Battle of Clontarf in Ireland in 1014, or the British

Secretary of State for War, Lord Horatio Herbert Kitchener, presumed lost with the sinking of the HMS *Hampshire* by a German mine in 1916.[7] Others are less immediately recognizable, their voices fading into the elemental strife of land and sea that Deleuze took to define the pre- and posthistorical character of islands.[8]

My aim in the poem is to evoke through writing a time-space of virtual simultaneity and coexistence in which pasts and presents, history and mythology, the human and the other-than-human might interact and reciprocally transform one another. I consider the poem anthropological because it seeks to explore the threshold(s) of emergence and dissolution of the human—of subjectivity, language, culture, and historical agency. I also consider it an overtly political work, but perhaps readers should make their own minds up about that.

Notes

1. Thompson, *New History of Orkney*.

2. Dennison, *Orkney Folklore and Sea Legends*; Marwick, *Folklore of Orkney and Shetland*; Towsey, *Orkney and the Sea*.

3. Eliot, *Four Quartets*; Joyce, *Ulysses*; Joyce, *Finnegans Wake*; Lispector, *Agua Viva*; Lovecraft, *Call of Cthulhu*; Lovecraft, *Shadow over Innsmouth*; Notley, *Songs and Stories of the Ghouls*; Mackay Brown, *Collected Poems*.

4. Laugrand and Oosten, *Sea Woman*.

5. Auton, Fletcher, and Gould, *Orkney and Shetland*; Ferguson, *Shipwrecks of Orkney, Shetland and the Pentland Firth*; Renfrew, *Prehistory of Orkney*.

6. Pound, *ABC of Reading*, 36.

7. Anonymous, *Orkneyinga Saga*; McCormick, *Mystery of Lord Kitchener's Death*; Phillips, *Loss of the H.M.S. "Hampshire."*

8. Deleuze, *Desert Islands*, 9.

14

WRITING OTHERWISE

LISA STEVENSON

If I could, I would write another poem in response to the next one. Another poem, another admixture of words that would fling us back into the sea— that would seem to be the most appropriate response. But instead of writing another poem I will begin again at the beginning of the one that follows—mostly because I am so interested in beginnings and also in the difficulty of beginning to speak. Walter Benjamin writes about the way photography opens up the optical unconscious just as psychoanalysis opens up the "instinctual" unconscious. But to illustrate his point he uses the example of walking: "It is possible, for example, however roughly, to describe the way somebody walks, but it is impossible to say anything about that fraction of a second when a person starts to walk."[1] Poetry, the way McLean does it, seems to let us feel what it means to begin to speak, the act of saying something when one beat before there was a kind of nothing.

But the beginning of the poem is where? The first word of McLean's "own" is the very title of the poem: "SEA," written in capitals. But before that there are two epigraphs. The first reads as follows: "The work of writing and reading and thinking is the tending of the otherwise." It comes from an interview with Myung Mi Kim in 2007, we are told. The second catapults us into a strange world of flat clapping fish with hands: "Let Ross, House of Ross, rejoice with the Great Flabber Dabber flat clapping fish with hands" is the line from Christopher Smart's religious poem, *Jubilate Agno*. As we will see, "SEA" is not a piece that provides any explanatory schemas; it is not a piece that claims mastery through providing the appropriate context for the information communicated. Who is Christopher Smart and what is a flat clapping fish? What about Ross, or the House of Ross? There are no summaries, plot diagrams, or outlines provided here.

Thus my first question, having progressed to the beginning that is already a beginning again: What is a title when it's not an explanatory scheme? A direction? A beginning? A gesture? A receptacle? A unity? Is this poem "about" the sea? If so, what could we mean by "about"? If not, what does the SEA in capitals do for us? Let me leave this question for a moment and come back to it below.

Returning to the poem, to the first line of the poem, the moment when McLean starts to speak again, we read:

I could never be an aardvark because
                            Moved inside as the weather
                            worsened

Here, in this very first line we are introduced to an "I" that is not an aardvark— but even more than that, we meet an "I" that could never be an aardvark. And moving down and across the page, we get "Moved inside as the weather worsened." What just happened? The "I" has disappeared! Who moved? The reader definitely moved, across the page, and the mood moved too, from the hypothetical to the declarative. But where is the writer? How did he slip so effortlessly from the poem?

Such disappearances, discontinuities, open spaces, absences, and beginning-agains litter McLean's poem. As a reader I find in them spaces for the "tending of the otherwise," as Myung Mi Kim puts it. There is room in this poem for writers to disappear, for voices to come and go, for the dead to commingle with the living. There is no narrative thread that allows our voices to slide along unwittingly, thus avoiding what might have been if we had only stopped for a moment to look around, then begun again. There is no seamless story being told here. No summing up of the facts. The otherwise is breaking through in the possibility that beginning to walk, or beginning to speak again, presents. On this question of narrative structure, the poet Aase Berg has said, "This chronology—time passes and things have to happen and there has to be a narrative—is an element that reminds me of male sexuality. It's a patriarchal invention I want to avoid."[2] And so too it seems does McLean. McLean's use of absence—the different kinds of empty space on the page, the disappearance of the subject of a sentence—make

it seem like he is always beginning again, allowing the reader to find reso-
nances rather than trajectories, fleeting possibilities rather than glorious
predictions and summations.

And sometimes these possibilities are dangerous, difficult, disturbing—
the tending of the otherwise is not only about holding out for utopias. In
Section II—perhaps the most disturbing stanza of the whole piece—there is
no I. Instead "the world" shifts across the page, even as it says that it has
always been as it is now. It goes like this:

> The world has
>
> always been
>
>   as it is now
>
>   The residue is thrown
>
>   in some place
>
> where no one goes

The schooled reader in me rebels. We should not be going back there, should
not be reading right to left, it's not right, it's not where one goes! We are
being carried back out to sea, with a dangerous tide, and then thrown back
up, disoriented, water filling our ears . . . left to make a life in the place
where no one goes. I get the sense, in reading just these first two stanzas of
Stuart's poetry, that the sea is spitting at us. Or perhaps spitting us. Or perhaps we are spitting. The sea, as title, then, is not an organizing principle but
perhaps also a disorganizing principle, in the sense of a foaming, moving
froth. Words become the detritus, the residue, the sea spits back at us, that
we find on the beach in the morning. (But still, that's not quite right either,
this is not [emphatically not] a poem about beaches: the only sunglasses are
Lady Gaga's, and the text remains somehow in the water, of the sea.)

Often, in anthropology, knowledge is understood to be dependent on the
possibility of providing the relevant context, the backstory that will explain
everything properly. Have we given the necessary context, our reviewers
ask—do we have a cat for poor Alice's grin? We, as anthropologists, are
constantly pressed for the context that will determine definitively what something "is." "SEA" refuses that kind of mastering context, and with it the
anthropologist's performance of the mastery. Instead the poem calls what
it means to say that something "is" into question. Where are the coordinates, the boundaries, of something being something and not something

else, is the question McLean seems to ask. Take Section XXI, where he writes:

Islands are

Until the sea

Covers them

Again

Is there a context that can do justice to the cosmological time of islands, of continents that are islands? Is there a way to talk about the context of non-existence? Of something being until?

In the penultimate stanza of the poem, McLean seems to wonder aloud—not what context would have determined once and for all what the islands are or are not, or what the stanzas say or do not say—but instead what might have kept them alive. He asks, with a kind of melancholy:

What other context
Might have kept these verses alive?

And so the question for anthropology, as for writing, comes back again to this question of "tending the otherwise." It is not that there is a singular, definitive context that will resolve all of our doubts about how to understand what is and what isn't, what works or what doesn't. We write and begin to write again, just as we walk and then begin to walk all over again.

Notes

1. Benjamin, "Short History of Photography," 7.
2. Aase Berg, "Response & Bio," translated by Johannes Gorannson, *Double Room*, no. 4 (Spring/Summer 2004), http://www.webdelsol.com/Double_Room/issue_four /Aase_Berg.html.

15

Origami Conjecture for a *Bembé*

TODD RAMÓN OCHOA

Movements of the Dead

In Cuba, the dead provoke. An attentive ear, and soon the island lifts from the sea, not on ancient coral terraces but on the burbling murmur of the dead. Those indistinct communications, taken for important and paid attention to, provoke. The dead provoke the living to speech, though perhaps not to discourse. In others, the dead provoke writing.

This is hardly unique to Cuba. A glance at the Caribbean and Latin America, if not most of the world, shows similar provocations by the dead. The dead have moved me in Havana and in the Cuban countryside, where they insinuate themselves over and over into the lives of people I know.

The Wilson Library in Chapel Hill at the University of North Carolina (UNC) is a good place to write and a good place to brood. How to communicate the energy of the dead in the Cuban countryside? How to move the dead toward the living, especially the living who will read these words? Wilson is not a bad place to confront this problem. It was once a great research library. A professor in the Department of Religious Studies at UNC, Ruel Tyson, recalls scrambling through the stacks as an undergraduate, where he chased the specter of Kant through its singular collections. UNC then built the hulking Davis Graduate Library, visible through the massive east-facing windows of Wilson's reading room. Left behind, this library slowly became defunct. On its walls are the portraits of long-dead university fathers, and on its ground floor is a huge room dedicated to displaying the Southern Historical Collection, complete with Civil War artifacts, lace doilies, and reproductions of antebellum interiors. You wouldn't want to get locked in here

for the night. The librarians seem to glide by, wispy and pale, as they disappear into the narrow stacks that are now off-limits, even to faculty. The
old town cemetery, which is a short walk out those big east-facing windows,
seems attractive by comparison. Like a giant, silent pump, Wilson primes
this writing for the dead.

Sierra Morena

Sierra Morena is two-thirds of the way between touristy Varadero Beach and
the city of Sagua La Grande, further to the east along Cuba's north coast.
Coming from Varadero, Sierra Morena is beyond the hot springs and a little
further than the town of Corralillo. This is where the highway hooks south
before hooking dramatically north again. If you're from anywhere west of
Varadero you probably don't have a real good idea of where this is, except
"that way, along the north circuit," as the highway is called. It is Cuba's only
road traveling this piece of the coast. This is fallow sugar country, with lots
of farmers trying to figure out how to make the best of a go in the quickly
shifting economy, which, no matter what, doesn't let them get ahead.

At the hook, which is a couple miles inland, Sierra Morena sits at the
narrow steppe of a low hill, for which the term *mountain* (sierra) is tongue-
and-cheek, the joke long lost. At Sierra Morena the road seeks high ground as
it dodges farmland that was once swampland that still goes under when a
hurricane hits, which is pretty regularly. Climbing the low hill, the North
Circuit runs straight at town before it veers suddenly away, ultimately acknowledging Sierra Morena at but a couple glancing points. The little grid
of streets that is the town is just beyond, out of view.

Not that there is much traffic along the North Circuit to notice. Today,
dump trucks, tractors, slow-moving diesel engines ply it a few miles at a time.
In 1999 you could spend most of a morning sitting on the side of the road
and not see a single car. There were plenty of horse-drawn carts and people
walking. In 2014, maybe ten cars went past in an hour, most of them government cars ferrying people midway up the ladder at the Ministry of Agriculture
(MINAG) or the Ministry of the Interior (MININT). The MINAG guys, dressed
in snappy polo shirts and artificially distressed jeans, chase the ever-elusive
production quotas stressed by the government, while the MININT people,
in their two-tone olive uniforms, chase the equally elusive (though more

frequently found) inner-tube refugees setting out for Miami. This is all local travel between towns strung along the coast, or inland to despondent little crossings in the middle of state-run pineapple and citrus farms. Gas is scarce in Sierra Morena, but these days you can hire a local driver to take you the 216 miles to Havana for sixty dollars, which is madness only a visitor like me could afford.

My teacher Isidra has been bringing me here for fifteen years, and little by little I've gotten to know her family. Isidra's younger sister, Elsy, is a lot of fun, always the sidekick. She lives in Cienfuegos, five hours by bus to the south. Like Isidra, she has been living away from town for decades. Along with their older brother, Pedro, they were recruited (*captados*) as teenagers by the Revolution in the earliest moments after its triumph. Their lives were spent on the projects the Revolution unfurled over the decades, and they only occasionally make it back to town. Another brother, Tomás, was likewise recruited, but he was to stay behind and run revolutionary programs and politics in town, like the once-robust Committees for the Defense of the Revolution. Other people in town have become friends, like Tomás's father-in-law, the ninety-one-year-old Lázaro Medrano.

Isidra and Lázaro Medrano are the people I talk to most about life in Sierra Morena, especially about the ubiquitous parties called *bembés* that people throw for the dead and for the *santos* and *orisás*. The santos and orisás are always synonymous and used interchangeably. For the sake of ethnographic pragmatics I will call them *santos-orisás*. Isidra brought me here to look at one particular bembé, a feast for the beggar-saint and sovereign over illness called San Lázaro-Babalú Ayé. Isidra and Lázaro Medrano both host parties for this santo-orisá, and it is for Lázaro's feast that I keep going back to town.

The Matter of a Bembé

"Cuba?" the librarian at Wilson asks. "I've always wanted to go to Cuba." This is a common response when people manage to draw me out on what I do. Everyone wants to go to Cuba. Many are revolutionary dreamers who have somehow managed a peaceful slumber through several very bad decades. Others are easygoing adventurers for whom the forbidden island offers just the right mixture of danger and security. And there are the misanthropic tourists drawn to the crumbling buildings and creaking cars as much as to the misery and despair. The librarian seems a combination of the first two: a beat-down liberal for whom a week on the beach in Cuba would do much to lift her spirits. In a few sharp questions she has got me talking about my writing.

"So, a bembé is like a party?" she asks.

"It is a party," I reply. "In town anyone can throw one. You need a drum, someone to sing, and someone to dance—that is all it takes. It helps if you have three drums and a hundred singers and dancers, then it will be a good party. But you can do it with three or four. The dancers are crucial, because it is the dancers who will be mounted by the dead and the orisás."

She lets a fleeting look of surprise cross her eye.

"Dancers who have a close relationship with the dead or the orisás are said to be their steeds," I say by way of an explanation. "Dancers are said to be the horses of the dead and the orisás, who mount up on the dancers' backs. 'Mounting up' is how what we call 'possession' is talked about at a bembé."

"So, it is a . . . religion," she says.

"You could call it a religion that thrives on the north coast of Cuba, and in other places that aren't Havana," I assure her. I have been down this path every time I talk about Sierra Morena and the parties there. "But it isn't like Protestantism, or Catholicism, or even Pentecostalism, because in a bembé there are no priests or leaders. Bembés don't happen in churches or anything like them. A bembé is a *party* and only has good singers, drummers, and dancers who lead, like good musicians and dancers lead at any party."

She seems surprised by the informality I'm describing, by the lack of leaders or buildings. It is five o'clock and the reading room is emptying. She peeks over her glasses and asks, "Does it have books?"

In the lovely, gloomy gallery just outside the reading room an exhibit of Diderot's Encyclopedia fills the glass cases.

"No, there are no books. People are literate, but there are no books," I say. She seems a little vexed. She knows as well as I do that without a book, or writing, there is no doctrine, there is no fixed law. This is significant for my writing about bembés, because it makes for a story of openness and change, or growth and transformation, where fixed rules are hard to come by, if they belong at all. Without fixed leaders and fixed rules, a bembé has only the figments of a hierarchy. I'm sure she is putting all this together but just to make sure, I say, "There are no initiations, no one who does divination, no one is really in charge."

She gets it just in time. The late winter light dies against the green marble columns towering over us and reminds me that I had better get going. I walk down the tunnel-like grand staircase to the campus, thinking how this very simple thing, that a bembé has no fixed hierarchy, makes the parties so nice for me. Because there are only drummers, singers, and dancer-mounts, a bembé remains a party, and it is fun.

To enjoy a bembé you have to like singing and dancing and also have a taste for "participatory theater," where you play a part in lifting the play and music to an excited sustain. It helps if you have a taste for rivalry as well, and if you enjoy helping singers, drummers, and those who impersonate the dead and the santos-orisás to overcome themselves, and one another. The musicians and dancers like to play together, just as much as they like to show one another up. A bembé is for this reason a lively, if not tense, affair, where players bring their best game or end up on the sidelines watching others join the fun.

A good bembé will have three drums, and drummers will vie with one another for a chance to play. Each drum has a different role, and only the very best drummers can get behind la caja (the box), a big bass drum where a player can improvise. If a person, almost always a man, sits down at the big box and can't match the sustain, or take the party higher, then they are quickly dragged off and replaced by someone else. Everyone who dances sings but very few people want to lead, or "call," songs. In town there are only three or four people who vie for the role of gallo (rooster, or caller) at a bembé. These callers know one another well; town is small and everyone knows everyone well, and for a feast to go all night at least two of them will be on hand. This doesn't stop them from keeping up a sometimes ugly banter. Dancers also compete, though again less so than the drummers. A bembé is full of dancers, and anyone willing to step out and have a try at a flourish is welcome, though they are not spared jokes or slights.

Without books, laws, or leaders, bembés are more in the way of "happenings" and "events," which is just what parties should be. This is why I have tried not to speak of bembé in the abstract, as if there were more to the parties than the parties themselves, with their drumming, singing, dancing, and mounting up of the dead and the sovereign santos-orisás. Each feast is as singular as the actual place and time where the dead and the santos-orisás are engaged. A bembé can spill out of the house and into the yard, the street, the cemetery, or the countryside, especially once the dead and the santos-orisás arrive. These santos-orisás, all of them esteemed by proper name, are the reason bembés happen at all. Those who drum, sing, and dance do so to please the dead and sovereign santos-orisás, to entice them with their music and movements, so as to draw them into encounters with the living. If the dead and the santos-orisás come, they will do so on the backs of their preferred dancers, their "horses" and "mounts." Then the pleasure is mutual, because there is nothing so lively for those at a bembé as sharing the attention of those sovereigns who hold your fate in their hands and who can change your life in a word.

One way I describe a bembé is as "praise." Perhaps better would be to call it a "style of praise," where what is praised is fate-shaping and fate-breaking. By style, I mean that a bembé is an active, superficially dynamic process. It moves to, and is moved by, outside forces. It is receptive to outside forces and seeks them, thus regularly churning out new versions of itself. In its play with these forces, and with the santos-orisás and the dead, a bembé recombines the cultural resources that make it possible with unforeseen differences from the outside. This is high-stakes style.

"Praise" is foremost joy and release: singing, dancing, and playing. The point of a bembé is to have fun until the dead and the santos-orisás mount up. Then the fun becomes joy because such effective and magnanimous powers join the party. The dead and the santos-orisás, like San Lázaro-Babalú Ayé, are the reason you attend a bembé, and the reason you host one. They are the guests of honor because together they shape and break fated lives, making the impossible seem possible again. To shape fate, the basic pieces of a stuck situation are turned in new directions.

The dead and a santo-orisá like San Lázaro-Babalú Ayé look for experienced mounts who can bear the weight of their influence, so that they can linger with the gathered crowd. So held, a santo-orisá like San Lázaro-Babalú Ayé will take time to consult people in their troubles. Fates are shaped in these conversations. Fate-shaping means changing what is given, petrified, or fixed, into something new, yet still connected to what has been. Santos-orisás, especially the beggar Lazarus, are beloved for working with what people in town have, since they have so little. A santo-orisá like San Lázaro-Babalú Ayé will take the situation you're given and make something new out of it, something no one was able to imagine. A bembé is meant to be very pragmatic in this way.

Fate-breaking is reserved for the dead. These are usually Kongo-inspired. They tend to mount up late in a bembé, if situations persist unchanged. When drummers and singers and dancers together turn their music toward Kongo rhythms and songs, then more urgent kinds of fate-working are being asked for. What the santos-orisás can't resolve, the dead will take in hand and push fated situations with hard-sounding counsel. The dead seek out difficult relationships and their interventions can feel precipitous and dangerous. There is no less joy for this in a bembé, and what is praised is fate-breaking power sufficient to change a life.

As far as I can tell, bembés happen all over Cuba, in towns along the north coast, and also outside of Cienfuegos, and throughout Cuba's east. In Sierra Morena, bembés look in some ways like Haitian Vodou as this is described both ethnographically and in travel accounts. Bembés share with Vodou the recombination of West African sources and Kongo sources, together at the same feast. Bembés and Vodou feasts share a history of reaching out on the part of the African people and their descendants. A history of reaching out—across language, across custom, and fear, and massive cosmological divides, always under conditions of maximum duress—in order to reach the outside and make a new day happen.

On a small plantation not far from Sierra Morena, these slaves were people from a city called Alladá, in what is now Benin. In Cuba, people from Alladá and its surrounding land came to be called *arará*. This is a creolized pronunciation of this once-powerful city. Today we know Alladá people by their ethnic name, this being Fon. In the Cuban countryside, especially around and within the great sugar plain south of Sierra Morena, Fon people came to live alongside their formidable political and military rivals, these being Yoruba people from the city of Oyo and its lands, in what is today Nigeria. Alladá and Oyo people had warred and slaved one another into their situation in tragic alliances with the Spanish, Portuguese, and French. These were people who might have hated one another but who shared experiences with one another prior to Europeans coming to their lands in West Africa. Once in Cuba it was their shared architecture for fate-making through the sovereign orisás that brought them together.

Neither Fon nor Yoruba had much experience with yet another people brought to Cuba as slaves, these being BaKongo people from central Africa, what are today Congo and the Democratic Republic of Congo. BaKongo people praised the dead, and their fate-making was more direct and physical than orisá fate-making. BaKongo people also had a confident and fluid healing practice through which cures for fated situations were pursued by activating the dead clinging to branches, stones, and roots, and to animal and human remains buried in the earth.

Together, these people labored and struggled as slaves on Cuba's sprawling and multifarious sugar plantations, some large, some tiny. Slavery continued in Cuba for twenty years longer than in the United States, with abolition finally complete in 1888. What can be surmised today is that in the plantation communities south of what is today Sierra Morena Fon people and BaKongo people made bembés together, with Yoruba people adding to the feasts. What they praised were orisás, the Kongo dead, and Catholic saints—the very matter of bembés today.

Origami Conjecture for a Bembé

A question I ask myself at this point in adding up a bembé is, "Why do bembés thrive?" The answer, of course, is in the bembés themselves, which, like dance parties anywhere, will last only so long as people continue to come. Dance parties are a limited analogy, though they do have in common with bembés music and dancing and the expectation that the extraordinary could happen. That it is African-inspired music moving them both is surely no coincidence. Bembés quickly exceed the analogy, however, in that you don't have to pay to attend a bembé and that those attending are integrally part of the development of a bembé. Which is to say, many more people play an active role. In a bembé the singers, drummers, and dancer-mounts are more than active-passive recipients of musical inspiration. It is for the extravagant dancers among them that bembés happen at all, in the expectation that they will receive the fate-breaking power of the dead, as well as the fate-shaping santos-orisás, mounted on their backs. In a bembé they are all jammed together: musicians, singers, and dancers in extravagant play with one another. This is how a bembé thrives, with musicians and dancers jamming Catholic saints, and santos-orisás, with the Kongo dead.

A bembé becomes an ethnographic problem at this point, because figuring out how all these sources get added together starts to become dialectically difficult to sustain, if only because none of the sources of a bembé are necessarily subordinated to any other. Subordination is a basic function and result of dialectical operations, the goal being the stabilization of opposed entities under the superordination of one of them. A bembé does something other than stabilize through subordination, and this choice sustains the complexity of encounters that a bembé hosts. One shape this takes in a bembé is the absence of leadership in feasts. It also has the consequences that Fon, Yoruba, Kongo, and Catholic resources are not "reconciled" in a bembé, but rather are competitively encountered with one another. Their relationships are unresolved.

Can all this really be added together, with nothing pushed down or falling out? Doesn't one thing subordinate another? In what order are they in? The dialectician will ask, "Isn't there a synthesis?" When does it stabilize? This is the first phrasing of a problem a bembé presents to ethnography, a problem not to be solved or explained, but rather to be made more delightful and precise, through conjecture. How do bembés resist synthesis? How do they continue to grow? How are bembés jammed?

The problem might start to find a shape if we ask what it means to jam a bembé. I would keep it simple and say that to jam is to *add to*, more and more: to bring one more in, to let another in the door, add one more to the point of breaking. In a bembé this will be sound-voice-movement, everything together, one thing added to the next: Fon and Yoruba santos-orisás, the Kongo dead, and Catholic saints. Drummers, singers, and dancers, animal killing, and fate-making forces received on the backs of those who become their bolting steeds, intensively energized but fully under the control of the sovereign santos-orisás and the Kongo dead who mount them. A bembé grows louder, faster, fuller, until you think it can't hold more. To the drumming, singing, and dancing add the ritual theater of santo-orisá impersonation, add the family and romantic dramas that the dead and the santos-orisás engage in, then add the musicians, the singers, even the santos-orisás themselves, vying with one another to determine the greatest stakes of life. A bembé expands precipitously, then it rolls over itself. Rather than exploding or spilling, time and again a bembé starts to roll, its surfaces of sound and movement roll up together rather than oppose one another. By rolling when things get intense, a bembé expands to include "everything forceful": the santos-orisás, the Kongo dead, and the Catholic saints.

A bembé keeps growing because its players find how to fit more in. A bembé rolls because it grows, and rolling is among the modes of expanding without exploding that a bembé follows. Rolling allows a bembé to carry outside forces slowly inside, wrapping them up in tiny gaps between layers that come to rest one-upon-the-next. These layers do not simply stack but curl around one another, twisting into coils. Bembés are added to by playing with santo-orisá forces, the forces of the Kongo dead, and Catholic forces, rolling them back and forth.

Inside forces are also carried outside, and soon a bembé has given rise to a torqued threshold, where inside and outside shift back and forth. What was once a line, a fixed limit in Catholicism, or "straight Yoruba Ifá divination," in a bembé becomes more of a running helix, actively moving back and forth. Those who jam forces in a bembé are arrayed unevenly along its quickly multiplying surfaces. This is one way of thinking inside and outside in a bembé, where such a distinction doesn't make a lot of sense, so open to the outside is a bembé. Interiority in a bembé is at best a rolled-up exteriority, what is inside having shortly before been outside, and likely to spill out again.

The roll, especially its thresholds, remits us to lines, relatively straight ones: limit lines, horizon lines. These are Plato's lines and Kant's lines and Hegel's lines; they are the limit lines of dialectics and of the laws it inspires. These are the lines that appear where the lip of a seashell casts a shadow across its mouth, and the curious want only what lies in the darkness. Inside and outside are conjured out of dialectical fantasies and almost simultaneously conjure "the self" and "the other." This is, in fact, how santo-orisá, Kongo, and Catholic forces see one another in bembés. The forces presently being drummed, danced, and mounted are in the "self" position, while those becoming what is actually happening, either through singers or dancers, are in the position of "other." A bembé at its fullest will engage all three sources, finding ways to embrace the outside, often along a rolling threshold. A bembé, among many things it does, could also be called a "practice of rolling with others."

On the reverberations of the drums, on the high falsetto cries of San Lázaro-Babalú Ayé when he takes his steeds, and in the limping impersonation of him, the sources of a bembé roll with one another. Later in the bembé the Kongo dead will come and shake the fates of the forsaken. Fon, Kongo, and Yoruba intensities, together with Spanish ones, roll and recombine because of the excessive mounting of forces. Together they will move those gathered across the mouth of the realm of possibilities.

Mounted forces—it is for them that bembés roll. These are the forces that make and unmake people's lives. A bembé generates them and also gathers them and keeps them. Kongo, Catholic, and Fon forces are kept in great stacks, as if inside the players of a bembé, but really only ever outside them, in the party. Pleated up, these forces are pushed one against another. Impossibly large amounts of energy tucked up into tight stacks, momentarily stashed away. The narrative greatness of Fon, Kongo, and Spanish Catholic sources is like a vast body of water, where the waves are heaped instead of dissipated. They lie one against the other, their undertow tails spreading out from the piled stack.

Pleats of Kongo, Catholic, and Fon forces can be deceptive. They can look repetitive and ordered, and apparently under control, stored, like a closed fan. A bembé can get boring, and the limited mix of drummers, singers, and dancers can start to look routine. Fans are famous for hiding things, and they are synonymous with images of nineteenth-century plantation gentility, where the world of things hidden was surely greater than the world of things seen. Keeping things hidden is an old trope that writers have used to approximate the music and healing of Caribbean and Latin American people, but in a bembé there is nothing essentially hidden. Forces stacked, or folded away, are expected to splay out again. The only questions are "when?" and "by whom?"

In a bembé, you can't see what is stacked up until the fan is on top of you, spreading and undulating as it expands. The great pleats of African and European sources that order a bembé like to come undone. In a moment, a rush of santo-orisá sovereignty, or the Kongo dead, comes running out of invisible tucks, where it was momentarily out of view among other pleats and rolls. When a pleat of energy—of santo-orisá playfulness, or Kongo fury—is released at a bembé, it fans out in a great or subtle display as it spreads its particular rhythm across the face of a feast. It will extend until it encounters another pleat of santo-orisá, or Kongo, or Catholic intensity, itself coming undone and spreading out.

Just as pleats of forces can fan out to overtake a bembé, so they are folded back up again. Like the many curtains of a stage furled high out of sight, they are displayed and rolled back again as the people at play on the stage encounter one another. Fans will return to the positions they previously occupied, just as they will change shape as a result of their extension upon opening, then contract upon closing. This is how Catholic forces start to sound Fon, Fon forces start to feel Kongo, and Kongo feelings take on European shades (of good and evil). Spreading and retracting are operations with consequences for the forces released, as much as for the bembé itself. Pleated stacks often return to place in a different orientation, giving a bembé a new shape.

Pleats and folds can as easily run against one another, just like santo-orisá and Kongo forces are seldom in rhythm or sync. In Havana people look down at bembé parties because they include both santo-orisá and Kongo forces, different as these are. What Havana-based feasts oppose is rolled-with in a bembé. Players in a bembé work with "opposing" forces by moving them in two or three directions at once, twisting and braiding them together. The tension in the braid is palpable, and it takes on the long shape of a twisting wave.

Forces in a bembé, be these Fon, Kongo, or Catholic, are not opposed so much as rolled, stacked, and braided. Their very shapes are a genealogy of their encounters with one another. One of the great pleasures of a bembé is to witness these genealogies being pragmatically played with. A bembé will twist forces around playfully and unexpectedly, almost as if looking for new, mischievous shapes to emerge from the jam. In the jam, the relation of forces is not a head-to-head, one-against-another affair. Rather, jammed-up forces move in multiple directions at once and relate to one another simultaneously, intimately, and luxuriously. The curls and pleats of their meeting are the life of a bembé and emerge from the matter of a bembé itself.

The play of a bembé is always consequential, at times monstrously so. Drummers, singers, and dancers push forces around, engaging one another through them. Santo-orisá rhythms are shaped by a drummer twisting time in a Kongo way, this gesture then opposed by the caller of the moment, who joins the drummer on the big drum to recruit Catholic time in turning the bembé back toward the santos-orisás. The failed bid for a Kongo turn rolls back against itself, and the moment is a monstrous little instant, where santos-orisás tangle up with the Kongo dead in perverse time, with twisted verse. A bembé is alive when expected shapes momentarily become unrecognizable and alien.

Bembés are over-full attempts to handle, momentarily, the great energies of people gathered to praise their saints, their santos-orisás, and their dead. In the course of a bembé jam, the energies of these sources are shaken to the boiling point, and the great and monstrous consequences are engaged. In a bembé people play with more energy than they can possibly hold, and it is not surprising that thresholds are moving and warped in a bembé. It is no surprise that its forces mount and twist into unstable, rolling waves.

Moving so, the energy and potential mount precipitously, in speeding coils that hold so much more than what can be held against the limit line of dialectics or European dualism. If you play bembé you realize this and begin to look for the mounted forces, more than you could ever imagine, undulating down from the barely visible tip of a twisted coil.

Not everything in a bembé is rolled, fanned, twisted, and coiled. Huge amounts of force go "nowhere" and do not return to mount or pleat back up. Forces are lost in a bembé perhaps more than they are stacked and mounted. When a fan of Kongo, santo-orisá, or Catholic forces is unleashed across a bembé, profligate amounts of energy are scattered and run away. That shift toward Kongo rhythm, that disjointed lash of Babalú Ayé's arms, in those movements forces will always become incongruous and dissipate into uselessness. At the fringes of profligate uselessness, a bembé comes undone and slips out of itself.

A bembé spills beyond identification. I can only treat it in the singular for this reason: "a bembé." This is preferable to any attempt to define something bigger, like a *religion*—"bembé itself." The excesses of a single bembé—the gathered forces, the jammed sources, the twisted waves and stacked arrays all waiting to spring out and coil around—give rise to a large variety of shapes, new shapes for a bembé. Each and every bembé is different, and its movements escape the demand that it be identifiable. This is an ethnographic conundrum for which it is sufficient to say that a bembé is growth, encounter, and twisting forces recombining in a splay of singularly Cuban life.

A bembé will come to a close with the slam of a bucket, mouth down. Lázaro Medrano, the last time I was at his feast, could feel that the forces unleashed and the stakes at play hardly merited the attention of the mounted dead and the santos-orisás who had rambled among his guests. Gently, taking care with his ninety-one-year-old frame, they took the bucket of seasoned water, swung it round and round before the drummers, then walked off to dump it on his doorstep. The mounted dead and santos-orisás, if there were any left, took their cues and were either sitting to be fanned and blown off their mounts, or were out the back door, fading into the thickets of countryside. Singing as he walked in, joyful to be putting a close to something that had been so sweet, Lázaro smashed the bucket down. The thumping boom brought even the drummer on the big box to rest.

16

ETHNOGRAPHIC EXCESS

DANIELLA GANDOLFO AND TODD RAMÓN OCHOA

Todd sits to write inside Wilson, an old, forlorn university library. It is a gloomy winter afternoon. He is thinking of *bembé* feasts in the central Cuban countryside, of their fluidities and their open ferment, which keep the dead vitally energized, uncontainable in their eagerness to mount singers and dancers. Todd broods. "How to communicate the energy of the dead in Cuba?" But surrounded by portraits of the university's dead fathers, antebellum paraphernalia, and even a cemetery just outside the library halls, Todd's thinking is suddenly fixed on the dead. "Wilson, like a giant, silent pump," he writes, "primes this writing for the dead."

Daniella commutes to work along the parkway, listening to talk radio, as always. The road is bland in its familiarity, but the flow of cars is not as it swerves and slows down in response to more roadkill than she has ever seen. She slows down too. Some of the animals are still agonizing. They fascinate but also ward off. The conversation on the radio turns to killing, to the yearly bear hunt in the state of New Jersey. Speaking in favor of it, a hunter tells of the significance hunting has for him: he loves nature, immersing himself in it and fulfilling his role as predator. He loves, and he kills. Millions of animals are killed every day in this country, but few claim to love them. There is a difference that matters here.

Todd and Daniella are both intruded upon in their respective encounters with the dead: Todd with the dead haunting his fieldwork and his library, Daniella with dead animals, some loved, some not. Are these intrusions of the life around us impelled by the power of "mediation" or of "immediacy"? How are we to explain the way our surroundings direct us, work on us as we think and write? What does this relationship with the things and beings that surround us have to do with ethnography, with writing, with the "craft" and "storytelling" of ethnography?

Since graduate school, we have been in an ongoing conversation about the matter of ethnography. Ethnography is writing, we have agreed many times; it appears in the middle of writing and cannot be conceived outside of it, let alone above it. But isn't this writing that produces ethnography also urged on by what appears to stand outside of writing? This includes the "work" that it takes, that writing calls for, pulls from us and requires, which is never commensurate with the writing that results from it. The work overflows this product, and the better the latter is, the fewer the traces of toil it contains. We like to think of this work as a kind of "excess," then, in the sense of Bataille's *dépense*, entailing the giving away, the expenditure of time and energy. There is no writing, no ethnography, without this expenditure, this surrender and heedless giving.

In one valence, the words on the page are the shifting linkages between life (fieldwork, the world) and text (as if text were something different from life itself). Text is linked to life but those links are not stable; they come and go, emerge and submerge, but can be cultivated with care. We think of "craft" as involving such cultivation, the vexing combination of labor and surrender. The repetition and painstaking lingering with writing and rewriting open up time to reflect and respond to the changes we effect on the words in front of us and the changes the words effect on us and our world. You might say that craft is lingering, slow, meticulous activity that at times rolls into creativity only to roll back out of it, toward the repetitive mulling of slow work.

Can craft be conceivable separate from an object? Is text our object, like we might think of mud being the object of a potter? Or is our object the world that impinges upon us, prompts us to write this or that way, putting demands on us, freeing but also limiting? Might we think of craft as mutually embroiled transformation, with our text changing us and our world just as we and the world change it? For our part, the writing of ethnography is as likely to work on us as the fieldwork that produced it.

We see ethnography as epistemologically "confused" by a mutual relationship with both mediation/negation and immediacy/affirmation. Ethnography communicates or translates one reality through another and for this reason is inescapable from the terms of mediation. Ethnography stands between worlds, bridges them, makes them communicable to one another.

But ethnography is also, and simultaneously, craft and storytelling, remitting its practitioners and readers to the affective realm of nonidentifiable transmission, which escapes the confines of mediation and tends toward immediacy. This is ethnography's visceral dimension, its nervous, electric, ecstatic possibilities: the dead on wall portraits nudging at a brooding but receptive ethnographer of bembé feasts; the volatile combination of love and death letting a student of hunting peer into a depth that is fascinating as much as it is terrifying.

Mediation and immediacy also find their way into our texts through storytelling. Our interest in writing has to do with the movement of life-into-text-into-life through the medium of the story and the care to tell a decent, readable story. Ethnography struggles with stories, which are its very lifeblood. Do we know of a genre of writing that is so at odds with its lifeblood? Stories told by people who, by design or chance, we meet in the course of fieldwork often don't fit into social scientific conventions or the instrumental reason of routine social scientific thought. Most stories are heterogeneous, incompatible with the logical accountability or demand for verifiability that social science continues to serve, if only spectrally. Stories told to us will continue to be told in congruent or antagonistic ways by other people, by the things surrounding them and us, by anticipated or unanticipated occurrences. So a good story, stumbled upon in the course of conversation, will likely grow and contort, explain as much as confuse, and threaten the demand to comprehensibility that ethnography, as translation, seems to require. That is what we mean when we say that ethnography struggles against its very lifeblood.

We ask, how to envelop a reader in a life? How to bring them along, to include them, in the lives we have inhabited and been invited into in the course of our fieldwork and our writing, even when this life is incomprehensible, inconsistent, or inconceivable? Even when it is uninteresting? Readers are treacherous, especially readers of ethnography. We are trained in ways of reading that seek to destroy or undermine, to negate what is written on the "ethnographic page." It seems to us that readers of ethnography frequently start out bored and only leave this state if they can undermine the text they are reading. To address these readers we look to storytelling that imports life into the reader. Detail is crucial in this, but more important are the relays of evocation and deferral, provocation and irresolution to which every detail must belong and that make detail not only bearable but also fascinating.

Each in our own way, we embrace the inevitability of ethnography as a minor form, ultimately lost, not quite insignificant enough to forever disappear. More important, we see ethnography as necessarily fraught with its own ambiguities and impossibilities, inevitably destined to confuse the social sciences.

The too-muchness that laughs at our capacity to bear it, to write it, to enclose it: ethnography is too much, always too much. For itself, its history, its practitioners, and its readers, ethnography escapes limitation, again and again. This excessive dimension is struggled against by the more reductive and institutional versions of ethnography, which seek to contain it under the sign of symbolic representation. But ethnography is doomed by its excesses, to minority, to becoming strange and misunderstood.

17

Conversations with a Hunter

DANIELLA GANDOLFO

Taboo fashions the pleasure at the same time as it condemns it.
—GEORGES BATAILLE, Erotism

> CALLER: I'm just calling on behalf of hunting in general. I think most
> people have a misconception that hunters are evil people that go
> into the woods and kill innocent animals just standing there. Hunt-
> ers themselves, by the nature of being a hunter, you're naturally a
> conservationist because you want to be able to do a hunt the follow-
> ing year. I don't know anybody who goes out into the wilderness and
> kills something just for the sake of killing. . . .
> HOST: You say that people don't just go out to shoot . . . How did you
> put it? For the fun of it? And I understand the conservation argu-
> ment, but don't most people who hunt actually literally go out and
> do it for the fun of it? This is a sport; this is . . . one of their hobbies,
> and people do it for fun.
> CALLER: Well, maybe I didn't represent exactly what I wanted to say.
> They go out for the camaraderie, for being in nature, for the fun of
> the hunt. It's not a bloodthirsty sport, is what I'm trying to explain.
> People don't go out there to kill an animal just because they can kill
> something.[1]

It was an early December morning. A blanket of old, hardened snow flanked
the asphalt, the pale sun bouncing off it all the way to where it ended, and
tall, thick woods rose up like a screen splitting the parkway corridor from

the sprawl of towns beyond. The forests this road intersects are not hunting grounds, but they teem with wildlife.

I had been commuting on this Connecticut parkway for four years, and I had never seen so much roadkill as this particular morning: deer, opossums, and raccoons, formless lumps of flesh on the side of the road, the strangest hues of purple and red. I puzzled over the reasons when the conversation on the radio began. The state of New Jersey had officially reinstated the black bear hunt after thirty-three years, and with the season already into its third day the waters of controversy hadn't yet settled. Even though nearby states like New York and Pennsylvania have held annual black bear hunts uninterruptedly all those years, New Jersey's decision to readopt hunting as a form of bear population control was all over the news. Black bears are native to the forests of northwestern New Jersey; with ever-growing developments pushing their way into the farthest reaches of bear country (and multiplying the sources of food), the bear population had doubled since 2001, expanding its range southward and eastward.[2] Who hasn't heard of New Jersey residents' encounters with black bears, the animals prowling in their back patios, rummaging through their garbage cans, breaking into their homes and cars? For the bear hunting event that December, which would take place over the course of six days, the state had issued over seven thousand permits, limiting the hunt to one bear per individual hunter, regardless of the animal's gender, age, or size. By the morning the radio talk show took place, 426 bears had been killed out of an estimated population of 3,400.[3]

Opposition to the New Jersey black bear hunt as a barbarous method of bear population control was vociferous as were the retorts affirming hunting as inherently conservationist. But what struck me as exceptional about the discussion that morning on the radio, which involved the show's host, a hunter, and regular folks calling in to voice their opinion, is that for brief but crucial moments it veered in the direction of arguments about hunting that weren't as instrumental as the conservationist appeal, that weren't as obvious or easily expressible; it veered, in other words, toward a less restricted or less reserved exploration of the allure of hunting and the hunting experience, carefully circling around what the philosopher José Ortega y Gasset refers to as hunting's in-itself—*la mismidad de la caza*.[4]

"I don't know anybody who goes out into the wilderness and kills something just for the sake of killing," the caller had said. "It's not a bloodthirsty sport. . . . People don't go out there to kill an animal just because they can kill something." If not killing for the sake of killing, then what kind of experience are hunters after?

> HOST: Listeners, if you have taken part in the New Jersey bear hunt, give us a call. Why do you do it? What's the fun of shooting a bear? Explain to those of our listeners who are going, "Oh my god, I could never do this!" . . . [To the hunter:] Is the bear hunt the best way to control the bear population in New Jersey?
>
> HUNTER: Yes, it absolutely is. . . . Certainly part of the issue is bears having conflicts with human beings. . . . But it's a bigger issue than that. It is about balancing the population of the animals with the care and capacity of the land. The simple fact is New Jersey is the most densely populated state in the country; there is not a whole lot of wilderness left for bears. I'm very happy they're thriving now . . . but the simple fact is that they don't have enough to eat because the land can't support them. . . . Part of [the problem is] that they haven't been hunted, quite frankly. . . . It's sort of the natural reaction of populations not being controlled and bears doing what they do: reproducing and spreading.
>
> CALLER: I am not a hunter myself, but I'm in full support of this bear hunting. As we slowly enter our way into their environment, there's going to be a crossing of cultures here, and all it will take is one bear to injure an adult or injure a child. . . . If we just let them keep breeding, what are we going to do, be living with the bears?

As the conversation unfolded on the radio, I drove by two deer carcasses on the side of the parkway. I thought, "A crossing of cultures." It is estimated that about a million vertebrates die each day on road collisions in the United States. Sometime in the last three decades cars overtook hunting as the leading human cause of animal mortality on land.[5] But while we become appalled at the sight of a fatally maimed raccoon wriggling in pain on the road's shoulder or of a dying buck heaving against a median wall, we view these deaths as accidental. We take them to have none of the calculated deliberateness and predictability of the hunt.

Roadkill and hunting. But in what ways do these forms of human-animal encounter converge other than in their tenuous, momentary coincidence in this piece of writing? Or is it writing alone that links them as a sort of compulsion that grows at the contemplation of violence, of life expiring, of an intimacy that links us humans to the agonizing animal in a relation that is marred by ambivalence and failure?

Eduardo Figueroa Alonso-Martínez, Count of Yebes, opens his book on big-game hunting—for which Ortega y Gasset wrote his much-cited prologue—with the scene of his first kill and with an apology. "It was a smooth and tender morning in the last month of the year," he writes. "It had rained overnight, and the sierra smelled like glory." Two deer entered his field of vision "like two exhalations," sweeping through the brush with that unmistakable rumbling that "shortens our breath and sends our heart galloping." A scramble for the guns followed, then some missed shots, the stumbling of a wounded deer, and the final bullet that put an end to the chaos. "I had killed my first *res*," Yebes writes, using the Latin term for *thing* or *property*, which is also frequently used in Spanish to refer to four-legged game.[6]

At that moment, a deep, pained humility descends upon the text, which contrasts sharply with the exalted passion for hunting that Yebes says grew out of this first experience. It also contrasts with the life of privilege—led among dukes, marquises, and other counts—that shimmers through his hunting stories like a magnificent, well-lit backdrop. If the need or desire to write about his life as a hunter is consuming, it never feels justified. The scale of the endeavor is overwhelming, defeating "for that who is not a writer," Yebes says as he nevertheless presses on, writing "with an audacity that the reader ought to forgive." He cannot *not* write. "I ask, again, for indulgence for my hopeless literature,"[7] he goes on—hopeless, it is understood, in light of the irrepressible here and now of the actual hunt, the intensity of the passion, the inexpressibility of the love, the beauty, the anguish, the pain, the sacrifice, and the fear.

Yebes's strained compulsion to write—"the doubts and vacillations"—is linked to his aspiration to show the practice of sports hunting as higher and nobler in concept than vulgar understandings allow. "It isn't a sport for butchers," he states. "It isn't a sport in which the interest is aimed exclusively at killing."[8] Killing: the contours of Yebes's narrative are firmly outlined by its imperative, but the reader is surprised to find that in the book's 525 pages relatively little of it takes place. The book is above all an exaltation of the Spanish landscape, an homage to its ruggedness, its impossible escarpments, its immensity and remoteness, sparsely populated by cliff-loving creatures to whose beauty and cunning one never gets accustomed. In this setting the hunter is but a speck, a barely discernible presence amid the jumbled topography of the sierra, which hides in plain sight, in a "terrible mimicry."[9] It produces a feeling of nothingness that both weakens and fortifies, belittles and uplifts.

Ortega y Gasset's prologue to the book zeroes in on this irony. He argues that modern sport hunting must be understood both from the perspective of what makes humans different from other animals and from the perspective of what we still have in common. "Life," Ortega y Gasset writes, "is given to us empty."[10] The dawning of human self-consciousness opens up before us an expanse of time—a "space of time," he calls it—that is terrifying on account of its sheer emptiness and utter finitude. Human life is an insipid, simple "being there," he writes, anticipating Heidegger, haunted by purposelessness and death. We ought to picture Ortega y Gasset penning these thoughts in 1942, in the wake of the Spanish Civil War, which brought about dizzyingly rapid social changes, especially for the aristocracy. Rushing to fill up our lives with focused, productive activity, with what we call "work," we gain a sense of purpose that never feels completely ours, that we thus constantly try to escape. "What most torments us about work," Ortega y Gasset explains, "is that by filling up our time it seems to take it away from us; . . . life used for work does not seem to us to be really ours, which it should be, but on the contrary seems the annihilation of our real existence."[11]

This is, for Ortega y Gasset, a thoroughly contemporary human dilemma—that in achieving purpose, we annihilate existence—and he argues that, unless we grasp this dilemma's real implications, we don't stand a chance of understanding the appeal of experiences that happen at the limits of human rationality, like modern sports hunting. For while, in its emptiness, human existence is "brief and urgent," we live it attentive to what Ortega y Gasset says is "an intimate little voice that . . . from the innermost secret folds of our depths"[12] entices us to project beyond this life and to escape it by living it as a "poetic task."[13] This intimate little voice tugs at our self-consciousness, compelling it to recognize our animal reality, which we purportedly have left behind. Hunting, in this scheme of things, only makes sense if understood as taking place within a zoological scale. For the meaning and appeal of hunting are rooted, says Ortega y Gasset, on "the complete extension of this immense fact": the equality of "the beast's predatory zeal and any good hunter's almost mystical agitation."[14]

CALLER: First of all, it's a natural, human thing to hunt. We're hunter-gatherers, so it's part of who we are. Secondly, it's the camaraderie of your fellow hunters, being in nature. Most of the time, when you go out, the odds are against you as a hunter. You're not going to come back with game, so most of the time you're out there enjoying nature. Like, for instance, two weekends ago I was deer hunting. I didn't see a single deer, but I saw twenty or thirty turkeys roaming around. And you know, for me, that was a wonderful thing, you don't get to see that in Westchester.

HOST: Did he hit the nail on the head [about why people hunt] as far as you're concerned?

HUNTER: Yeah, [he] did an excellent job explaining some of the appeal of hunting. . . . We don't do it because it's fun to kill, but it's fun to hunt. To me, it's part of immersing myself in nature in a way that I can't get from other activities. I backpack, I camp, I canoe, I do a lot of things outdoors. But when I'm hunting, I'm part of the ecosystem, fulfilling my natural role as a predator. And then when I bring home the game and feed my family this wonderful meal of wild meat, it's something that's very special, very hard to replicate. Hunting is certainly fun, but it's a lot more than that. It's also very meaningful and kind of powerful to people who do it. . . . It's wonderful to go out and camp and to go to sit on a ridge top and look at the world around you. But hunting gets you in a little deeper, I think. It just does for me. . . . I find that the more I'm in nature, the more I love it, the more I want to protect it, the more I understand it.

Cars on the parkway slowed down, some dangerously so, until traffic came to a full halt. Drivers felt compelled to take a look, to contemplate the deer carcasses from up close. What is it about the blood, the agony, the life expiring? Violent death, including that of animals, revolts but in that sort of ambivalent way in which it also fascinates. It "shortens our breath and sends our heart galloping," Yebes says. The moment of its proximity—"the supreme moment," in his words—is incomparable, powered by the subtle affinities, the flashes of identification that link hunter and prey as well as reader and hunter, as his experiences are related in the second person for us to relive and embody. "With your five senses on the stag," Yebes writes, "you hear a rustling between you and him. Somewhat alarmed, you look and notice two does that, ahead of the stag, approach in the same direction. . . . The does are already three meters away, and you don't dare to even blink. You see with clear detail their long ears; you can count the lashes in their big, sorrowful eyes, in which the dilated tear duct betrays an anguished expression."[15] But we learn that, as the stalking progresses and life hangs in the balance, the hunter is himself—and, by extension, us?—full of anguish, full of apprehension. Body tense, mouth parched, "You don't know what to do," whether to shoot or wait.

The situation is precarious in the extreme, riddled with uncertainty and dread. The encounter and its outcome hinge on a delicate choreography, the fragile cooperation of the most insubstantial of elements, like the sunlight, sound, fog, and wind, which, together with the hunter's unpredictable nerves, can abruptly redirect the wary animals. But as one reads along, it becomes clear that the anguish that pervades the scene and that Yebes believes afflicts even his prey grows out of a prohibition on violence—the ban on aggression and killing that, according to Georges Bataille, makes possible ordinary, productive human life.[16] He calls this type of prohibition "taboo":

> Prohibitions eliminate violence, and our violent impulses . . . destroy within us that calm ordering of ideas without which human awareness is inconceivable. . . . We must know, we can know that prohibitions are not imposed from without. This is clear to us in the anguish we feel when we are violating the taboo . . . when the taboo still holds good and yet we are yielding to the impulsion it forbids. If we observe the taboo, if we submit to it, we are no longer conscious of it. But in the act of violating it we feel the anguish of mind without which the taboo could not exist.[17]

The anguish matches the intensity of the desire that is fulfilled in the taboo's infringement. Desire and horror thus come together, like in the gory magnetism drivers feel toward a bloody carcass, as it disrupts and at the same time enthralls our drab routine rides to work.

Ortega y Gasset puts forth a rather narrow understanding of hunting as an activity. He echoes Yebes when he states that killing is not the exclusive or even the main purpose of a hunt. Hunting has maintained much of its general structure since ancestral times. The most obvious difference is in the weapon used, he says, which today is the rifle. But as weapon technology was improved, made more efficient, hunters made sure to impose new limitations on themselves so as to preserve the crucial but delicate disequilibrium that must exist between hunter and hunted, the calculated disparity in power without which the hunt ceases to be a hunt. To disrespect the subtle inequality in this relationship, Ortega y Gasset argues, is to destroy the meaning of hunting, to turn it into pure killing and destruction.[18]

The limitations sport hunters impose on themselves take the form of injunctions, long lists of often complicated prescriptions and proscriptions by which they must abide. But these are not designed just to prevent a free-for-all; they also drastically restrict their sphere of action, generating the conditions of possibility for the experience, magnifying the desire and the pleasure—in Yebes's words, "conjuring the danger" itself[19]—and thus heightening the significance of what is at stake. A glance at the 2015 *New Jersey Hunting and Trapping Digest*, which contains the official regulations for all hunting in the state, makes this clear. In addition to firearm permits, hunters must obtain licenses for each kind of animal they want to hunt; these licenses are valid for only one season and limited to a relatively small geographical area, whose boundaries they must study and be able to identify as they roam the woods. For each animal, hunters are allowed to use only some kinds of weapons and ammunition and must follow strict rules regarding ground blinds, tree stands, baiting, animal decoys, and other devices. Rigid "bag limits" are often imposed based on the age and sex of the animal, which presuppose hunters' near-expert knowledge of the subtle physical differences within each species (i.e., body size, shape of antlers, number of antler points, color variations, etc.), the ability to recognize these at a distance and while in motion, and an acute, masterful self-control to stop themselves from shooting an attractive but banned animal.[20]

These legally binding regulations undergird an ethics that, the philosopher Brian Luke notes, have turned the modern experience of hunting into a "highly ritualized" pursuit.[21] In this pursuit, hunters deliberately and voluntarily maintain some of the animal's margin of advantage, deliberately and voluntarily renounce their technical superiority with which they could quickly annihilate most animal species. Rather than doing this, Ortega y Gasset remarks, hunters restrain their destructive power, temporarily refusing the supremacy of human rationality in order to affirm their equality in dignity with animals. When he states that the superiority of the hunter cannot be absolute, Ortega y Gasset means that the distance in aptitude between hunter and hunted must be measured, precise, not too close or too far apart, but a precise and narrow distance within which "the game" of hunting—"su juego"—can take place. For this "game" to be possible, "for this precise event that we call hunting really to happen," in Ortega y Gasset's words, "it is necessary that the hunted animal have his [sic] *chance*, that he be able, in principle, to avoid capture; . . . that he possess means of some degree of effectiveness to escape from the pursuit, because hunting is precisely the series of efforts and skills which the hunter has to exercise to dominate with sufficient frequency the countermeasures of the animal which is the object of the hunt. If these countermeasures did not exist, if the inferiority of the animal were absolute . . . the peculiar fact of the hunt would not exist."[22] Ultimately, Ortega y Gasset writes, the object of the hunt is "a conscious and almost religious humbling of man which limits his superiority and lowers him toward the animal. I have said 'religious,'" he then remarks, "and the word does not seem excessive to me."[23]

CALLER: I'd love to engage the last guest at a cocktail party and not waste your time, but I just want to alert everyone to the realities of the hunt. I own about five hundred acres of land in upstate New York and have for at least forty-five years. When my wife and I go for a walk in the fall or the early winter, we're constantly confronted with seeing the carcasses of rotting deer and, on unfortunately two or three occasions, smaller black bear. What happens is, you have a singular license [that] permits you to make one kill. A hunter goes out for, call it the fun, the blood sport, whatever you want to call it, they go out and they kill a 250-pound bear. Well, it is early in the morning when you do this because they're really not running around at two in the afternoon. Comes the evening, you see a 350-pound bear. You have a single license. What do you do? You let the 250-pound bear go, and you kill the 350-pound bear.

HOST: Let me get a reaction. . . . Is this a big problem?

HUNTER: No. I'm not going to deny there aren't bad actors out there. Of course . . . but the vast majority of hunters would never do something like that, would be revolted by something like that, and would turn in one of their buddies if they did that. You know, we have game wardens who go out and patrol, and they certainly do find people who poach, but to me they're not a hunter, they're a poacher, they're a criminal, who's taking the wildlife that belongs to all of us in an illegal, unethical way.

———————

The talk show's host said that bear rights groups, in their protests, had referred to the bear hunt as "the black bear massacre."

From a point of view, it is indisputable that the killing of hundreds of bears, however ritualized the manner of killing, amounts to carnage. But any serious effort to approach the "interiority" of hunting, "su mismidad," says Ortega y Gasset, must grasp the difference between the individualized, restrained actions of a hunter and those of, say, a fisherman who poisons a mountain brook to mass-kill the trout in it.[24]

A veteran of the civil war and not one to balk at destructive force, Yebes insists that, irrespective of their levels of skill and confidence, hunters must marshal their best technique for a clean kill at the first shot. He finds it reprehensible to employ automatic weapons; not only are they "excessively lethal" but they frequently lead to extreme bodily damage or to a protracted, miserable death when a wounded animal gets away "with a broken jaw or a shattered hoof."[25] The concern with avoiding plain butchery and even minimizing suffering reveals a rationale that exceeds the anthropocentric values of safety, lawfulness, fairness, and pleasure, notes Luke. It exposes hunters' qualms about the violence inherent in what they do and their complicated feelings regarding suffering. "The sportsman's code," writes Luke, "by enjoining hunters to minimize the infliction of pain, recognizes that less violence is better than more."[26] It recognizes that hunting, as a practice, teeters on the brink between right and wrong. Hunting, Luke writes, "is hedged by an elaborate network of restrictions, conditions, and guidelines to prevent it from lapsing into a completely unacceptable activity."[27] These injunctions unequivocally point to hunters' misgivings about violence and killing, a symptom of "the ethical tension internal to hunting."[28]

Yebes is candid as to how he lives this tension. By turns petrified, rattled, delighted, anguished, in a fear-induced sweat, exhilarated, satisfied, and mortified, he is candid about how difficult it is, in that feverish moment, to rein in his emotions and overcome his hesitations, how difficult to control his ambition and resist the urge to cross the line into despicable or careless behavior, all this despite being a respected hunter and a terrific shot.

In his account, he dwells in the deep, quiet fulfillment that follows a clean kill, particularly if in the wake of strenuous personal effort, as much as in the crass, frenzied exertions that often are the fallout of a bad, impatient call that leaves an animal shrieking in pain. He takes his time to describe the unwavering, uncontainable urge to possess he feels upon sighting a gorgeous stag or roebuck as well as the loving appreciation that grows out of the silent contemplation of an equally lovely specimen, which "makes you forget your rifle, relish in the ineffable, and, frequently, with a remorseful conscience, think in the possibility of killing such a beautiful animal . . ."[29]

Luke concludes that "the moral burden of killing,"[30] hunters' awareness of their deeply paradoxical desire for an ethical kill should compel them to renounce it. But what Yebes's account makes so brilliantly clear is that this "moral burden," the permission to commit a violent act that would be condemned under most other circumstances, the nearly seamless fusing of right and wrong, is precisely what makes hunting so alluring. The limitations self-imposed on hunting delineate not just the definitional boundaries beyond which hunting ceases to be hunting; the system of restrictions, preconditions, and dictums constitutes the limits within which the violation of the taboo on killing engenders for hunters an experience they passionately seek, one that depends on the simultaneous respect and transgression of the taboo on violence.

The "transgression [of taboo] outside well defined limits is rare," writes Bataille in reference to forms of licensed violence and killing, like hunting. When an object or action is forbidden under normal circumstances, the prohibition fuels the desire for it and instills in its transgression the significance of a religious violation.[31] In imposing limits, taboo controls the form that its violation may take. Such is what happens with hunting: what hunters seek is precisely to inhabit the subtle, fragile traces of what those limits both encourage and condemn.

Taboo "is never anything but the means of cursing gloriously whatever it forbids," writes Bataille. "It is always a temptation to knock down a barrier; the forbidden action takes on a significance it lacks before fear widens the gap between us and it and invests it with an aura of excitement."[32] Legal and ethical injunctions surely work to ensure that the hunter's margin of advantage is limited, intensifying the thrill. But they are also, if not primarily, a recognition that hunting is killing and that lodged at the heart of the experience hunters desire is the violation of a prohibition on this type of violence. In this situation of proximity, even of intimacy with the animal, the kill takes the form of a transgression. This and nothing else but the heightened awareness of a crossing of limits is what brings about what Ortega y Gasset calls the "delights in hunting" and provokes in the hunter the "mystical agitation" he also writes about, the mix of anguish and awe that approximates the hunter's experience to what he calls "religiosity."

HOST: Let me just touch the Sarah Palin story before we run out of time. The fourth installment of her reality show, *Sarah Palin's Alaska*, was all about hunting. She went on a two-day caribou-hunting trip with friends and family and shot and killed a caribou. It took her six shots with three different guns. Are hunters pleased with the depiction of her hunting in this series?

HUNTER: Well, any time that hunting can get play in front of a national audience on a big channel like that . . . that's a good thing for hunting. Would it have been better if she shot better and killed the caribou on the first shot? Certainly. Hunters pride themselves on being very proficient, making quick, humane, clean kills. Certainly, [if] you hunt long enough, everybody misses. It's unfortunate. That's why you spend time at the range; you shoot and hone your skills, and try to do it as well as possible.

HOST: Missing five times. Is that considered worse than an embarrassment, somehow bad form or a danger even?

HUNTER: It's not a danger as long as you're following the rules of gun safety. . . . Sure though, no one would want to miss six times. That's a bad day. Every hunter would be disappointed with themselves if they did that.

I noticed that not a single woman called in to the show to express herself either in favor of or in opposition to the bear hunt. Women, of course, have hunted throughout the history of the West, but it is unclear, and quite a bitter point of contention among hunters and scholars, if what is at stake for them in the hunt is the same as it is for men. Is the violence of the hunt expressive not so much of our human ambivalence toward animality as of a particularly masculinist yearning for its domination?[33]

If so, pure domination and unquestionable superiority are at a cross-purpose. For how often does a hunter prevail? "That's the matter," says Yebes. "I think it is precisely the low frequency with which such complete [successful] days occur that makes us savor them when they happen." He goes on:

> To fully appreciate them it is necessary to have undergone many [days] in which the cold, rain or fog have ruined *a mancha* [a hunting spot] for us; in which the adverse wind has undercut the deer racing in the right direction; in which the move into the *mancha* has been a mistake from beginning to end, and helpless from our posts we have witnessed the game turning away, staying put or fleeing where nobody was, or in which—as is frequently the case—we have shot like a shoe, and such days, reader, I don't say this to dissuade you, occur with an excessive frequency.[34]

If hunting is about reaffirming masculine self-identity, what to make of such domination predicated on failure? Yebes speaks of the "vital resistance" of each species, its recurrent ability to avoid being hunted down, as keeping the hunter's desire aflame. Then there is the ruggedness of the landscape, the sheer challenge of coming "face to face with the sierra," the life-threatening risks it demands, which often leave hunters spent even before a single shot has been fired. Hunting in "the most magnificent and terrible places of creation"[35] is, again, simultaneously humbling and uplifting. Is taking on this struggle a mark of masculinity? If so, even when successful, certainty eludes him.

Ortega y Gasset notes that, in his writings, Yebes recalls more than once seeing a splendid animal within shooting range and being overcome by doubt. The hunter, Ortega y Gasset claims, envisions the scene that will ensue, the animal's fine, lavish fur tainted with blood, its handsome and agile body inert. "Is it licit to do this?" the hunter is prone to ask.[36]

The idea that such a slender life is going to be annulled surprises him for an instant. *Every good hunter is uneasy in the depths of his conscience when faced with the death he is about to inflict on the enchanting animal.* He does not have the final and firm conviction that his conduct is correct. But neither, it should be understood, is he certain of the opposite. . . . This says nothing against hunting, but only that the generally problematic, equivocal nature of man's relationship with animals shines through that uneasiness. Nor can it be otherwise, because man has never really known exactly what an animal is. . . . The animal remains too close for us to not feel a mysterious communication with it.[37]

If hunters are predators, they seem to be predators of a conflicted kind.[38] Humans' relationship with animals is problematic and equivocal. They are an enigma to us, one from which we ourselves emerged. The charged, conflicting meanings of hunting affirm at once our distance and our proximity.

Memoirs of hunting often belie the fact that the exhilaration of the hunt is interlaced with feelings of sadness and guilt: a boy's first kill is frequently spoiled by grief and anxiety; merely wounding an animal is mortifying; and around 20 percent of hunters who hunt in their youth eventually give it up because they feel it is "wrong." Even seasoned hunters will often "express regret, remorse, sadness, and shame over the killing that they do."[39] Unlike other forms of killing, where the desire to kill is usually rooted in rage, hatred, or indifference, hunters, like Yebes, normally profess love for the animals they kill. They are moved by their beauty and grace, seek to understand their preferences and habits, and admire their astuteness and agility to the point of identification, notes Luke.[40] Ortega y Gasset refers to this identification as a "mystical union" with the animal, which results from the hunter's intimate knowledge of its movements, his necessary willingness during the hunt to adopt its point of view, to mimetically assimilate into its surroundings and unite with the animal in a sort of tragic intimacy. It is nothing short of "a drama" that unfolds in hunting, says Ortega y Gasset: in each kill, "a minor zoological tragedy."[41]

HOST: Alright, we will leave it there. . . . Do you want to tell us in ten seconds what your favorite animal is to hunt and why? You have one?

HUNTER: Yes, my favorite animal to hunt is white-tailed deer. You can find them anywhere; they are very smart, cunning, very difficult to hunt. They are a beautiful animal, delicious. When I come back in the fall with a white-tailed deer, I know my family will eat it for months to come.

HOST: Alright, thanks for joining us. We appreciate it.

———————

To know, love, and kill, to kill what you know intimately and love. The Spanish term *querencia* is related to *querer*—to want or to love—and Yebes consistently uses it to refer to the inclination animals have to inhabit a particular spot or place, or to the pull—in the form of fondness, attachment, or love—that such a spot or place exerts upon those animals. The hunter must develop a sensibility, through habit and study, to be able to identify such *lugares querenciosos*, such places of attachment. The hunter must habituate to the animal's love of its home, its attachment to the landscape, and in the process must grow attached himself.

In contrast to human life, Ortega y Gasset imagines animal life as never empty or undetermined. He argues that this imagined lost condition is what motivates hunters to hunt. "The principle which inspires hunting for sport," he writes, "is that of artificially perpetuating, as a possibility for man, a situation which is archaic in the highest degree: that early state in which, already human, he still lived within the orbit of animal existence."[42]

But if at the heart of the hunting experience is transgression, this, however, does not return humans to the intimate continuity of animal life. "It opens the door," Bataille writes, "into what lies beyond the limits usually observed"—into the violence, excess, and exuberance we associate with animals—"but it maintains these limits just the same."[43] If we oppose the human world of work to the world of violence that, in the course of everyday life, we reject for its association with unbridled animality and unreason, what the passion aroused by activities like hunting brings to the fore is that rational, productive work does not absorb us completely; our obedience to reason is never unlimited. We belong both to the world of work and to the world of violence, "and between them willy-nilly [our] life is torn."[44]

The irony in hunters' desire to ethically hunt and kill, then, would make it an eminently *human* desire, a response to that "intimate little voice" tugging at their self-consciousness. It is a deliberate bracketing of reason—as *ratio*—for the sake of the experience of temporarily and "artificially" reaching beyond the human condition to the actuality of life outside of productivity as the "here and now." Through hunting, hunters look to distract themselves from being human. "This is the superlative diversion," Ortega y Gasset writes, "the fundamental diversion." Propelled by their inevitable progress away from their ancestral proximity to animals, hunters take pleasure in an occupation that permits them "something like a vacation from [their] human condition."[45]

Notes

1. WNYC, "On the Hunt," *Brian Lehrer Show*, December 9, 2010.

2. WNYC, "On the Hunt"; New Jersey Department of Environmental Protection, "Know the Bear Facts," http://www.state.nj.us/dep/fgw/bearfacts.htm.

3. WNYC, "On the Hunt." Over the six-day hunting period, 592 bears were killed. New Jersey Department of Environmental Protection, "New Jersey 2010 Black Bear Hunting Season Results," http://www.nj.gov/dep/fgw/news/2011/bearseason10_results .htm.

4. Ortega y Gasset, *Sobre la caza*, 31–32. Howard B. Wescott translates "la mismidad de la caza" as "the essence of hunting" in Ortega y Gasset, *Meditations*. I rely on Wescott's translation unless otherwise indicated.

5. Forman and Alexander, "Roads."

6. Yebes, *Veinte años*, 93. All translations of this book from the Spanish are mine.

7. Yebes, *Veinte años*, 94.

8. Yebes, "Breve Historia de un prólogo histórico," in *Veinte años*, 7; Yebes, *Veinte años*, 95.

9. Yebes, *Veinte años*, 347.

10. Ortega y Gasset, *Meditations*, 27.

11. Ortega y Gasset, *Meditations*, 28.

12. Ortega y Gasset, *Meditations*, 29.

13. Ortega y Gasset, *Meditations*, 28.

14. Ortega y Gasset, *Meditations*, 54.

15. Yebes, *Veinte años*, 126.

16. Bataille, *Erotism*, 35–48.

17. Bataille, *Erotism*, 38.

18. Ortega y Gasset, *Meditations*, 53.

19. Yebes, *Veinte años*, 371.

20. New Jersey Department of Environmental Protection, *New Jersey Hunting and Trapping Digest*, http://www.njfishandwildlife.com.

21. Luke, "Critical Analysis of Hunters' Ethics," 36.

22. Ortega y Gasset, *Meditations*, 57.

23. Ortega y Gasset, *Meditations*, 111.

24. Ortega y Gasset, *Meditations*, 53.

25. Yebes, *Veinte años*, 292–93.

26. Luke, "Critical Analysis of Hunters' Ethics," 41.

27. Luke, "Critical Analysis of Hunters' Ethics," 34.

28. Luke, "Critical Analysis of Hunters' Ethics," 34, 43.

29. Yebes, *Veinte años*, 197.

30. Luke, "Critical Analysis of Hunters' Ethics," 39.

31. Bataille, *Erotism*, 71–72.

32. Bataille, *Erotism*, 48.

33. Studies on hunting and its relation to gender identity include Fitzgerald ("Emergence of the Figure"), Smalley ("'I Just Like to Kill Things'"), and Stange ("Women and Hunting in the West"; *Woman the Hunter*). Fine ("Rights of Men, Rites of Passage") emphasizes the historical and class-cultural specificities of hunting's impact on masculinity. She writes, "Even though the activity of hunting has a trans-historical, trans-cultural dimension to it (men and women everywhere have hunted since the beginning of recorded history and undoubtedly before) the activity, regulation, ideas about, and those who could, couldn't, and did engage in hunting have a history" (808). Ecofeminism's critique of hunting emphasizes the link between sexism and the exploitation of and violence toward nature and animals, of which hunting is an example. In other words, male violence toward women is coterminous with violence toward animals. See Adams ("Bringing Peace Home"), Gaard (*Ecofeminism*), Kheel ("Killing Game"), and Luke ("Violent Love"). Luke ("Violent Love") also discusses the "erotics" of hunting, that is, hunters' experience of the exhilaration of hunting as sexual arousal. I find ecofeminist critiques of hunting extremely compelling except for lines of argument that dismiss hunters' narratives as conceited strategies to merely legitimize their desire to hunt in light of hunting's "image problem" (Kheel, "Killing Game"; see Luke's criticism of this stance in "Critical Analysis of Hunters' Ethics") and those that uphold the untenable distinction between "subsistence hunters" and sport hunters. Kheel ("Killing Game") affirms this difference but also recognizes that utility, pleasure, gender identity, and other "social rewards" are probably involved in hunters' motivations to hunt cross-culturally.

34. Yebes, *Veinte años*, 129.

35. Yebes, *Veinte años*, 223.

36. Ortega y Gasset, *Sobre la caza*, 68. My translation.

37. Ortega y Gasset, *Meditations*, 102.

38. See also Luke, "Critical Analysis of Hunters' Ethics," 35.

39. Luke, "Critical Analysis of Hunters' Ethics," 44. Luke provides a wealth of references to firsthand accounts of this aspect of hunting. See also David Stout's amazing "The Sadness of the Hunter," *New York Times*, December 10, 1995.

40. Luke, "Critical Analysis of Hunters' Ethics," 43.

41. Ortega y Gasset, *Meditations*, 142.

42. Ortega y Gasset, *Meditations*, 129.

43. Bataille, *Erotism*, 67.

44. Bataille, *Erotism*, 40. The vast and rich literature on hunting, including the works by Ortega y Gasset, Bataille, and Luke, sheds light on the great appeal that other human activities reliant on violence have, most obviously other activities including animals, like bull- and cock-fighting, but also human-only contact sports like American football and hockey. McGrath ("Does Football Have a Future?") discusses the ambivalence players and fans feel toward the role of violence in football.

45. Ortega y Gasset, *Meditations*, 129.

18

ON WRITING AND SURVIVING

LISA STEVENSON

A conversation about bear hunting during a regular commute to work, punctuated by the fleshy carcasses of roadkill: sport hunting is inextricable from the realm of make-believe, from the realm of the game, of *play*. The deaths are real and predictable, but we tell ourselves, as hunters or as highway drivers, that they can be avoided. That is, during the hunt, before the kill, hunters "restrain their destructive power, limit and regulate it"[1] in order "that the hunted animal have his *chance*, that it be able, in principle, to avoid capture."[2] For José Ortega y Gasset, as Daniella Gandolfo reminds us, this is what makes the hunt the hunt. Hunters temporarily bracket their superiority and affirm their equality in dignity with animals. They humble down to them, play at fairness and equality.

It's a strange way to think about play. More often when I think about play, especially in D. W. Winnicott's psychoanalytic sense, I think of playing at omnipotence or plenitude—but as hunters we pretend that we aren't as strong as we really are, that the animal can always get away. There is a blurring between the hunter and the hunted: the hunters see themselves in the animal body of the hunted and want very much to believe in the possibility of escape. I want to draw an uneasy parallel between writing and this type of play: the writer as hunter and hunted, the writer playing with the possibility of escape. I suggest this, fully cognizant of the "difficulty of reality"[3] that hunting presents, a difficulty that seems to shoulder us out of our everyday worlds into a reality that is almost too much to bear. *A being that was alive dies at our hands.*

In Inuktitut the word for survival, *annaktujuniq*, literally means the state of one who escapes from sickness, hunger, danger.[4] But the base of the word, *annaktuq*, is also used to describe an animal or quarry that gets away, escapes a death. Human survival is etymologically linked to escape from death in a hunt. The intimacy of the other death, the death that one somehow escapes, is crucial to Inuit lifeworlds—the other death imagined as one's own, but a death that one has, *for the time being*, escaped. The bear hunter, in Gandolfo's piece, also escapes, first, the insipidness of servile, productive existence, and, second, the hunter's own mortality, which is embraced but only through the animal that is loved and killed. The animal dies, and the hunter, for the time being, escapes death.

Is it possible that to be able to write about, to render, other lives we enter a make-believe world where, if only for a moment, there is such a thing as escape for our prey, and thus also for our fragile bodies, for ourselves? Perhaps this possibility of escape (which always means to witness the death of another, a death you know will someday be your own) is what we mean by a lifetime or a lifeworld. That without that possibility of some kind of escape we might as well not bother to write? That through writing we create a world in which we diminish our powers, on purpose, so that our prey has a chance of escape. Of course, in the end, with writing, as with hunting, someone always dies or must already be dead. Surviving, like writing, entails witnessing that other death that is also our own.

Notes

1. Gandolfo, this volume.
2. Ortega y Gasset, *Meditations*, 57.
3. Diamond, "The Difficulty of Reality and the Difficulty of Philosophy."
4. Stevenson, *Life beside Itself*.

19

A Proper Message

LISA STEVENSON

A voice involves the throat, saliva, infancy, the patina of experienced life, the mind's intentions, the pleasure of giving a personal form to sound waves. What attracts you is the pleasure this voice puts into existing . . .
—ITALO CALVINO, "A King Listens"

In the midst of a Thanksgiving dinner, with people splayed out on the floor—a middle-aged man with his back against the legs of a chair recounting a road trip across the southern United States, a teenager twisting her hair around her finger and gazing inertly in front of her, a couple of kids lying on their stomachs, engrossed in their own densely laid world of right and wrong—and everyone eating and talking and bickering as most families, happy or sad, eat and talk and bicker. In the midst of all that, two women face each other, the younger one kneeling on the floor at the knees of the old woman, a woman whose legs can no longer support her weight, a woman who has been lifted from a car into the house and placed on the living room couch. The two women bring their faces close together, so close they are almost touching, their arms resting on each other's shoulders. They sway slightly as they begin to *kataq*. The younger woman starts, and the sounds she makes come from the back of her throat, low and thick, almost growling.

Ham ma ham ma, ham ma, ham ma—she breathes in and out in a steady rhythm, intensely, her vocal cords bruising each other. Buzzing, panting, the older woman's voice comes in and moves up and down as if plucking the lower rhythm, teasing it almost. The sounds and rhythms pass from body to body, echoing and playing with each other, growling, buzzing, yelping.

There's something machinelike and modern in sounds that are also archaic and guttural.

> Ham me, ham ma, ma, ham ma, ham ma, ham ma
> Ha ha ha, ha he he, ha he he, ha he he ha ha ha ha

Then the old woman breaks off and cackles loudly, hooting almost, in pleasure. The younger woman laughs too and wipes away tears. People smile, clap, and go back to what they were doing.

A few months later the old woman dies in her sleep. I am in the house when the young woman returns, but I've already heard the news. I hear her shutting the door, putting down her purse. The ordinariness of the sounds is hard. "She's gone," the young woman tells me, thinking I don't know. "My *anaana* is gone." In my memory it's as if she is swaying, but not rhythmically, rather as if she might fall over.

In one sense these *katajjaiit* are not well understood even by the women who perform them (and these days they are performed all over the world, at the Olympic Games in Vancouver, at the World Conference on Women in Beijing). Between cry and language,[1] many katajjaiit have no discernible words whatsoever. Just the breath—rhythmic, guttural, staccato—being passed from one body to another. Some have titles like *Kitturiat* (Mosquitos) or *Qimmiruluapik* (The last little puppy). Some people say that the sounds voiced in katajjaiit were words used by the remote ancestors of modern-day Inuit, and that what the words mean is forever lost.[2] Others say that katajjaiit can only be understood by the dead or their ambassadors—the northern lights, for example, who make their presence felt by whispering or whistling, or the *tunnituarruit*, the flying heads without bodies, that occasionally descend to earth.[3]

A Son Listens

On August 10, 1956, an Inuit woman named Kaujak left the Canadian Inuit community of Arctic Bay,[4] on a ship known as the CD *Howe*, to begin her journey to the Mountain Sanatorium in Hamilton, Ontario. For months Kaujak had been getting weaker and weaker. She was increasingly unable to hunt and fish as she once had, and the medical personnel on the patrol ship had diagnosed her with tuberculosis. Her grandson, Sakiassie, standing on the shore, followed the ship with his eyes until it passed out of sight beyond Uluksan Point. He never saw her again.

In June 2008 I received an email from Anna, Sakiassie's daughter, who had been trying for several years to figure out what happened to Kaujak.[5] "My name is Anna," she wrote, "a few years ago I was in search of my dad's grandmother that passed away on the train to Hamilton, they unloaded her body before reaching Hamilton." The only trace Anna has been able to find in her search for Kaujak is an index card from the municipal offices with Kaujak's name and disc number typewritten on it. Handwritten in ink are the words "Dead" and "1956."

Kaujak raised Anna's father, Sakiassie, as a son, after his own father drowned in a hunting accident when Sakiassie was only one year old. Anna told me that Sakiassie was very attached to his mother-grandmother and that "Kaujak was able to do things a man could do, she was a very good fisher, she would go fishing, dry fish." Each spring when Sakiassie goes fishing "a lot of the techniques [he uses] he learned from her." Anna tells me, "She was a very able woman . . . she was [capable] of doing things that men were capable of doing. She was able to build $qaumaqs$ [sod houses]. The year before she left she couldn't build the qaumaq and she developed an infection on her stomach and on her back. . . . When the ship came in to screen people for TB they screened her and that's when they sent her away."

Sakiassie was fourteen years old when Kaujak was sent away on the CD Howe. I ask him whether he remembered the day of his mother's departure. "Yes, I remember very clearly," he tells me. Her illness had been getting worse and she began to pay visits to family members, even distant relatives, saying she might not live long enough to see them again. Sakiassie was very worried. "It was very painful when the helicopter came from the ship to pick her up to move her," he tells me. Kaujak was taken from her camp outside of town to the ship where the medical team was waiting. Kaujak tested positive for tuberculosis.

Generally when the x-ray technician discovered a shadow on the lung Inuit weren't allowed to return to shore for fear they would never return to the ship. But for some reason they made an exception for Kaujak. She made a last trip to shore in a small skiff. Sakiassie didn't get to speak to her. He was unloading the ship's supplies at the time, and he saw his mother smiling and posing for a photograph—all from a distance.[6]

That fall, in October sometime, Sakiassie doesn't remember the exact date, the Hudson's Bay Company manager called him on the radio to let him know that Kaujak was dead. Nothing else was said.

For years after that, when the ship returned on its yearly patrol, Sakiassie would go to the beach, where people were loading and unloading its cargo, and patients were disembarking after being at the sanatorium, and listen. He listened for his mother's name; he listened in the hope that someone would someday mention her, her death, or anything about her. As Anna described it, "Each year whenever the ship came in to do a screening, he would rush over to where the patient's area was near the ship to see if he could overhear anyone talking about his grandmother. He was afraid to ask about her so he wouldn't ask. He would just hang around to listen to see if anyone would mention her—to see if they've seen her or there's any news of her and he would check to see if she was on the boat. . . . He did this for many years." I am confused and try to clarify. "Each year when the ship came . . . he still didn't know if she was alive or not?"

"She left in August and in October they heard she had died and that's all that was said. No mention of where her body was, how she died, nothing, they were just informed that she had passed away. That's all the news that they got."

Sakiassie knew she was dead but didn't know.

A few days after my interview with Sakiassie, I went with his daughter Anna, to interview Laisha, a man who was on the train with Kaujak when she started her journey to the sanatorium. Laisha had also been headed to the Mountain Sanatorium in Hamilton, but he was just a boy. Sakiassie did not come with us to the interview, and he had never spoken directly to Laisha about what happened to his mother. In those days, Anna explains to me, people didn't ask questions. In those days, Laisha tells me, "They [the Inuit] didn't know what anger was." Laisha's trip to the hospital was a "sad experience." He was put in a hospital room by himself. He did not speak any English and didn't know where the toilets were, or even how to ask. When he fell asleep he soiled his pants and the nurses treated him badly when they found him in the morning, covered in his own shit.

Laisha tells Anna what she already knows—that Kaujak died on the way to the hospital. When the train finally pulled into a station, her body was unloaded. Neither he nor the other Inuit on the train spoke enough English to know where they were, what the name of the station was. I listened carefully as he tried to reproduce the foreign sounds—La-pa-lis, Lap-au-s— struggling to form his lips to a distant sonic memory, hoping to give me some clue in our search for the story of Kaujak's death.

Laisha says that as Kaujak was dying she began to speak in the voices of animals, and the nurses were offended, telling her to stop. "But she is dying!" an Inuit woman on the train tried to explain to the nurses. "She is not trying to be disrespectful!"

Once Kaujak was gone they laid her body on a stretcher in the corridor. Laisha remembers having to pass her body on the way to the bathroom.[7] Later he watched from the window as her body was unloaded from the train.

The Lights Were So Bright

Muktar Akumalik is a man in his early sixties, a hunter of some renown who lives in a sparsely decorated house with windows that give onto the bay. He tells the story of his journey, in the late 1950s, to the Distant Early Warning (DEW) Line station where they had arranged to meet the ship that would take his father down south to be treated for tuberculosis. At the time Muktar's whole family was uneasy. They had started to hear stories, that people weren't coming back, weren't returning from the sanatorium down south. And so as they traveled by dogsled team toward the DEW Line station, his father began to teach Muktar and his brother things. He tried to teach them as much as he could—about ice conditions, hunting techniques—anything he could pass on verbally that would help them survive.

When they got to the DEW Line station, Muktar and his brother tried to convince the administrators to let one of them go with their father to the hospital. Their father spoke no English, they explained. They gave the nurse all his information, his E number—everything they could think of. But they were not allowed to go with him.

That winter, during the dark season when the sun doesn't rise around Arctic Bay, Muktar was traveling by dog team and he saw the most wonderful northern lights, beautiful lights—blue, red, and white—lights like he had never seen before. There were so many. The lights were so bright that he could even see to travel—with those lights he could follow the tracks of the sled dogs.

Muktar knew, when he saw those lights, that there would be bad news. The next day they told him that his father had passed away in the hospital in Ontario. His body stayed down south. Later they found out that he had been buried in an unmarked grave in a cemetery near the sanatorium.

In 1957 R. A. J. Phillips, the director of the Arctic Division of Canada's Department of Northern Affairs, responding to the critiques that his department was insensitive to the plight of Inuit hospitalized in the South with tuberculosis, stated, "Our present means of keeping relatives in touch with patients is by letters, tape recordings and by photographs."[8] Earlier he had declared, "We would like to get tapes and messages into every settlement and area from which Eskimo patients come."[9] Phillips was not satisfied with the idea that only people in the larger Inuit settlements visited by the CD *Howe* would be able to receive messages.

The archival record contains a flurry of letters back and forth about the creation and disposition of taped recordings by Inuit in the hospital to their family up north and vice versa. How feasible was it to play such taped recordings to Inuit in communities that could not be reached by ship and had no source of electricity?[10] The reel-to-reel tape players were bulky and cost upward of $300. Listening to the tapes was an event, as people crowded around the ship's player to see if there was a message for them.

Although Inuit unquestionably longed to communicate with their relatives and despite the fact that countless letters were sent by Inuit to the Department of Northern Affairs asking for news of particular patients, and pleading with them to stop sending Inuit to the hospital, it was not always easy for hospital staff to get Inuit to comply with their tactics for keeping Inuit in touch. Included in the correspondence of R. A. J. Phillips there is a letter from a hospital administrator at the Hamilton Sanatorium concerning an Inuit patient, Mrs. A:

> In accordance with your letter we have had our Hospital Photographer photograph this Eskimo in four (4) different poses which we enclose herewith.
>
> We had some difficult [sic] in getting Mrs. A. to overcome her shyness enough to record messages. However, the enclosed recording tape will give you the story.
>
> We started off recording in her room where there were three other patients and it was not until we had moved her into a room by herself that she gave a *proper message*.[11]

One night in the fall of 2003, three teenagers I knew were hanging out with me at my latest house-sit. We were in the living room—that standard Iqaluit living room with a tightly stuffed blue couch and matching armchair, glass coffee table, and a television. Government housing. We were talking about one thing and then another, arranging ourselves on the couch, on the floor, moving back and forth to the kitchen to bring out plates of food. One of the teenagers, a thirteen-year-old girl, still besieged by the death of her best friend, tells me a dream she had just after her uncle died. She dreamt about seeing him in the Northmart, the local store for groceries and supplies where he had worked on and off before his suicide. In her dream, she keeps looking toward a bookshelf that obscures the steady stream of customers coming in the front door of the Northmart. She tells us, "For some reason I kept looking towards that way. You know, you can't really see people coming. . . . So I was walking and I kept looking there. And I saw my uncle passing by. He was just looking at me, we didn't smile or anything. We looked at each other till we couldn't show."

Till we couldn't show. The dreamer, like the dreamed, disappears from sight, soundlessly, without remainder. Nothing shows.

As if in response to the soundlessness of that dream, one of the other teenagers tells a dream she had about her aunt, Sabrina, who died of cancer. In the dream the phone is ringing and my friend picks it up. It's her aunt, Sabrina, trying to locate someone called Olutie.

"Where's Olutie?" asks her aunt, peremptorily.

"Who's this?" my friend asks, ignoring her aunt's question. But the aunt insists, "Where the fuck is Olutie?" she yells into the phone.

"Is this Sabrina??" asks my friend, recognizing her aunt's voice. "Hey, Sabrina!"

"Fuck, I gotta go," says her aunt and hangs up quickly.

A little later in our conversation the girl whose best friend died tells me a dream in which that friend appears. The dream doesn't make sense to her, but she tells it to me anyway. A bunch of people are sitting in a restaurant, and her friend is there too, but she won't look at her, won't make eye contact. Then, as if out of nowhere, her dead friend looks at her and says, "Trade spots?"

"So yeah, we just traded spots. And then this other dream just showed up that we were outside—it was just me—outside of Convenience crying and

I *knew* that she passed away. And I was like, 'This doesn't make sense.' *Or something. And . . . I don't know.* I was writing or drawing stuff on Styrofoam. 'Cause there was lots of Styrofoam outside."

In dreams of the dead, voices can seem muffled, muted, as if the volume has been turned down, sonority denied. Instead of speaking, my friend writes on Styrofoam. Lots and lots of Styrofoam.

Dislocating Children

Maybe you will hear this or maybe you won't. Anyway, do not worry about me. I do not fret at this end.

—From a message recorded by a patient in 1956 in the Hamilton Sanatorium for her mother living in Pangnirtung, Northwest Territories

Getting messages from Inuit in the hospital to their families was difficult.[12] Inuit being treated for tuberculosis often spent several years in southern hospitals. Inuit who died in the hospital were buried in unmarked graves in the nearby cemetery. Although hospital staff tried to inform the families of their deaths, there was often much confusion about the identity of the Inuit in the hospital, especially the children. Hospital administrators could not speak Inuktitut, had no clear sense of Arctic geography. Which was why they had started giving out disc numbers in the first place. By giving each Inuit a number embossed on a leather tag they hoped to keep track of them better. But there were stories of children being removed from the hospital and not being sent back to their parents, being placed instead in foster homes without the permission or knowledge of the parents. There is a letter in the archives from Mr. Cunningham petitioning the department's legal counsel to advise him on this practice. Cunningham writes,

> Several instances have come to my attention over the past few months where Eskimo children have been placed in foster homes or in residential schools without the consent or knowledge of their parents or this department. . . . I will cite two examples.
> A nine year old Eskimo boy on discharge from Moose Factory Hospital last year was sent to the Fort George residential school. His parents at Port Harrison had no knowledge of this arrangement and had assumed

the boy was under continuing treatment. The boy was located after they had begun to make enquiries about his whereabouts.

Last summer, a five-year-old Eskimo girl was removed by a Fort Smith man from the Charles Camsell Hospital. He later reported to us that he had spoken to the child's mother and stated that she had agreed to this arrangement. As the Department had not participated in this plan, we have no idea as to what the wishes of the mother actually were.

I would like your advice on whether under existing North West Territories Ordinances this dislocating of children in the instances described can be considered legal.[13]

The stories seem to have no end. One man I interviewed in Arctic Bay returned home to find out his name had been given away—his parents believed he was dead and his soul-name had been given to another child. Another young boy returned home and realized he could no longer speak to his parents. He had forgotten how to speak Inuktitut.

The Assertion of Gentleness

In 2008 I visited the archives of the McMaster Health Sciences Archives in Hamilton, Ontario. I had read that one of the taped messages from Inuit to their family members in the hospital had been preserved there. I wanted to hear the tape, and I wanted to see the hundreds of photographs of Inuit in the hospital that had been collected. Soon after arriving, I arranged with the archivist to send the audiotape, a huge reel that looked more like a filmstrip than anything else, to the National Archives in Ottawa to be digitized.

The tape, recorded in 1961, is entitled simply "Eastern Arctic Patrol" after the patrol of the Royal Canadian Mounted Police (RCMP) patrol that took place in the Eastern Arctic each year once the ice had moved out of the bay. The Eastern Arctic Patrol visited as many of the Inuit communities, Hudson Bay outposts, and RCMP detachments as time and weather conditions permitted. Beginning in the 1940s, a team of doctors, x-ray technicians, nurses, and finally a social worker accompanied the RCMP patrol, screening the inhabitants of each settlement for tuberculosis and overseeing the passage south for anyone who tested positive.

The tape "Eastern Arctic Patrol" contains five messages from family members in the communities of Lake Harbour, Arctic Bay, Pond Inlet, and

Clyde River to patients in the Hamilton Sanatorium in Ontario over two thousand miles away. Each message, recorded in Inuktitut, is introduced by the voice of a nurse, speaking in English. Quietly, with a voice made silvery from smoking, she puts things in order, contains things. There is, to borrow a phrase from Barthes, a certain "assertion of gentleness" in her voice. Each message is numbered, each speaker is identified by his or her Inuktitut name along with a government-issued disc number. The intended recipient of the message is also named, and a disc number also given. Her Inuktitut is good enough: she doesn't butcher the names. She is deliberately kind.

Voices in the Archive

Many of the Inuit being recorded had a hard time finding words to speak into the recorder. A mother says to her son: "S. your mom speaking. I'm just going to say 'Bye' to you right now." And then her voice breaks off. "What was it?" She says softly, as if searching for a scattered thought. Then briskly she starts again, as if there had been no problem. "I don't know what to say. Just listen and do as you're told. That's all." She ends abruptly, the same way you would end a call on a CB radio. *Taima!* Over and out.

A father says to his daughter, "This is your father speaking, E5-283. However, I don't have much to say." He continues to speak and finds some words—more in fact than many of the other speakers. "Though I'm not with you and can't see you physically I would like to say to you that although I don't know how you are I try not to worry about you too much. Just as I don't want you to worry either while we live here on earth . . ."

A daughter says to her mother: "I don't know what to say, Mom, so I'm just going to say hello and bye, Mom."

A very small child says in a frightened voice: "Good-bye." And then, with a little coaching, he says, "Big brother, good-bye."

Three Packs of Gum

One of the speakers on the tape, Ittuq, a man from Arctic Bay, is less reticent than the others. Once again, the nurse's measured voice provides the frame: "Message Number Three: This is Ittuq E5-213 of Arctic Bay speaking to his wife Akikiakjuq E5-214 in Mountain Sanatorium Hamilton."[14]

And then we hear Ittuq begin to speak. "This is Ittuq," he says into the microphone, then clears his throat. His voice is humble, thickened with age. As he speaks, he picks up speed: "Speaking to my wife, E5-213: I think of you a lot. There are times when I don't think of you as much as I used to when you were first away. Last year just after you went away I nearly went out of my mind, but I'm now able to cope better. I get lonely for you very much." Then firmly, almost with a hint of defiance, he says, "I miss you very much." He pauses and adds, "I love you very much." At this point there is a long silence interrupted only by the faint sounds of weeping. When he begins to speak again, he struggles with the words, his voice rising in pitch, as if it might split. "I worry a lot though. I don't know what else to say at the moment so I'm just going to say bye for now."

As I listened I decided I would try to find his family, to hear more of the story that his voice designated. It wasn't hard. My sister-in-law in Iqaluit called someone from Pond Inlet, who called someone from Arctic Bay and within twenty-four hours I had a phone number for Ittuq's daughter, a thirty-five-year-old woman named Sandy. Ten months later I would be tenting with Ittuq's children in a summer camp a fifteen-minute drive from town. At that time of year it was all rock and sun and snow. We drank tea with pilot biscuits in the yellow light of canvas tents and ate barbecued seal on the rocks by the shore. The teenagers played golf over the hills with makeshift holes in patches of artificial grass and the kids skipped stones on the bay that the ice hadn't yet left. It was there that I learned that one of Ittuq and Akikiakjuq's sons was in prison. Later that summer I asked the prison administration permission to interview Peutagok Ittuq.

Peutagok Ittuq, the son of Ittuq and Akikiaqjuq, was seven years old when his mother was taken down south to be treated for tuberculosis. He didn't see her again, or hear from her, when she returned from the hospital. I met with Peutagok in the Baffin Correctional Center, in Iqaluit where he was an inmate. I never asked him why he was there, and he didn't tell me. The prison, located in the industrial outskirts of Iqaluit, near the airport, mechanic shops, and the old military buildings, is a gray podlike building made out of corrugated metal. After giving up our IDs and passing by the television monitors flickering in a darkened office and through the usual clanking doors, we were escorted to a windowless meeting room stuffed with two rectangular tables and a dry erase board. An Inuit social worker joined us. She was reassuringly round and smiling, with frizzy permed hair. Peutagok looked apprehensive, his compact frame leaning forward as he sat down at the table.

I played him the tape from my computer, letting him listen through some headphones. Listening to his father's voice does something strange to time: "I go back to when I was a kid," he tells me. When I ask him what he remembers, he tells me about the time, a year before his mother went away, when he and his parents rowed the fifteen miles from their outpost camp to meet the CD Howe in Arctic Bay. It took them two or three days.

"Yeah, it was a very nice time," he says. "Blue sky. No wind. And ice, and birds. . . . That was very special, that day. I remember. And in the morning my dad was making fire, making tea, coal stove, only fire, early in the morning. Yeah . . . I remember that. That was beautiful."

He tells us that just before his mother got on the boat to go down south, she gave him three packets of gum. He struggles to remember the brand of the gum but remembers the yellow package. Then he gets it: "Juicy Fruit!"

Peutagok remembers he wanted to keep that gum forever. "Yeah. 'Cause my mom was special to me. So much." He was the youngest child and, as he remembers it, was still breastfeeding when she left. So at night, when he went to bed he would put the gum under his pillow. So that no one could take it from him.

———————

"A Proper Message" is an experiment with textual montage. It was actually written before the publication of my book Life beside Itself, but due to the vagaries of academic publishing it is appearing much later. In some ways I see this piece as the distillation of that much longer—perhaps more convoluted—argument. In many ways I prefer its economy. To create this piece, I cut out each thought image and laid it on the floor and then began to play around with the order of the images. Images that I thought were inextricably paired got separated. I wanted to stay away, as much as possible, from abstraction and social science explanation, although there are a couple of moments where I succumb to the temptation to comment. As with cinematic montage I wanted the juxtaposition of images to suggest a "third thing"—something that wasn't contained in either image. The piece would think itself through images and not in a standard discussion section. In the end the thought images from "A Proper Message" found their way into Life beside Itself and are dispersed throughout its pages.

Notes

1. Saladin D'Anglure, "Entre cri et chant."
2. See Margaret Uyauperk Aniksak, quoted in Bennett and Rowley, *Uqalurait*, 108.
3. Saladin D'Anglure, "Entre cri et chant."
4. Arctic Bay is located on the northern part of the Borden Peninsula on Baffin Island, Nunavut.
5. Anna contacted me because she had heard about my work collecting the photographs and audiotapes of sanatorium patients and their families that are held in the archives of Hamilton Health Sciences and McMaster University's Faculty of Health Sciences in Ontario.
6. Years later he found that photograph on the wall of the high school in Pond Inlet, and he asked for a copy.
7. "It didn't anger him," Anna explains to me, "but he felt uncomfortable about it."
8. Eskimo Economy and Welfare General Policy File, memorandum for the director of Welfare of Permanently Hospitalized Eskimos, Ottawa, September 20, National Archives of Canada, Record Group 85, Vol. 1473, File 251-1, pt. 5, 1957.
9. Eskimo Economy and Welfare General Policy File, G. W. J. Fiddes (Moose Factory) to R. A. J. Phillips, June 13, National Archives of Canada, Record Group 85, Vol. 1473, File 251-1, pt. 5, 1956.
10. The Medical Superintendent of Moose Factory Hospital protested that the RCMP do a patrol approximately once a year to these places but certainly they would not take along a tape recorder, and if they did there would be no electrical supply with which to use it (Eskimo Economy and Welfare General Policy File, Fiddes letter to Phillips, June 13, 1956).
11. Eskimo Economy and Welfare General Policy File, W. McAtchison (Administrative Assistant of the Montreal General Hospital) to R. A. J. Phillips, June 13, National Archives of Canada, Record Group 85, Vol. 1473, File 251-1, pt. 5, 1956. Emphasis added.
12. Epigraph for this section: Eskimo Economy and Welfare General Policy File, B. G. Sivertz, memorandum to R. A. J. Philips, October 25, National Archives of Canada, Record Group 85, Vol. 1473, File 251-1, pt. 5, 1956.
13. Eskimo Economy and Welfare General Policy File, F. J. G. Cunningham, memorandum for Mr. We. Nason, Chief, Legal Division, National Archives of Canada, Record Group 85, Vol. 1473, File 251-1, pt. 5, 1956.
14. Eastern Arctic Patrol, Messages to Patients in Mountain San. Hamilton, ON, McMaster University's Faculty of Health Sciences Archives, domain CMH, James Sylvia, Series: Inuit Patients, Box 1.

FIDELITY AND INVENTION

ANGELA GARCIA

I fell into a kind of anguish while participating in the seminar that resulted in this book. During the day, I was anxious and teared up easily, while at night I was exhausted but unable to sleep. My mind kept wandering north, into the houses of people I knew and missed. It was late April, the fourth week of Easter, and I recalled the corresponding birthdays, death anniversaries, and their accompanying prayers. Restless, I'd tiptoe past my colleagues' bedrooms and step outside to look at the stars, only to find that the bright moonlight had washed the constellations out from the sky.

I hadn't told my relatives or friends that I was back in New Mexico. If they knew that I was in Santa Fe, they would start calling and show up unannounced. Messages from home would have weighed on me, collapsing the distance I thought was necessary to participate in the seminar. But the space of privacy that I tried to keep didn't facilitate greater clarity or creativity. On the contrary, it expanded the absence that my essay, and the letters contained within it, hoped to close.

I wrote *The Pastoral Clinic* "in the field," within reach of my subjects. The pitched-roof adobe house that I rented for three and a half years loomed above my neighbor's trailer. Joe and his eleven siblings were born and raised in the house I rented, and they were the third and last generation of his family to live there. Shortly after I moved in, Joe told me that he tried to buy the house from his grandmother, who was forced to sell it to pay off family debts, but he couldn't afford the $50,000 she needed. I never told him that my landlady, an artist who lived in Santa Fe, offered to sell me the house for $275,000, what she called "a steal."

Back then, my writing desk was located in the attic, in front of a westward-facing window. It offered a view of the Black Mesa, a huge volcanic plug sacred to the nearby Pueblos. Looming over the Rio Grande, the Black Mesa casts its dark memories over the villages below: memories of the Spanish Conquest, the Pueblo Revolt, the Spanish Reconquest, Tsave Yoh, duende, basalt mining, land disputes, heroin overdoses. The list goes on. Sometimes I imagined the house I rented was a different kind of Black Mesa, one that cast painful shadows for Joe.

Peering out the attic window in a downward direction, I could see my other neighbors' house, a young couple with a small child. I often observed their fights and the constant stream of their customers, in and out, day and night, buying bags of mota and chiva. When their fights grew in intensity, I moved downstairs but could still hear them—the bitter accusations and intimidations, the passionate wailing; their child in quiet conversation with his imaginary friend, trying to drown it all out. The voices and troubles of my neighbors unsettled my writing, became a force within it. It is a force that still urges me to increase the clarity and hurt in every word. And it reminds me that these words will never say enough.

On the first day of the seminar in Santa Fe, Michael Jackson raised the issue of literary technique as being either a mode of invention or a mode of fidelity; in both cases, betrayal is inevitable. Part of the work of literary ethnography, as I see it, is the perpetual search for words and forms of writing that seek fidelity to the people with whom we work, or fidelity to our own ideas. Invention is a vital element for fidelity to construct itself. At times, invention runs the risk of obscuring this fidelity (although this is not necessarily a bad thing). Other times, invention succeeds in unsettling and expanding the limit of what can be seen and felt, changing the terms upon which fidelity is rendered and understood.

Lisa Stevenson's "A Proper Message" can be read as a meditation on fidelity and invention. The chapter is not a chapter in the traditional sense of the word; it doesn't offer straightforward exposition and explanation of any particular subject. Rather, it proceeds through vivid and fragmentary images: singing, dreams, listening, friendship, a child's voice on tape, to name a few. These images disappear almost as quickly as they are written. Yet, in Lisa's words, they "seem to have no end." It's not just the other images that the chapter could draw upon, but that each of the images Lisa offers us already has too much to say.

"A Proper Message" recalls Derrida's theory of writing as fragmentation, where to write is to acknowledge fragmentation and to become fragmented. Derrida describes the act of writing as the "anguished choice" of one word or meaning from the plurality that exists.[1] In making this choice, only a fragment of what could be expressed is actually written. Lisa's essay makes this unsettling process explicit. What's more, her writing takes on the sentiment of anguish that Derrida identified, but never in a way that obscures the hurt and fragmentation experienced by the people with whom she worked. She writes,

> A daughter says to her mother: "I don't know what to say, Mom, so I'm just going to say hello and bye, Mom."
> A very small child says in a frightened voice: "Good-bye." And then, with a little coaching, he says, "Big brother, good-bye."

The rejection of knowing what to say, of only being able to say good-bye, unsettles the possibility of a proper message. Instead, the fragmented voice on the tape becomes writing that carries the distance between words and life. Lisa's essay, as a metonymical object of the child's voice, does not bring the meaning of the message to completion, but lets its untold possibilities haunt us. This too is a mode of fidelity.

Note

1. Derrida, *Writing and Difference*, 9.

Epilogue

KATHLEEN STEWART

This volume skids into view against the doldrums of the usual ethnographic writing conversation. Against the endless incantations of the difference between fact and fiction. Against the, by now, anachronistic, and even odd, habit of detouring into a tired critique-of-representation mode. The writing here is not an evaluative critique weighed down by its own assumptions and deposited into something like big-box stores of the good and the bad. Instead, like experience itself, writing here is an experiment of being in some kind of world. It is an effort to attune to, to respond to, actualities and potentialities, enclosures and excesses. It sits in a pause against the usual nervous gestures to foreclose the problematic of writing ethnographically with an empty recitation of mantras of ethical decontamination or a quick surge to find a high ground.

Here, instead, writing is a mode of approaching ethnographic scenes that are both solid and flighty, variegated and scripted. Scenes the ethnographic writer has to follow as they seep into human and nonhuman labors and split off in tendrils of their own. Scenes that buoy people and weigh on them in ways that give pause. These scenes of ethnographic attention are speculative objects; their poesis calls for a response. Writing aimed at bringing generative, moving objects into view takes care and skill.

So, for example, we enter the scene of a Cuba where the dead provoke. A *bembé* starts as a party, a participatory theater of impersonations of the dead jammed into music, song, and dance. The event described becomes a rolling threshold of self and other, inside and outside, a running helix of multiplying surfaces. The pleats of forces fan out and fold back up again. People ruminating on it are hit by thoughts and reactions; a woman lets a fleeting look of surprise cross her eye, seems surprised by the informality, asks basic orienting questions: "Does it have books?"

Or we are driving on a Connecticut parkway suddenly peppered with roadkill. Talk radio is onto the topic of hunting because New Jersey has just begun a sanctioned bear kill. The now hypervisible roadkill consists of formless lumps of flesh on the side of the road, the strangest hues of purple and red. The conversation unfolding on the radio has its own strange cadences of outrage and pleasure, an insider's vocabulary. Some questions of hunting ethics are foregrounded. Something about the experience of human/nonhuman existence itself emerges. Then the essay pulls into a border zone of what is deliberate, what is unavoidable. It raises the specter and possibility of efforts to fill the lonely state of being-in-a-world with lines of some kind—some line of action, some encounter, some purpose. Meanwhile, the cars on the parkway keep slowing down to take a look at the deer carcasses as if magnetized to the horror and fascination of death and life. A speculative state of being in a speculative world. Some kind of autonomic divergence from the encounter of death in life that is also a little bit of dwelling in death for a minute, like a salting of food. In the chromatically multiple potency of things, there is also a sheer, flat, empty distraction without motive or intention. Wow! No wonder roadkill is surprising.

In this little volume, ethnographic writing gets a moment to pull itself into the compositional variations of form and event, word and world. It slows to home in on the barely legible or the submerged, what's pleasurable and painful in what happens. The writing has the presence of mind to stop at the murky pooling-up of things. Or it speeds to perform the condensation of a pile of elements in a scene. Or it flattens itself and spreads out to follow the prismatic lines of a node folding and unfolding, expanding and contracting. It follows its objects, which are not adequately described as simply ethnographic encounters but have the qualities of refrains registering across a field, or thresholds of expressivity appearing, cuts that throw a trajectory off-course, or forms of attunement or disorientation that come of being somehow in, or proximate to, or aware of a coming or receding situation.

The essays gathered here register the tunes on which people venture out, a worlding captured in a shared gesture or a kind of haircut, or the arc of a threat resonating in a routine. It matters to note the way that bodies are situated and splayed around a Thanksgiving dinner table and the sounding of an Inuit *kataq* in the corner of the room: two women, their bodies almost touching, a wordless almost growling, buzzing, panting, a rhythmic plucking, teasing. Or the suddenly unbearable ordinariness of sound right after someone dies: "She's gone."

Voice gets foregrounded here. The power of a voice in itself; the connection people feel to the recorded voice of a missing person, the qualities of a voice made silvery from smoking or one that giggles on the side. Ethnographic writing steals voices, betrays them, tries to become and remain true to them, stops and starts and starts again, homes in on the act of saying something when one beat before there was a kind of nothing. Language is always already a beginning again, borrowed language doubly so, doubling back on the charges it carries. A voice is so literally and materially *of* a body, a family, a place, some vast array of fictions, some grooves of imagined somethings scored into saliva and the sound of waves.

There is room in this writing for voices to come and go. Room made by the writing buckling back on itself, hamstringing its own first anthropological impulse to lose itself in a hardline narrative and explanatory context. Necessarily recursive, it fashions itself like a tuning fork that learns its note through small, incremental experiments made in fits and starts. It lurches or sails into some kind of capacity to be with matter-practice-thought-feelings that stretch beyond the representational register of signification to etch uses and forms, frictions, constraints, motions, and lines leading out onto a landscape of sociality and dream.

Full-bored ethnographic writing tries to let the otherwise break through, to keep it alive, to tend it. Worlds and lives unsettle what social science has considered settled, and they open a path into what science has left unexplored and unspoken. There are returns, through the language of literature and poetry, to the compositions of reals. Ethnographic writing can be a portal into a weird, swollen realism far from the deadness of the literal. A side angle onto the telling details, the horrors and beauties, of affective-material-social-political registers of living. We see a refugee get off a plane. "The church ladies took him to a store, bought him fresh sneakers soft and white as wedding cake. The next day he walked through whole aisles of dog food." Then, in another moment, after the fanfare and fractured expectations have passed and his situation is still dangerous and abandoned in new ways, he "sits inside his apartment, heat cranked up to 80, curtains closed, a pile of chicken boiling on the stove, slides another Kung Fu movie into the VCR, settles back into the smelly, swaybacked couch, a Budweiser between his legs. He giggles."

Ethnography thinks and writes at the limit of what it is possible to say. This means it has to be nimble, patient, but jumpy. In some cases it might turn itself into a viscosity like the deliberate opacity or muddiness of poems moving "blindly, but well-intentioned, amidst the irresistible mud" of a Vermont pond. The writing might become a kind of catchment area. In Chennai, on a film shoot, "everywhere else . . . the sun rises in the morning and sets at night, but not here, things here, they suddenly happen, all at once," and "there is rain more rain and even more rain in Chennai, drowning out their plans for another scene, and by the time the rain lets up the actor is gone, the director's back to editing another project, and the actress who knows as they've hardly let me speak to her for more than a minute at a time . . ." As if to keep up with all of this, the writing in this volume becomes an ambient atmosphere with tempo, tone, and mood. It propels into the affordances of a situation, the characteristics of a thought-ecology, a sociality-pause, or a state of matter. It is itself a path on which things amass and accrete; it arrives at stalemates, speeding shoots, a shady spot, a treacherous impasse, an unwilling audience.

Each essay pulls into alignment with the consubstantiality of subject-object-world relations: mud, a drug world, the deep sea, the rolling thresholds of rituals, filmmaking, a hypervalent performativity, a childhood memory, a poetic rumination, a hunt, a game of make-believe, an apparatus of rules and restrictions that enthralls. These are not just images in a representational order of things but modes of copresencing. Visceral imaginaries that make demands on the sensorium. Materialities that swell into modes of address, thought feelings venturing into an incipiency.

Like the objects it pulls into relief, ethnographic writing is lodged as much in bodies, circulations, and the shock of a sensory recognition as it is in words. The essays gathered here approach this situation of writing through sharply precise but careful, gentle engagements with questions of experience, what it means to be a person in a world and writing of a world, how ethnography can render other and unfamiliar the everyday world, how a person caught up in a speculative poesis can imagine emergent events, can size up in a glance what's blowing through a scene or be transported back to another scene at a sound or a quality of the air, can recognize another's copresence to events or the possibility of events as a limited connection, a gesture at connecting.

Writing, here, is pictured as a passage, an interval, a bridge, a transitional space, a holding environment for a scene that surrounds and presses but is not only for the writer's eyes or ears. It has a fidelity to what is overheard from a solitary perch in the attic window or read in a letter from prison, to the limits of connection or to the discontinuity of experience, to the inability to reach a settled state. It dreams; it is language almost in trance, a story that cannot be told completely in a state of waking.

The writer is taken to a moment of startling unexpectedness. Or the rhythm of writing becomes the rhythm of mourning, absence. The writer tries to speak to those who spoke with her or it becomes impossible not to write in a certain way. There is always the sense that much more could be said, that things could be said differently and that that would matter, that everything we do is on the side of someone or something else. Description is so freighted by positing a palpable relation to an otherness. "There's the old man selling watermelons blessed by Jesus, the old woman with the live chickens squawking in their metal cages. Heat bounces off the black tarmac." Or, "I heard the muffled cor coro coo of a ringdove and declared aloud, 'My God, it's the south of France!'"

Pushed to perform scenes and objects that preexist and exceed it, ethnographic writing can become a condensation that brings out a real: the knot of a something else that swells with expressivity, that could be conveyed in so many ways, and that remains partially undisclosed in what gets said and what gets done. The real of the ethnographic object here exists in mixed material-aesthetic registers that are at once emerging and deflating. It tries to pull forms into partial view, gives them textures, makes them sensate or dreamy or abstract, gives them density to show how the actual is not simply there, flatly coincident with its notion, and the language aimed at approaching it is a bit of bark, a sliver of rock.

Writing, in these essays, is a flickering resource used to reopen subject-object-world ontologies. The essays lean into their objects, sidle up to other people's attunements, hardenings, iron-clad investments, and failures to endure. They look to the engagements and distractions of living through something as if they're lessons in effort. They try to move in the manner of things slipping in and out of an existence. The artful complicity of ethnography with its objects and scenes becomes an impetus for thought and action, a prism of projects and momentarily might-have-beens throwing together and falling apart.

The essays collected here present a series of differing and linked accounts of ethnographic writing's familiarity with and estrangement in the singularities of worlds. They make a method out of ontologically curious writing. Far from a writerly excess that obscures the real, as such efforts are sometimes taken, this is a speculative performance of the qualities of subjects, ecologies, and force fields in the things that happen. It functions as a hinge, a magnet, a diffuser, or a detour as it follows what pushes matters and subjects into energetic states of being and what begins to take place, what folds back on itself and recombines, what goes nowhere and is lost.

The authors, using sensate, ontologically mixed modes of transformative encounter, turn these essays into a problematic of what writing does to thought. They note that writing is the materiality of ethnography, both in the field and in the process of writing up or cooking down field notes. The movement of life-into-text-into-life is foregrounded as a visceral and energetic mode that impels us, works on us.

In mobilizing the materialities and motions of ethnographic writing we learn something about the creative energy of worlds. We also learn about kinds of excess and expenditure, kinds of surrender, or denial or hypervigilance, the possibilities and threats of building conceptual bridges between phenomena and scales, or the importance of remembering that actuality is never just coincident with itself and the real is always a relation of difference.

We might learn to fly under the radar of categorical knowledge. We might imagine dissolving into the matter of the world or a landscape littered with words hardened into rock or trash. In the unresolved relationship between being and thought, in the active effort to do justice to lived experience with conceptual thought and perception, there are costs, betrayals, pleasures, violence, returns, alternatives, a commingling, a gesture, an unexpected collective energy.

BIBLIOGRAPHY

Adams, Carol. "Bringing Peace Home: A Feminist Philosophical Perspective on the Abuse of Women, Children, and Pet Animals." In *Bringing Peace Home: Feminism, Violence, and Nature*, edited by Karen J. Warren and Duane L. Cady. Bloomington: Indiana University Press, 1996.

Adorno, Theodor W. "The Essay as Form." In *Notes to Literature*, vol. 1, edited by Rolf Tiedemann. New York: Columbia University Press, 1991.

Agamben, Giorgio. "Aby Warburg and the Nameless Science." In *Potentialities: Collected Essays in Philosophy*. Stanford, CA: Stanford University Press, 2000.

Agee, James. *Let Us Now Praise Famous Men*. Boston: Houghton Mifflin, 2001.

Ali, Daud. "Anxieties of Attachment: The Dynamics of Courtship in Medieval India." *Modern Asian Studies* 36 (2002): 103–39.

Anonymous. *The Orkneyinga Saga*. London: Penguin, 1978.

Arendt, Hannah. *The Human Condition*. Chicago: University of Chicago Press, 1958.

Auton, Clive, Terry Fletcher, and David Gould. *Orkney and Shetland: A Landscape Fashioned by Geology*. Edinburgh: British Geological Survey, 1996.

Barthes, Roland. *Camera Lucida*. New York: Hill and Wang, 2010.

Barthes, Roland. *Mourning Diary*. New York: Hill and Wang, 2009.

Bataille, Georges. *The Accursed Share, Volumes II and III*. New York: Zone, 1993.

Bataille, Georges. *Erotism: Death and Sensuality*. San Francisco: City Lights, 1986.

Bataille, Georges. *The Impossible*. San Francisco: City Lights, 2001.

Behar, Ruth. *The Vulnerable Observer: Anthropology That Breaks Your Heart*. Boston: Beacon, 1996.

Benjamin, Walter. "A Short History of Photography." *Screen* 13, no. 1 (1972): 5–26.

Benjamin, Walter. "The Storyteller: Observations on the Work of Nikolai Leskov." In *Selected Writings*, vol. 3: 1935–1938, edited by Howard Eiland and Michael W. Jennings. Cambridge, MA: Belknap Press of Harvard University Press, 2002.

Bennett, John, and Susan Diana Mary Rowley. *Uqalurait: An Oral History of Nunavut*. Montreal: McGill-Queen's University Press, 2004.

Berg, A. Scott. *Maxwell Perkins: Editor of Genius*. New York: Berkley, 1978.

Berger, John. *Keeping a Rendezvous*. New York: Pantheon, 1991.

Biehl, João. *Vita: Life in a Zone of Social Abandonment.* Berkeley: University of California Press, 2005.

Blanchot, Maurice. *L'espace littéraire.* Paris: Gallimard, 1955. English translation by Ann Smock. *The Space of Literature.* Lincoln: University of Nebraska Press, 1982.

Blanchot, Maurice. *The Work of Fire.* Stanford, CA: Stanford University Press, 1995.

Blanchot, Maurice. *The Writing of the Disaster.* Lincoln: University of Nebraska Press, 1995.

Brown, Julia Prewitt. *The Bourgeois Interior: How the Middle Class Imagines Itself in Literature and Film.* Charlottesville: University of Virginia Press, 2008.

Calvino, Italo. "A King Listens." In *Under the Jaguar Sun.* San Diego: Harcourt Brace Jovanovich, 1986.

Canetti, Elias. *Crowds and Power.* London: Penguin, 1992. First published 1960.

Carr, David. "Translator's Note." In Edmund Husserl, *The Crisis of European Sciences and Transcendental Phenomenology.* Evanston, IL: Northwestern University Press, 1970.

Castaing-Taylor, Lucien, and Verena Paravel, dirs. *Leviathan.* Harvard University, Sensory Ethnography Lab, 2012.

Chittick, William. *The Sufi Path to Knowledge: Ibn al-'Arabi Metaphysics of Imagination.* Albany: State University of New York Press, 1989.

Clifford, James. *The Predicament of Culture: Twentieth-Century Ethnography, Literature, and Art.* Cambridge, MA: Harvard University Press, 1988.

Clifford, James. *Routes: Travel and Translation in the Late Twentieth Century.* Cambridge, MA: Harvard University Press, 1997.

Clifford, James, and George E. Marcus, eds. *Writing Culture: The Poetics and Politics of Ethnography.* Berkeley: University of California Press, 1986.

Colebrook, Clair, ed. *Extinction.* Ann Arbor, MI: Open Humanities, 2012.

Colla, Elliot. "The Ladies and the Eye: Figure and Narrative in the Porter's Tale." In *Scheherazade's Children,* edited by Philip Kennedy and Marina Warner. New York: New York University Press, 2013.

Condominas, Georges. *Nous avons mangé la forêt.* Paris: Mercure de France, 1957.

Conrad, Joseph. *Lord Jim.* New York: Dover, 2011. First published 1900.

Cotera, Maria. *Native Speakers: Ella Deloria, Zora Neale Hurston, Jovita Gonzalez, and the Poetics of Culture.* Austin: University of Texas Press, 2008.

Crapanzano, Vincent. "Hermes Dilemma: The Masking of Subversion in Ethnographic Description." In *Writing Culture: The Poetics and Politics of Ethnography,* edited by James Clifford and George E. Marcus. Berkeley: University of California Press, 1986.

Crapanzano, Vincent. *Imaginative Horizons: An Essay in Literary-Philosophical Anthropology.* Chicago: University of Chicago Press, 2004.

Crapanzano, Vincent. *Tuhami: Portrait of a Moroccan.* Chicago: University of Chicago Press, 1980.

Daniel, E. Valentine. "Culture/Contexture: An Introduction." In *Culture/Contexture: Explorations in Anthropology and Literary Studies,* edited by E. Valentine Daniel and Jeffrey M. Peck. Berkeley: University of California Press, 1996.

Daniel, E. Valentine, and Jeffrey M. Peck, eds. *Culture/Contexture: Explorations in Anthropology and Literary Studies.* Berkeley: University of California Press, 1996.

Das, Veena. *Life and Words: Violence and the Descent into the Ordinary*. Berkeley: University of California Press, 2006.

Debaene, Vincent. *Far Afield: French Anthropology between Science and Literature*. Chicago: University of Chicago Press, 2014.

de Certeau, Michel. *The Writing of History*. New York: Columbia University Press, 1992.

Deleuze, Gilles. *Bergsonism*. New York: Zone, 1990.

Deleuze, Gilles. *Cinema 2: The Time Image*. Minneapolis: University of Minnesota Press, 1989.

Deleuze, Gilles. *Desert Islands and Other Texts, 1953–1974*. Cambridge, MA: MIT Press, 2004.

Deleuze, Gilles. *Expressionism in Philosophy: Spinoza*. New York: Zone, 1992.

Deleuze, Gilles. "Literature and Life." *Critical Inquiry* 23, no. 2 (1997): 225–30.

Deleuze, Gilles, and Félix Guattari. *Anti-Oedipus: Capitalism and Schizophrenia*. Minneapolis: University of Minnesota Press, 1983.

Deleuze, Gilles, and Félix Guattari. *Kafka: Toward a Minor Literature*. Minneapolis: University of Minnesota Press, 1986.

Deleuze, Gilles, and Claire Parnet. "Dead Psychoanalysis: Analyse." In *Dialogues II*. New York: Columbia University Press, 2007.

Deloria, Ella. *Waterlily*. Lincoln: University of Nebraska Press, 1988.

Dennison, Walter Traill. *Orkney Folklore and Sea Legends: Studies of Traditional Life and Folklore*. Kirkwall: Orkney Press, 1995.

Derrida, Jacques. *Archive Fever: A Freudian Impression*. Chicago: University of Chicago Press, 1998.

Derrida, Jacques. *Margins of Philosophy*. Chicago: University of Chicago Press, 1982.

Derrida, Jacques. "This Strange Institution Called Literature." In *Acts of Literature*, edited by Derek Attridge. London: Routledge, 1992.

Derrida, Jacques. *Writing and Difference*. Chicago: University of Chicago Press, 1978.

Dewey, John. *Experience and Nature*. New York: Dover, 1958. First published 1925.

Diamond, Cora. "The Difficulty of Reality and the Difficulty of Philosophy." In *Philosophy and Animal Life*, edited by Stanley Cavell, Cora Diamond, John McDowell, Ian Hacking, and Cary Wolfe. New York: Columbia University Press, 2008.

Diamond, Stanley. Preface. "Poetry and Anthropology," special issue, *Dialectical Anthropology* 11 (1986): 131–32.

Didi-Huberman, Georges. *L'image survivante: Histoire de l'art et temps des phantoms selon Aby Warburg*. Paris: Editions de Minuit, 2002.

Edwards, Jorge. *Persona non grata*. Madrid: Letras Hispánicas, 2015. First published 1973.

Eisenstein, Sergei. "A Dialectical Approach to Film Form." In *Film Form: Essays in Film Theory*. New York: Harcourt, 1977.

Elias, Norbert. *The Civilizing Process: The History of Manners and State Formation and Civilization*. Oxford: Blackwell, 1994.

Eliot, T. S. *Four Quartets*. New York: Harcourt, 1943.

Fassin, Didier. "True Life, Real Lives: Revisiting the Boundaries between Ethnography and Fiction." *American Ethnologist* 41 (2014): 40–55.

Fassin, Didier. *When Bodies Remember: Experiences and Politics of AIDS in South Africa.* Berkeley: University of California Press, 2007.

Favret-Saada, Jeanne. *Deadly Words: Witchcraft in the Bocage.* Cambridge: Cambridge University Press, 1980.

Feld, Steven. "Pygmy POP: A Genealogy of Schizophonic Mimesis." In *Yearbook for Traditional Music,* vol. 28. International Council for Traditional Music, 1966.

Ferguson, David. *Shipwrecks of Orkney, Shetland and the Pentland Firth.* Newton Abbot, UK: David and Charles, 1988.

Fine, Lisa M. "Rights of Men, Rites of Passage: Hunting and Masculinity at Reo Motors of Lansing Michigan, 1945–1975." *Journal of Social History* 33, no. 4 (2000): 805–23.

Firth, Raymond. *We, the Tikopia: A Sociological Study of Kinship in Primitive Polynesia.* Boston: Beacon, 1965.

Fitzgerald, Amy. "The Emergence of the Figure of 'Woman-the-Hunter': Equality or Complicity in Oppression?" *Women's Studies Quarterly* 33, nos. 1/2 (2005): 86–104.

Forché, Carolyn. *Blue Hour.* New York: Harper Perennial, 2004.

Forman, Richard T. T., and Lauren E. Alexander. "Roads and Their Major Ecological Effects." *Annual Review of Ecology and Systematics* 29 (1998): 207–31.

Forsdick, Charles. "*De la plume comme des pieds*: The Essay as a Peripatetic Genre." In *The Modern Essay in French: Movement, Instability, Performance,* edited by Charles Forsdick and Andrew Stafford. Oxford: Peter Lang, 2005.

Freshwater, Helen. "The Allure of the Archive." *Poetics Today* 24 (2003): 729–58.

Frykman, Jonas, and Orvar Löfgren. *Culture Builders: A Historical Anthropology of Middle-Class Life.* New Brunswick, NJ: Rutgers University Press, 1987.

Gaard, Greta, ed. *Ecofeminism: Women, Animals, Nature.* Philadelphia: Temple University Press, 1993.

Garcia, Angela. *The Pastoral Clinic: Addiction and Dispossession along the Rio Grande.* Berkeley: University of California Press, 2010.

Geertz, Clifford. *Works and Lives: The Anthropologist as Author.* Stanford, CA: Stanford University Press, 1988.

al-Ghazali, Abu Hamid. *Al-munqidh min al-dalal, al-Ghazali's Path to Sufism, His Deliverance from Error.* Louisville, KY: Fons Vitae, 2000.

Gillies, Malcolm. *The Bartók Companion.* Portland: Amadeus, 1994.

Goethe, Johann Wolfgang. *Elective Affinities.* Harmondsworth, UK: Penguin, 1971.

Goffmann, Alice. *On the Run: Fugitive Life in an American City.* Chicago: University of Chicago Press, 2014.

Hamdouni Alami, Mohammed. *The Origin of Visual Culture in the Islamic World: Aesthetics, Art, and Architecture in Early Islam.* London: I. B. Tauris, 2015.

Hecht, Tobias. *After Life: An Ethnographic Novel.* Durham, NC: Duke University Press, 2006.

Hegel, Georg W. F. *Phenomenology of Spirit.* Oxford: Oxford University Press, 1977.

Hrabal, Bohumil. *Dancing Lessons for the Advanced in Age.* New York: Harcourt Brace, 2005.

Hurston, Zora Neale. *Dust Tracks on a Road.* Urbana: University of Illinois Press, 1984.

Hurston, Zora Neale. *Mules and Men*. Philadelphia: J. B. Lippincott, 1935.

Husserl, Edmund. *The Crisis of European Sciences and Transcendental Phenomenology*. Evanston, IL: Northwestern University Press, 1970.

Illich, Ivan. *Tools for Conviviality*. London: Caldar and Boyars, 1973.

Ingold, Tim. *Being Alive: Essays on Movement, Knowledge and Description*. London: Routledge, 2011.

Jackson, Michael. *The Accidental Anthropologist: A Memoir*. Dunedin: Longacre, 2006.

Jackson, Michael. *Barawa, and the Ways Birds Fly in the Sky: An Ethnographic Novel*. Washington, DC: Smithsonian Institution Press, 1986.

Jackson, Michael. *Between One and One Another*. Berkeley: University of California Press, 2012.

Jackson, Michael. *Latitudes of Exile: Poems 1965–1975*. Dunedin: McIndoe, 1976.

Jackson, Michael. *Lifeworlds: Essays in Existential Anthropology*. Chicago: University of Chicago Press, 2013.

Jackson, Michael. *The Other Shore: Essays on Writers and Writing*. Berkeley: University of California Press, 2013.

Jackson, Michael. *Wall*. Dunedin: McIndoe, 1980.

James, William. *Essays in Radical Empiricism*. New York: Dover, 2003. First published 1912.

Joyce, James. "Daniel Defoe." *Buffalo Studies* 1 (1964): 1–27.

Joyce, James. *Finnegans Wake*. London: Faber and Faber, 1939.

Joyce, James. *Ulysses*. New York: Vintage, 1990. First published 1922.

Keats, John. *The Letters of John Keats, 1814–1821*, vol. 1. Edited by Hyder Edward Rollins. Cambridge: Cambridge University Press, 1958.

Khatibi, Abdelkebir. *La blessure du nom propre*. Paris: Denoel, 1974.

Kheel, Marti. "The Killing Game: An Ecofeminist Critique of Hunting." *Journal of the Philosophy of Sport* 23 (1996): 30–44.

Kilito, Abdelfattah. *L'oeil et l'aiguille: Essai sur les milles et une nuit*. Paris: La Découverte, 2010. First published 1992.

Kofman, Sarah. "Beyond Aporia." In *Post Structuralist Classics*, edited by Andrew Benjamin. London: Routledge, 1988.

Kristeva, Julia. *Tales of Love*. New York: Columbia University Press, 1987.

Kumar, Amitava. *Lunch with a Bigot: The Writer in the World*. Durham, NC: Duke University Press, 2015.

Kusserow, Adrie. *Refuge*. Rochester, NY: BOA Editions, 2013.

Lacan, Jacques. "Ecrits 'inspirés': Schizographie." In *La psychose paranoiaque dans ses rapports avec la personnalité*. Paris: Editions du Seuil, 1975. First published 1932.

Lacan, Jacques. *The Four Fundamental Concepts of Psychoanalysis*. New York: W. W. Norton, 1977.

Lasch-Quinn, Elizabeth. "From Inwardness to Intravidualism." *Hedgehog Review* 13, no. 1 (2011): 1–5.

Latour, Bruno. *An Inquiry into Modes of Existence*. Cambridge, MA: Harvard University Press, 2013.

Laugrand, Frédéric, and Jarich Oosten. *The Sea Woman: Sedna in Inuit Shamanism and Art in the Eastern Arctic*. Fairbanks: University of Alaska Press, 2008.

Lavie, Smadar, Kirin Narayan, and Renato Rosaldo, eds. *Creativity/Anthropology.* Ithaca, NY: Cornell University Press, 1993.

Lévi-Strauss, Claude. "Jean-Jacques Rousseau, Founder of the Sciences of Man." In *Structural Anthropology,* vol. 2. London: Allen Lane, 1976.

Lévi-Strauss, Claude. *Tristes Tropiques.* New York: Penguin, 1992.

Lispector, Clarice. *Agua Viva.* New York: New Directions, 2012.

Lovecraft, H. P. *The Call of Cthulhu.* Richmond, ON: Prohyptikon, 2010.

Lovecraft, H. P. *The Shadow over Innsmouth.* Everett, PA: Visionary Publishing, 1936.

Lucretius. *On the Nature of the Universe.* London: Penguin, 2005.

Luke, Brian. "A Critical Analysis of Hunters' Ethics." *Environmental Ethics* 19, no. 1 (1997): 25–44.

Luke, Brian. "Violent Love: Hunting, Heterosexuality, and the Erotics of Men's Predation." *Feminist Studies* 24, no. 3 (1998): 627–55.

Luria, Alexander R. *The Making of Mind: A Personal Account of Soviet Psychology.* Edited by Michael Cole and Sheila Cole. Cambridge, MA: Harvard University Press, 1979.

Mackay Brown, George. *Collected Poems of George Mackay Brown.* London: John Murray, 2006.

Mahdi, Muhsin. *Ibn Khaldun's Philosophy of History.* London: Ruskin House, 1957.

Malinowski, Bronislaw. *Argonauts of the Western Pacific.* Prospect Heights, IL: Waveland, 1984.

Malinowski, Bronislaw. *A Diary in the Strict Sense of the Term.* Stanford, CA: Stanford University Press, 1989.

Marcel, Gabriel. *Being and Having.* Boston: Beacon, 1951.

Marcus, George E. "The Legacies of Writing Culture and the Near Future of the Ethnographic Form: A Sketch." *Cultural Anthropology* 27, no. 3 (2012): 427–45.

Marcus, George E., and Dick Cushman. "Ethnographies as Texts." *Annual Review of Anthropology* 11 (1982): 25–69.

Marcus, George E., and Michael M. J. Fischer. *Anthropology as Cultural Critique: An Experimental Moment in the Human Sciences.* Chicago: University of Chicago Press, 1999.

Marcuse, Herbert. "The Affirmative Character of Culture." In *Negations: Essays in Critical Theory.* Boston: Beacon, 1968.

Marwick, Ernest. *The Folklore of Orkney and Shetland.* Edinburgh: Birlinn, 2000.

Mauss, Marcel. *The Gift: Forms and Functions of Exchange in Archaic Societies.* London: Cohen and West, 1954.

McCormick, Donald. *The Mystery of Lord Kitchener's Death.* London: Putnam, 1959.

McGrath, Ben. "Does Football Have a Future?" *New Yorker,* January 31, 2011.

McLane, Janice. "The Voice on the Skin: Self-Mutilation and Merleau-Ponty's Theory of Language." *Hypatia* 11 (1996): 107–18.

The Meaning of the Holy Qur'ān. Edited by A. Yūsuf 'Alī. Betsville: Amana, 1989.

Merleau-Ponty, Maurice. *The Phenomenology of Perception.* New York: Routledge, 2002.

The Message of the Qur'ān. Edited by Muhammad Asad. Bristol, UK: Book Foundation, 2003.

Mitchell, Don, and Lynn A. Staeheli. "Turning Social Relations into Space: Property, Law and the Plaza of Santa Fe, New Mexico." *Landscape Research* 30, no. 3 (2005): 361–78.

Montaigne, Michel de. *The Essays: A Selection*. Harmondsworth, UK: Penguin, 2005.

Narayan, Kirin. *Alive in the Writing: Crafting Ethnography in the Company of Chekhov*. Chicago: University of Chicago Press, 2012.

Nietzsche, Friedrich. *The Will to Power*. New York: Vintage, 1968.

Notley, Alice. *Songs and Stories of the Ghouls*. Middletown, CT: Wesleyan University Press, 2011.

Ochoa, Todd Ramón. "Versions of the Dead: Kalunga, Cuban-Kongo Materiality and Ethnography." *Cultural Anthropology* 22, no. 4 (2007): 473–500.

Ortega y Gasset, José. *Meditations on Hunting*. New York: Scribner, 1972.

Ortega y Gasset, José. *Sobre la caza, los toros y el toreo*. Madrid: Revista de Occidente en Alianza Editorial, 1999. First published 1960.

Pandolfo, Stefania. *Impasse of the Angels: Scenes in a Moroccan Space of Memory*, part I. Chicago: University of Chicago Press, 1997.

Pandolfo, Stefania. *Knot of the Soul: Madness, Psychoanalysis, Islam*. Chicago: University of Chicago Press, 2017.

Pasolini, Pier Paolo. "The 'Cinema of Poetry.'" In *Heretical Empiricism*. Washington, DC: New Academic, 2005.

Phillips, William C. *The Loss of the H.M.S. "Hampshire" and the Death of Lord Kitchener*. London: Hepworth and Co., 1930.

Pound, Ezra. *ABC of Reading*. London: Faber and Faber, 1936.

Rapport, Nigel. *The Prose and the Passion: Anthropology, Literature and the Writing of E. M. Forster*. Manchester, UK: Manchester University Press, 1994.

Redfield, Robert. *The Little Community*. Chicago: University of Chicago Press, 1956.

Renfrew, Colin, ed. *The Prehistory of Orkney*. Edinburgh: Edinburgh University Press, 1993.

Rimbaud, Arthur. *Complete Works*. New York: Harper and Row, 1967.

Rosaldo, Renato. *The Day of Shelley's Death*. Durham, NC: Duke University Press, 2014.

Rudwick, Lois Palken. *Utopian Vistas: The Mabel Dodge Luhan House and the American Counterculture*. Albuquerque: University of New Mexico Press, 1996.

Saladin D'Anglure, Bernard. "Entre cri et chant: Les Katajjait, un genre musical féminin." *Études/Inuit/Studies* 2, no. 1 (1978): 85–94.

Schmidt, Nancy J. "Ethnographic Fiction: Anthropology's Hidden Literary Style." *Anthropology and Humanism* 9, no. 4 (1984): 11–14.

Serres, Michel. *Angels: A Modern Myth*. Paris: Flammarion, 1993.

Serres, Michel. *The Troubadour of Knowledge*. Ann Arbor: University of Michigan Press, 2003.

Shakespeare, William. *The Tempest*. London: Everyman, 1994.

Smalley, Andrea. "'I Just Like to Kill Things': Women, Men, and the Gender of Sport Hunting in the United States, 1940–1973." *Gender and History* 17, no. 1 (2005): 183–209.

Smith, Jane, and Yvonne Haddad. *The Islamic Understanding of Death and Resurrection*. Oxford: Oxford University Press, 2002.

Spinoza, Benedict de. *Ethics*. London: Penguin, 2005.

Stange, Mary. *Woman the Hunter*. Boston: Beacon, 1997.

Stange, Mary. "Women and Hunting in the West." *Montana: The Magazine of Western History* 55, no. 3 (2005): 14–21.

Stark, Gregor, and E. Catherine Rayne. *El Delirio: The Santa Fé World of Elizabeth White*. Santa Fe, NM: School of American Research Press, 1998.

Starn, Orin. "Introduction." In *Writing Culture and the Life of Anthropology*, edited by Orin Starn. Durham, NC: Duke University Press, 2015.

Steedman, Caroline. *Dust: The Archive and Cultural History*. New Brunswick, NJ: Rutgers University Press, 2002.

Stevenson, Lisa. *Life beside Itself: Imagining Care in the Canadian Arctic*. Berkeley: University of California Press, 2014.

Taminian, Lucine. "Rimbaud's House in Aden, Yemen: Giving Voice(s) to the Silent Poet." *Cultural Anthropology* 13, no. 4 (1998): 464–90.

Tarr, Roger L., ed. *As Ever Yours: The Letters of Max Perkins and Elizabeth Lemmon*. University Park: Pennsylvania State University Press, 2003.

Taussig, Michael. *I Swear I Saw This: Drawing in Fieldwork Notebooks, Namely My Own*. Chicago: University of Chicago Press, 2011.

Tedlock, Barbara. "From Participant Observation to the Observation of Participation: The Emergence of Narrative Ethnography." *Journal of Anthropological Research* 47, no. 1 (1991): 69–94.

Thompson, William P. L. *The New History of Orkney*. Edinburgh: Birlinn, 2008.

Thoreau, Henry David. "Walking." In *Walden and Other Writings of Henry David Thoreau*, edited by Brooks Atkinson. New York: Modern Library, 1992.

Tournier, Michel. *Friday: Or, The Other Island*. Baltimore, MD: Johns Hopkins University Press, 1997.

Towsey, Kate, ed. *Orkney and the Sea: An Oral History*. Kirkwall: Orkney Heritage, 2001.

Tyler, Steven A. "Postmodern Ethnography: From Document of the Occult to Occult Document." In *Writing Culture: The Poetics and Politics of Ethnography*, edited by James Clifford and George E. Marcus. Berkeley: University of California Press, 1986.

Van Maanen, John. *Tales of the Field: On Writing Ethnography*. Chicago: University of Chicago Press, 2011.

Walley, Christine J. *Exit Zero: Family and Class in Postindustrial Chicago*. Chicago: University of Chicago Press, 2013.

Waterston, Alisse, and Maria D. Vesperi. *Anthropology Off the Shelf: Anthropologists on Writing*. Oxford: Wiley-Blackwell, 2011.

Weigle, Marta. "From Desert to Disney World: The Sante Fe Railway and the Fred Harvey Company Display the Indian Southwest." *Journal of Anthropological Research* 45, no. 1 (1989): 115–37.

Winnicott, Donald W. *The Maturational Processes and the Facilitating Environment*. London: Hogarth, 1965.

Winnicott, Donald W. *Playing and Reality*. Harmondsworth, UK: Penguin, 1974.

Wulff, Helena, ed. *The Anthropologist as Writer: Genres and Contexts in the Twenty-First Century*. New York: Berghahn, 2016.

Yebes, Eduardo Figueroa Alonso-Martínez, Conde de. *Veinte años de caza mayor.* Prologue by José Ortega y Gasset. Seville: Ediciones Al Andalus, 1963. First published 1942.

Zahan, Dominique. *The Religion, Spirituality, and Thought of Traditional Africa.* Chicago: University of Chicago Press, 1970.

Zurita, Raúl. *Dreams for Kurosawa.* Chicago: arrow as aarow, 2012.

CONTRIBUTORS

DANIELLA GANDOLFO is Associate Professor of Anthropology at Wesleyan University. Her work, including *The City at Its Limits: Taboo, Transgression, and Urban Renewal in Lima* (2009), explores forms of sacred experience in everyday life and the challenges these pose for writing.

ANGELA GARCIA is Associate Professor of Anthropology at Stanford University. She is the author of *The Pastoral Clinic: Addiction and Dispossession along the Rio Grande* (2010).

TOBIAS HECHT, an independent scholar, is the author of *At Home in the Street: Street Children of Northeast Brazil* (1998, winner of the Margaret Mead Award), *After Life: An Ethnographic Novel* (Duke University Press, 2006), and *El Cerdito Pulcro/The Remarkably Clean Life of a Little Pig* (2016).

MICHAEL JACKSON is Distinguished Professor of World Religions at Harvard Divinity School. He is the author of more than thirty books of ethnography, poetry, and fiction, including the prizewinning *Paths toward a Clearing: Radical Empiricism and Ethnographic Inquiry* (1989) and *At Home in the World* (Duke University Press, 1995).

ADRIE KUSSEROW is Professor of Anthropology at St. Michael's College in Vermont. She is a cofounder of the Africa Education and Leadership Initiative (www.africaeli.org) and the author of two books of poetry, *Hunting Down the Monk* (2002) and *Refuge* (2013).

STUART McLEAN is Associate Professor of Anthropology at the University of Minnesota. The author of *The Event and Its Terrors: Ireland, Famine, Modernity* (2004), he is currently completing a book manuscript titled *Fictionalizing Anthropology: Encounters and Fabulations at the Edges of the Human.*

TODD RAMÓN OCHOA is Associate Professor in the Department of Religious Studies at the University of North Carolina, Chapel Hill. He is the author of *Society of the Dead: Quita Manaquita and Palo Praise in Cuba* (2010).

ANAND PANDIAN teaches anthropology at Johns Hopkins University, and he writes at the interstices of ecological, philosophical, and literary anthropology. His books include *Crooked Stalks: Cultivating Virtue in South India* (2009) and *Reel World: An Anthropology of Creation* (2015), both published by Duke University Press.

STEFANIA PANDOLFO is an anthropologist at the University of California, Berkeley. Her work centers on forms of life and subjectivity, imagination, memory, and the experience of madness. She is the author of *Impasse of the Angels: Scenes from a Moroccan Space of Memory* (1997) and *Knot of the Soul: Madness, Psychoanalysis, Islam* (2017).

LISA STEVENSON is Associate Professor and William Dawson Scholar in the Department of Anthropology at McGill University. Her book *Life beside Itself: Imagining Care in the Canadian Arctic* (2014) won the 2015 Victor Turner Book Prize.

KATHLEEN STEWART teaches anthropology at the University of Texas, Austin. Her books *A Space on the Side of the Road* (1996) and *Ordinary Affects* (Duke University Press, 2007) experiment with ethnographic writing to approach the variegated poesis of worlds in the making.

INDEX

Note: Page numbers in *italics* refer to illustrations.

art and madness in Morocco (*continued*)
imaginal border (*barzakh*), 105, 118;
Islamic tradition of the Imaginal,
94–95; melancholia and transformation, 112–14; passage or bridge (*'ibra*)
and, 95, 97, 111–12; "pictures that
contain a state" (*luḥat lly fihum ḥalā*),
101–6; "the sea-bride" (*'arusat-l-baḥr*)
painting, 101–3, *102*; snake painting,
97, *98*, 98–100, *108*, 109–14, 117; "tree
of life" (*shajarat al-ḥayat*) door painting, *103*, *104*, *106*; visual meaning
and imagination of the real, 109–12;
Warburg's bipolar images, 105–6,
114, 118
"Assertion of Gentleness, The"
(Stevenson), 217–18
authenticity, 13, 49–51, 60–62
authorial vantage point, relinquishing,
127–28
authority, 13, 20, 60–62
Ayirathil Oruvan (One in a thousand)
(film; Selvaraghavan), 121, 128
'ayn/evil eye/source motif, 115n19

Baffin Correctional Center, Iqaluit,
219–20
BaKongo people, 178–79
Barthes, Roland, 37, 218
Bartók, Béla, 49–50, 66n66
barzakh (imaginal border), 105, 118
Bataille, Georges, 17, 20, 186, 189, 195,
199–200
bear hunting in New Jersey, 190–91.
See also hunting
Behar, Ruth, 5, 9n10
bembés in Cuba: commentary, 185–88;
the dead and fate-breaking, 178;
drummers, singers, dancers, and
callers, 176, 180; Fon, Yoruba,
and BaKongo people and legacy
of slavery, 178–79; how it thrives,
179–80; leaderlessness of, 175–76;

"mounting up," 175, 177–78, 180;
movements of the dead, 172–73;
origami conjecture for (jamming,
rolling, pleats, fans, twist, and
coils), 179–84; as parties or religion,
174–75; *santos-orisás*, about, 174;
santos-orisás and fate-shaping, 177;
Sierra Morena, about, 173–74; singu-
larity of, 184; as style of praise, 177
Benedict, Ruth, 3
Benjamin, Walter, 20–21, 168
Berg, Aase, 169
Berg, A. Scott, 56–59
Berger, John, 51, 61
Bergson, Henri, 128
Bessire, Lucas, 9n10
Between One and Another (Jackson), 55
Biehl, João, 43n7
bipolar images, 105–6, 114, 118
Blanchot, Maurice, 13, 40, 94–98
Bohannon, Laura, 3
borderlands and liminality: *barzakh*
(imaginal border), 105, 118; ethno-
graphic poetry, movement, and con-
fusion, 74, 78; ethnographic writing
and policing the borderlands, 52;
poetry and, 92; transitional space
and, 46–47
Brown, A. R. Radcliffe, 25
Brown, George Mackay (GMB), 166
"Bucket, The" (Hecht), 139–41
Buñuel, Luis, 52
"Bus Station, Kampala, Uganda"
(Kusserow), 79–80

Calvino, Italo, 209
Cannetti, Elias, 118n2
Cape Town, South Africa. *See* fiction
about AIDS in Cape Town, South
Africa
care, writing with, 45–47
Carroll, Lewis, 48
Castaing-Taylor, Lucien, 21

ethics: hunting, ethical and emotional tension in, 198–204; madness, registering experience of, 97; reciprocity and unforeseen consequences, 93; refugees and, 80. *See also* responsibility

ethnographic writing: anthropology and writing, 12–15; closure, resistance to, 57–58; craft of, 5, 15–18, 186; death of the subject and, 65–66; deep intertwining of language and life, 8; excess and, 16, 186, 188, 230; as experimental form of being in a world, 225; form and event, word and world in, 226–27; incontinent writing, 26; islands and archipelagos of, 24–27; letters and, 43n7; at limit of what is possible to say, 228; materiality of expression, 13–14, 230; "minor literature" of, 16; ontologically curious, 230; the otherwise breaking through in, 227–28; "policing the borderlands," 52; postmodern ethnography as poetry, 10n20; radical possibilities for, 3–4; "reality" and, 18–21, 51, 229; responsibility of, 13, 21–24; Rimbaud's "Drunken Boat" and transformative passage, 1–2; scenes, mode of approaching, 225–26; subject-object-world relations, consubstantiality of, 228–30; suspicion of writing and critique of "politics of representation," 15–16; as transitional space, 46–47, 229; "uncanny" presence of literary impulse in anthropology, 3; unexpectedness, moments of, 229; world beyond itself, commitment to, 14; *Writing Culture* (Clifford and Marcus), 7, 9n9, 15–16. *See also* fidelity in ethnographic writing; poetry, ethnographic

ethnography: children, ethnographers as, 15; fiction and, 131, 145–47;

Heisenberg uncertainty principle and, 91; mediation/negation, immediacy/affirmation, and, 186–87; working as story, 20, 186–87. *See also* anthropology

excess and ethnographic writing, 16, 186, 188, 230

existential care, 46

experience: ambiguity of, 51; Eliot on modalities of, 67n34; multiple lived realities, poetry and condensation of, 81–82; "romantic science" and, 60–61; scientific vs. humanistic, 54–55

Exterminating Angel, The (film; Buñuel), 52

faithfulness and faithlessness. *See* fidelity in ethnographic writing

Fassin, Didier, 146, 147n3

fate-shaping and fate-breaking in Cuban *bembés*, 177–79

Favret-Saada, Jeanne, 3

Feld, Steven, 61–62

fiction about AIDS in Cape Town, South Africa: "The Bucket," 139–41; commentary, 145–48; death toll from AIDS, 130; denial, denialism, and imagination, 130–33, 147; generative apparatus of fiction, 131, 133; "In Translation," 137–39; "Upon Arrival," 132–37, 146; "Vice Itself," 141–44

fidelity in ethnographic writing: about, 48–49; anthropology, fidelity, and authenticity, 49–51; binaries and, 51–53; commentary, 68–70; dreams, death of the subject, and, 65–66; embourgeoisement of anthropology and practical means of going on, 61–64; epistolary friendship between Maxwell Perkins and Elizabeth Lemmon and, 56–60; intercessors and, 117; invention and,

223; natality, the new, and, 53–54; romantic authenticity vs. scientific authority and, 60–62; scientific–humanistic dialectic, mysteries, and aporia, 54–56; Stevenson's "A Proper Message" and, 223–24

Films in My Life, The (Truffaut), 122

Fine, Lisa M., 205n33

Firth, Raymond, 2–3

Fisher, Michael, 3

folksongs, Romanian, 49–50, 66n66

Fon people, 178–79

Forché, Carolyn, 21

Forsdick, Charles, 68

fragmentation, Derrida's theory of, 224

Gandolfo, Daniella, 185–88, 189–208

Garcia, Angela, 29–44, 46, 222–24

Geertz, Clifford, 18, 146

gender and hunting, 201, 205n33

al-Ghazali, 99, 101

Gift, The (Mauss), 93

Goethe, Johann Wolfgang von, 56

Goffmann, Alice, 7

Guattari, Félix, 126

Hancock, Herbie, 62

Hecht, Tobias, 130–48; "The Bucket," 139–41; "In Translation," 137–39; "Upon Arrival," 132–37, 146; "Vice Itself," 141–44

Heidegger, Martin, 193

Heisenberg uncertainty principle, 91

Hrabal, Bohumil, 125n8

humanistic experience, 54–55

humanness and hunting, 193–94, 203–4

hunting: Bataille on taboo and, 189, 195, 199–200; ecofeminist critiques of, 205n33; ethical tension and conflicted feelings around, 198–204; gender, masculine self-identity and, 200–201, 205n33; humanness and,

193–94, 203–4; in-itself (mismidad), 190, 198, 204n4; injunctions, regulations, and self-limitation, 196–98; New Jersey black bear hunt, 190–91; opposition to, 190; Ortega y Gasset on, 190, 192–94, 196–98, 200–204; radio call-in show excerpts, 189, 191, 194, 197–98, 200, 202–3; roadkill and, 190, 191–92, 226; violent death and the moment of proximity, 194–95; Yebes on, 192–93, 195, 196, 198–99, 201–3

Hurston, Zora Neale, 16

Husserl, Edmund, 50–51

Ibn al-'Arabi, 105, 109

ʿibra (passage or bridge), 95, 97, 111–12

"I is another" (Rimbaud), 2

imaginal ethnography of art. See art and madness in Morocco, imaginal ethnography of

imaginary space, 94–95

imagination: denial, denialism, and, 130–33, 147; fictional vs. ethnographic, 147n3; visual meaning and imagination of the real, 109–12

Ingold, Tim, 17

inner space of the world (Weltinnenraum), 95–96, 97

intercessors, 106, 113–14, 117–18

intersubjectivity, 24, 55

"In Translation" (Hecht), 137–39

Inuit presence of the dead, textual montage of, 209–20; "The Assertion of Gentleness," 217–18; commentary, 222–24; "Dislocating Children," 216–17; katajjaiit performance, 209–10; "The Lights Were So Bright," 213; "A Proper Message," 214; "A Son Listens," 210–13; as textual montage, 220; "Three Packs of Gum," 218–20; "Voices in Archive," 218; "Writing on Styrofoam," 215–16

literature, definition of, 166
"Lost Boy" (Kusserow), 71–74
Lovecraft, H. P., 166
Lucretius, 18
Luke, Brian, 196, 198–99, 205n33, 205n39
Luria, Aleksandr Romanovich, 60

madness. *See* art and madness in Morocco, imaginal ethnography of
Malinowski, Bronislaw, 2, 19, 25
Mande-speaking peoples, 60
Marcel, Gabriel, 55
Marcus, George, 3, 9n9. *See also* *Writing Culture* (Clifford and Marcus)
masculinism, 201, 205n33
"mastery of non-mastery" (Bataille), 17
Mauss, Marcel, 93
Mayakkam Enna (Why the tumult) (film; Selvaraghavan), 124
McLean, Stuart, 1–9, 48, 116–18, 126–29, 168–71; "SEA," 148–67
McMaster Health Sciences Archives, Hamilton, ON, 217–20
mental illness. *See* art and madness in Morocco, imaginal ethnography of
Merleau-Ponty, Maurice, 41
messengers, 116–17
migrants in Europe, 63–64
migrants in New England. *See* refugees, South Sudan, and New England, poetry about
"Milk" (Kusserow), 82–85
montage, textual, 220. *See also* Inuit presence of the dead, textual montage of
Montaigne, Michel de, 56
Morocco. *See* art and madness in Morocco, imaginal ethnography of
Mountain Sanatorium, Hamilton, Ontario, 210, 212, 214, 216, 218–20
mourning, rhythm of writing and, 31

"Mud" (Kusserow), 85–87
Music of the Ba-Benzélé, 62
mysteries, 55–56, 60

Narayan, Kirin, 5, 9n10
natality, 53
New England, refugees in. *See* refugees, South Sudan, and New England, poetry about
New Mexico, 45. *See also* letters archive, Española Valley, NM; Santa Fe, NM
newness and fidelity, 53–54
Nietzsche, Friedrich, 17, 20, 147
Notley, Alice, 166

Ochoa, Todd Ramón, 65, 116, 172–84, 185–88
opacity, 91–92
"Opening Day, Mukaya" (Kusserow), 88–89
Orkney Islands, Scotland, 166–67. *See also* "SEA" (McLean)
Ortega y Gasset, José, 190, 192–94, 196–98, 200–204, 207
Other Side (*l'autre coté*) (Blanchot), 95–96

Palin, Sarah, 200
Pandian, Anand, 1–9, 48, 68–70, 119–25, 145–48
Pandolfo, Stefania, 91, 94–115
Paravel, Verena, 21
Pasolini, Pier Paolo, 126, 128
passage: ʿibra (passage or bridge), 95, 97, 111–12; Rimbaud's "Drunken Boat" and transformative passage, 1–2
Pastoral Clinic, The (Garcia), 222
Peck, Jeffrey, 3
Perkins, Louisa Saunders, 57
Perkins, Maxwell, 56–60
phenomenology, 50–51
Phillips, R. A. J., 214